D0872112

Issues in Applying SLA Theories toward Reflective and Effective Teaching

Critical New Literacies: The Praxis of English Language Teaching and Learning (PELT)

Series Editors

Marcelle Cacciattolo (*Victoria University, Australia*)
Tarquam McKenna (*Victoria University, Australia*)
Shirley Steinberg (*University of Calgary, Canada*)
Mark Vicars (*Victoria University, Australia*)

VOLUME 7

The titles published in this series are listed at *brill.com/cnli*

Issues in Applying SLA Theories toward Reflective and Effective Teaching

Edited by

Mitra Zeraatpishe, Akram Faravani,
Hamid Reza Kargozari and Maryam Azarnoosh

BRILL

SENSE

LEIDEN | BOSTON

All chapters in this book have undergone peer review.

The Library of Congress Cataloging-in-Publication Data is available online at http://catalog.loc.gov

ISSN 2542-9396
ISBN 978-90-04-38086-8 (paperback)
ISBN 978-90-04-38087-5 (hardback)
ISBN 978-90-04-38088-2 (e-book)

This book is printed on acid-free paper and produced in a sustainable manner.

CONTENTS

PREFACE

We, language teachers, desire for commitment to unrelenting pursuit of our goals as reflective practitioners. We are responsible to take actions and make decisions as agents of immediate situations in line with the constant changes of the world. This spontaneous burst of situating ourselves in the immediate contexts won't be attainable without reflection. This book is an attempt toward practicing EFL teaching in a reflective way as a result of which we could train reflective learners too who can regulate their own learning, who can gain practical skills other than knowledge, who can become autonomous at the end. This book consists of two parts; the first part focuses on SLA theories and the second part is on reflective and effective teaching of language components and skills.

In the first chapter, Kargozari and Faravani introduce key figures of behaviorism and discuss the features of this psychological school of thought and the way it is put into practice in a language class. They end with the drawbacks of behaviorism. In the second chapter, Maftoon and Shakouri illustrate different reflections on cognitive approaches to SLA and discuss several pedagogical implications for L2 teaching and learning. In their paper, the controversy over nature/nurture is elucidated by juxtaposing both relying on some features of behaviorism along with some of those in cognitivism. In Chapter 3, Nassaji and Tian focus on two branches of constructivism, namely cognitivism and social interactionism and their application to second language learning. Dawson with his chapter on connectionism, introduces this concept as one consequence of the criticisms of classical cognitive science which assumes cognition in general, and language processing in particular. Loewen and Majorana in Chapter 5 elaborate on the interactionist framework and the main concepts it covers. The final chapter in the first part of the book written by Crookes is a focus on the critical theories of SLA and that how these theories can be used toward creative teaching.

The second part of the volume starts with Levis and McCrocklin's chapter on reflective and effective teaching of pronunciation. They refer to four characteristics of effective teaching of pronunciation. Finally they suggest some questions for teachers' reflection before and during their teaching. Reflective and effective teaching of Grammar is co-authored by Weaver and Gillmeister in Chapter 8, which is divided into two parts. The first part includes the theoretical scheme underscoring the role of equipping learners with comprehensible input in teaching grammar. The second part is on the application of the steps to be taken to teach grammar which was based on Richards and Rogers (2001). Nurmukhamedov and Plonsky start their chapter (Chapter 9) on teaching vocabulary with introducing four goals for vocabulary instruction, such as expanding learners' vocabulary size, raising their awareness about formulaic language, and developing their word knowledge.

To achieve these goals, they recommend the four strands of teaching vocabulary by Nation (2001), including: meaning-focused input; meaning-focused output; language-focused learning; fluency development.

Covering the reflective teaching of components of language, the second part continues with the pragmatic side of the language and language teaching. Liontas, in Chapter 10, introduces three general idiom tenets regarding the content, construction, and their dependence on the contexts in which they are uttered during conversations. Then he elaborated on a reflective and effective teaching of idioms through outlining specific pragmatic concepts for incorporating these three idiom tenets within conversational contexts.

Part 2 continues with the reflective and effective teaching of language skills. Chapter 11 is on teaching speaking. Relying on the idea that speaking is a combinatorial skill, Burns emphasizes the core skills learners have to gain. She also proposes a teaching-learning cycle including seven stages: focus learners attention on speaking, provide input and/or guide planning, conduct speaking task, focus on language/skills/strategies, repeat speaking task, direct learners' reflection on learning, facilitate feedback on learning.

Zeraatpishe and Azarnoosh co-author the next chapter on teaching writing. They suggest a reflective post-process approach to writing. They introduce some metacognitive and cognitive strategies and also propose an eight stage model for reflective an effective teaching of writing. These stages include teaching mechanics of writing, pre-task planning, drafting/writing task, teachers' feedback on the first draft, learners' reflection through monitoring and editing, learners' reflection through interactive feedback and self-assessment, teachers' direct feedback on the final draft, teachers' reflection on the whole procedure.

Chapter 13 by Goh and Vandergrift is on teaching listening which consists of two parts. In the first part, they discuss the cognitive processes that come into play during the process of foreign language listening comprehension. Then in the second part in the chapter, they point to the techniques and ways listening can be practiced reflectively and effectively.

In the final chapter, Day writes about reflective and effective teaching of reading. He puts forward an in-depth discussion of the nature of reading. Day highlights the concept of reading fluency and criticizes those approaches that just teach reading for the purpose of comprehension.

We hope this book will enlighten the ways of teaching and learning languages in an EFL or ESL context. Since each teacher is responsible for his/her own professional development, this book can be a tool to achieve self-regulating, self-evaluating, and self-improving abilities. This way, we hope teachers will become more effective in their professions and that through collaboration this will lead to the betterment of their colleagues and their own students.

We are so grateful to the contributors who honoured us writing the chapters and we owe a lot to Elias Sheybani, Fateme Motavallian, and Atefe Ghods who assisted in the formatting of the book.

FIGURES AND TABLES

FIGURES

TABLES

PART 1
THEORIES

HAMID REZA KARGOZARI AND AKRAM FARAVANI

1. BEHAVIORISM

INTRODUCTION

The early decades of the twentieth century witnessed a new school of thought in psychology. The emergence of this school happened in the United States. This innovation led to the rejection of consciousness in psychology and the accentuation of behaviors (Leahey, 2000). As the result, the main focus of this school was on observable behaviors and it was called behaviorism. At the turn of the century, since Darwin's theory of evolution was in vogue, behaviorists borrowed the idea that animal learning and human leaning were the same and attempted to develop their theories mostly based on animals' observable behaviors. In this way, proponents of behaviorism, as pure materialists, rejected the role of mind in learning and focused on materials such as behaviors.

Behaviorists' main concerns were stimulus and response. To them, conditions were parallel to stimuli and behaviors were parallel to responses. This is why behaviorist theories are called stimulus-response theories.

This chapter starts with introducing behaviorism and key figures of this psychological era, then it continues with its philosophical foundation and its application in language classes. Finally, it ends up with the drawbacks of behaviorism.

KEY FIGURES IN BEHAVIORISM

J.B. Watson is considered as the forefather of behaviorism. Watson suggested his classical conditioning based on Pavlov's studies. This theory focused on associations between stimuli and responses. Watson believed that people do not have any differences initially and are born with a limited number of reflexes that are the results of their experiences. This view is parallel with the ideas suggested by environmentalists (Mirhassani, 2003).

Ivan Pavlov, a Russian physiologist, is another key figure in behaviorism. Pavlov is considered as the originator of *classical conditioning*. He proposed that pairing unconditioned stimulus with unconditioned response repeatedly causes conditioned stimulus and conditioned response. This repeated pairing of stimulus and response leads to association that is called classical conditioning.

Edwin Guthrie's model of conditioning was in contrast with Pavlov's classical conditioning. This model was based on the idea that there is no need for repeated pairings of stimulus and response for association and learning. This model is a theory

© KONINKLIJKE BRILL NV, LEIDEN, 2018 | DOI:10.1163/9789004380882_001

called *one-trial learning*. Moreover, Guthrie believed that practice cannot affect the association between stimulus and response.

Edward Thorndike presented a different construal of conditioning referred to as *instrumental conditioning* in which response is performed to obtain the reinforcer (Ghaemi & Mirhassani, 2007). The reinforcer is analogous to stimulus in classical conditioning. The learning emerging from this type of conditioning is called *trial-and-error learning*.

Perhaps P.F. Skinner is the most prominent behaviorist and sometimes is synonymous with behaviorism. He is considered as an experimental psychologist who became the most influential behaviorist. Skinner, a radical behaviorist, led behaviorism to one of its extremes. He followed instrumental conditioning and called it *operant conditioning*. The same as other behaviorists, Skinner also believed that the analysis and study of external behavior was more productive than those of internal mind. For Skinner, 'reward' or 'reinforcement' play a significant role in conditioning. Unlike other behaviorists who focused on all events that happen before issuing response, Skinner put a great emphasis on those things that follow the response. This type of conditioning is called *operant conditioning*. On the other hand, if an operant (response) is supported by a reinforcing stimulus, response is strengthened. Operant conditioning theory is based on environmental conditions which form behaviors by adding or eliminating rewards or punishment that may leave a desired r undesired effect (Ghaemi & Mirhassani, 2007).

BEHAVIORISM AND LANGUAGE LEARNING

Language development is considered as an indispensible part of child development. Behaviorism is among the theories of language acquisition that was in vogue for a long time. It has contributed to both first and second language acquisition and has been considered the psychological foundation of some language teaching methods. Skinner's and Thorndike's notions might be the most prominent ones in this realm. Their ideas formed the earliest theories of language learning. Skinner stated that environmental factors regulate and control language development. He also considered imitation, repetition, reinforcement and conditioning as the key concepts for language learning (Weiten, 2004). In this way, language learning was different from other types of learning for Skinner. It means language acquisition was an association between the stimulus, response and environmental conditions (Samkange, 2015). Skinner elaborated how children can learn syntax and sentence construction by imitating adults' language (Weiten, 2004). By the same token, students learn all aspects of the second language through repetition and imitation. Moreover, the teacher is responsible to provide a perfect model and to monitor the correct imitation by the students. For Skinner, environmental factors play significant roles in language learning. Weiten (2004) proposes that language games, listening, training objects and tools are among tools in the classroom environments which help students to develop language. Samkange (2015) also claims that classroom environment should provide a conducive environment.

Hutchinson and Waters (1987) claim that the simplicity and directness of behaviorism had a great influence on language teaching. Audio-lingual Method (ALM) of the 1950s and 1960s was widely based on behaviorist ideas. This method laid down a set of methodological guidelines based on behaviorists' concepts of stimulus and response. The basic technique used in ALM was pattern practice, especially in the form of drills practiced in language laboratory. In this way, imitative habit formation might be valuable in language classes.

BASIC PRINCIPLES OF BEHAVIORISM IN A LANGUAGE CLASS

Demirezen (1988) provides a comprehensive list of behaviorists' principles in language classes. He states that spoken language is emphasized over written language in behaviorism. On the other hand, speaking and listening are acquired primarily and are more important than reading and writing. In this case, language is speech in behaviorism. This fact demonstrates the importance of spoken language and consequently the significance of drills in language classes. Moreover, the concept of habit formation as a key term of behaviorism in language classes is constrained to the acquisition of grammar. It means language learning is equal to language usage and language use is ignored.

Demirezen (1988) also adds that conditioning is a chain of stimulus and response. This chain is built from simple conditioned responses to more complex behaviors. As a result, language learning happens based on linear acquisition of clauses and sentences.

Skinner's operant conditioning is based on the concept of reinforcement that can be either positive or negative. Negative reinforcement happens in the form of punishment but positive reinforcement is represented in the form of rewards. Rewards can reinforce and fortify language learning. By the same token, language teachers can rely on reinforcement in their classes to facilitate language learning. Furthermore, behaviorists' socially-conditioned nature implies that learning is the same for all learners. It means all learners can learn equally and in the same way, provided that learning conditions are the same for each individual.

PHILOSOPHICAL FOUNDATIONS OF BEHAVIORISM

The close association between psychology and philosophy can be sought throughout the history of psychology. One of the most prominent connections between these two sciences is found in behaviorism because the originator of this school of psychology, Watson, was a philosopher originally (Sarkar & Pfeifer, 2006). This view fits with empiricists' idea that theoretical claims should be reduced to observational claims and this may happen only by providing operational definitions. Logical positivism which was later called logical empiricism was a movement in western philosophy which asserted that only statements that are verifiable through empirical observation are cognitively meaningful (Sarkar, 1996). The movement thrived in early 20th century in some European countries such as Austria and Germany. Two main attempts followed by the proponents of this doctrine included: good philosophy must be completely familiar with the most recent developments in all sciences; and metaphysics should be rejected for its lack of empirical significance. Empiricism sought to avoid confusion which was rooted in unclear language and unverifiable claims. This fact contributed to the achievement of the experimental and natural sciences in which materialistic factors became important. Moreover, it is claimed that empiricism holds an epistemological position in which the interrelations among different sciences concern claims to knowledge (Moore, 1985). In short, direct experiential contact with nature was insisted to be the foundation of claims to knowledge and experimental operations became synonymous for science. In this way, laboratory was considered as the best place for experimental operations. Zuriff (1980) claims that logical positivism has much in common with Skinner's radical behaviorism. Skinner drew attention to the rejection of the mental explanatory fictions by focusing on behaviors and immediate observations. This fact lent itself to the importance of description of observable phenomena rather than the explanation of supernatural and mystical powers (Skinner, 1938, cited in Moore, 1985). Therefore, quantitatively verifiable relations became important in psychology such as other sciences. This trend in psychology put a focal attention on practical and pragmatic matters by which manipulation, control and prediction became feasible. Moore (1985) sees this methodology "as the antidote to the problem of classical structuralism, in which the focal concern was with establishing an account of the realities of conscious mental functioning from the building blocks of introspective reports" (p. 58).

In summary, Skinner borrowed the assumption that science entails the behavior of scientists from logical positivism. In this way, the behavior of the scientist influences the science. The same as other positivists, Skinner highlighted the role of experimental methods as the mostly appropriate methods for any type of investigation. Moreover, interpretation and description of sensory experiences became important for him.

DRAWBACKS OF BEHAVIORISM

The behaviorists' rejection of instinct and innate abilities is considered as the main drawback of this theory. Contrary to Freudians who have demonstrated the existence of instinctive behaviors patterns and their complexity, antimental behaviorists ignored the role of mind and stressed observable behaviors. Titchener (1914, cited in Harzem, 2004) considers behaviorism's inability to explain psychological method of introspection as the negative aspect of this theory. Moreover, operational view of science, borrowed from positivists, which focused on predictions and rejected understandings and insights caused behaviorists to be able to describe observable behaviors and to ignore instinct behaviors.

Behaviorism's special attention to stimulus and response was also problematic (Harzem, 1996). Behaviorists claimed they could analyze all responses into simple connections of stimulus and response. This atomistic analysis of stimulus-response connections was contrary to Gestalt psychology's holistic analysis. Holism theory highlighted the importance of interconnected systems rather than separate connections. On the other hand, holistic analysis could describe psychological events more convincingly than atomistic analysis of stimulus and response.

Chomsky's (1959) notion of creativity was a serious critique of Skinner. Chomsky believes that people can understand and produce languages they have never heard before. This is against behaviorists' idea that learning happens by practice, repetition and imitation. Moreover Chomsky (1959) adds that language is unpredictable from stimulus. For Chomsky, language is not stimulus-bound, but it is stimulus-free.

Finally, behaviorists overemphasized the role of environment in language learning. But environment is full of impoverished data such as false starts, incomplete sentences, etc. that children never acquire them in that way.

REFERENCES

Chomsky, N. (1959). Review of B. F. Skinner verbal behavior. *Language, 35,* 26–58.
Demirezen, M. (1988). Behaviorist theory and language learning. *Hacettepe Universties Egitim Fakultesi Dergisi, 3,* 135–140.
Harzem, P. (1996). The craft of understanding the mind: Why it cannot be a science. *Mexican Journal of Behavior Analysis, 22,* 5–17.
Harzem, P. (2004). Behaviorism for new psychology: What was wrong with behaviorism and what is wrong with it now. *Behavior and Philosophy, 32,* 5–12.
Hutchinson, T., & Waters, A. (1987). *English for specific purposes.* Cambridge: Cambridge University Press.
Leahey, H. T. (2000). Control: A history of behavioral psychology. *The Journal of American History, 87*(2), 686.
Mirhassani, A. (2003). *Theories, approaches, and methods in teaching English as a foreign language.* Tehran: Zabankadeh Publication.
Mirhassani, A., & Ghaemi, F. (2007). *Language teaching theories, approaches, methods and skills.* Tehran: Kasa Kavosh Publication.
Moore, J. (1985). Some historical and conceptual relations among logical positivism, operationism, and behaviorism. *The Behavior Analysis, 8*(1), 53–63.
Sarkar, S. (1996). *Science and philosophy in the twentieth century: Basic works of logical empiricism: Logical empiricism at its peak: Schlick, Carnap, and Neurath* (Vol. 2). New York, NY: Garland.
Sarkar, S., & Pfeifer, J. (2006). *The philosophy of science: An encyclopedia.* London: Routledge.
Samkange, W. (2015). Examining Skinner's and Bandura's ideas on language acquisition: Implications for the teacher. *Global Journal of Advanced Research, 2*(11), 1858–1863.
Weiten, W. (2004). *Psychology theory and variations.* London: Wadsworth.
Zuriff, G. (1980). Radical behaviorist epistemology. *Psychological Bulletin, 87,* 337–350.

Hamid Reza Kargozari
Tabaran Institute of Higher Education
Mashhad, Iran

Akram Faravani
Islamic Azad University, Mashhad Branch
Mashhad, Iran

PARVIZ MAFTOON AND NIMA SHAKOURI

2. COGNITIVE APPROACHES TO SECOND LANGUAGE ACQUISITION

A Symbiosis between Nature and Nurture

INTRODUCTION

Cognitive approaches to second language acquisition (SLA) are mainly concerned with the individual's mind "as a processor of information rather than with the specificity of the linguistic information it contains" (Mitchell & Myles, 2004, p. 129). Although still research needs to be carried out, recent cognitive approaches and models have made well-developed proposals for situating their stance in SLA. The present paper, from the one hand, expounding reflections on the cognitive approaches to SLA, discusses several pedagogical implications for L2 teaching and learning. On the other hand, it declares that in cognitive approaches to SLA, a symbiosis between nature and nurture is shaped. In a sense, the dichotomy of nature and nurture needs to be abandoned because SLA is the byproduct of an interaction of the two.

The cognitive approach to SLA is a relatively new and innovative field of study, gradually becoming the mainstream domain of SLA investigation. The root of cognitive perspective on SLA takes its inspiration from Piaget's cognitive determinism (Owens, 1996) in that language development is mainly determined by one's cognition development. In other words, cognitive development is seen as a prerequisite for acquiring and using language (Nelson, 1991). However, cognitive approaches to SLA are not purely rationalist. In fact, cognitive perspectives on SLA attempt to find a middle path between rationalist and empiricist approaches. The rationalist aspect of cognitivism is more evident in formal approaches, such as Chomsky's (1957) Universal Grammar (UG), contending that "it is possible to study language as a formal or computational system, without taking into account the nature of human experience" (Evans & Green, 2006, p. 44). The empiricist aspect of cognitive approaches, in contrast, emphasizes that language cannot be investigated in isolation. Thus, truths about the world can be discovered through experimentation and observation (Ellis, 1999).

In this regard, Ellis (2003) asserts that SLA is governed by two general laws, that is, associative learning and cognitive learning. Associative learning is influenced by the doctrine that learning happens when connections are made between ideas. In contrast, cognitive learning occurs because human beings are born with innate knowledge.

© KONINKLIJKE BRILL NV, LEIDEN, 2018 | DOI:10.1163/9789004380882_002

The present chapter provides a theoretical debate concerning the stance of cognitive approaches to SLA. In order to accomplish this, the writers of this paper begin with the most general perspectives on SLA and gradually focus on more specific issues.

THEORETICAL LINCHPINS OF COGNITIVE APPROACHES TO SLA

Debates over cognitive approaches to SLA range across a slew of issues, but there is a consensus among scholars that language, per se, is part of cognitive development. H.D. Brown (2007) considers cognitive development "as a process of moving from states of doubt to certainty" (p. 67). Piaget (1952), in the same vein, cogently contends that cognitive development is the process of moving from the state of disequilibrium to equilibrium. Put differently, the developing mind is constantly seeking for equilibration – a balance between what is known and what is recently being experienced. Equilibration is accomplished by two complementary processes: assimilation (i.e., modifying incoming information to fit our knowledge) and accommodation (i.e., modifying our knowledge to include new information). These two processes contribute to what Piaget calls adaptation, a process of learning from the environment and adjusting to changes in the environment.

Another common explanatory scenario for cognitive development is suggested by McLaughlin (1987). In line with Piaget's assimilation-accommodation paradigm, McLaughlin's model regards language acquisition as the gradual automatization of skills through stages of restructuring and linking new information to old knowledge. Restructuring, according to McLaughlin, refers to the process of imposing a new organization on the information earlier stored in long-term memory. As to McLaughlin (cited in O'Malley & Chamot, 1990), an example "of restructuring in SLA [is] interlanguage, where individuals restructure transitional grammars that are seen to violate more recently acquired principles" (p. 67). Interlanguage is defined as "the interim grammars constructed by the second-language learners on their way to the target language" (McLaughlin, 1987, p. 60). "These mental grammars are perceived as dynamic and [are] subject to rapid change" (Ellis, 1994, p. 352).

Undeniably, interlanguage is variable (Ellis, 1985). "Variability refers to cases where a second language learner uses two or more linguistic variants to express a phenomenon, which has only one realization in the target language" (Song, 2012, p. 779). However, according to Ellis (1985), interlanguage is systematic, while it is variable. Although seems contradictory, the notion of variability and systematicity is reconcilable. That is, variability, per se, is either systematic or nonsystematic (Ellis, 1992). As Ellis remarks, the variability that can be predicted and accounted for is systematic variability. Ellis further holds that systematic variability results from linguistic, situational, and psychological contexts. In contrast, the variables which are not part of one's language competence, including false starts, slips of the tongue, changes of mind, and so on are unsystematic variability. In this regard, Song (2012) maintains that "non-systematic variation occurs when new forms are assimilated but have not yet been integrated into the learner's form-function system. Systematic variation [in contrast] occurs when the new forms have been accommodated by the existing form-function system" (p. 781).

PROPERTY THEORIES VERSUS TRANSITIONS THEORIES

Numerous theories have been proposed concerning SLA. Cummins (1983) makes a distinction between transition theories and property theories. In transition theories, the emphasis is laid on the changes that occur to a given system (i.e., a learner). In other words, transition theories explain how the learner "changes from a state of L2 ignorance to a state of L2 (probably imperfect) knowledge" (Gregg, 1997, p. 70). Put differently, transition theories entail causal relationship because it is concerned with explaining the changes between events or states (Wendt, 1999).

Property theories, however, are basically explanatory (Cummins, 1983). Put differently, property theories are concerned with such a question as *what the nature of a given cognitive faculty is*, while transition theories attempt to answer such a question as *how one acquires that faculty*. In sum, "transition theories explain a system's behavior [in terms of the] previous causes, whereas property theories explain behavioral capacities in terms of the system's internal organization" (Tonneau, 2008, p. 90).

One prominent type of property theories in SLA is Chomsky's (1957) UG. UG is mainly based on a set of assumptions: (1) grammar autonomy, (2) modularity, (3) poverty of stimulus, (4) language instinct, and (5) acquisition as parameter setting. Chomsky remarks that grammar of a language is constituted independently without reference to meaning, discourse, and language use. The term modularity, as to Chomsky, is based on the idea that a human brain is composed of a series of different modules, each one with a different function. Poverty of stimulus, according to Chomsky, refers to the notion of degeneracy of input; children do not receive enough input to infer the existence of core aspects of language. Besides, language is considered an instinct, and language universals are inherited. By language instinct, Pinker (1994) refers to the idea that human language is not an invention; rather children spontaneously create it. And finally, according to Chomsky (1957), acquisition as parameter setting refers to the assumption that a person's syntactic knowledge is composed of a finite set of parameters that are different in languages and determine the variability among languages. Besides, there are a finite set of principles that are common to all languages. In effect, one can make an infinite number of sentences with these finite set of rules.

Incompatible with Chomsky's conviction, several scholars (e.g., Halliday, 1973; Lakoff, 1971) claim that the form of language is determined by the use of language. The inseparability of form and meaning, i.e. construction (Ellis, 2003), is the cornerstone of language learning.

Unlike property theories that are concerned with how the knowledge of language is represented, cognitive approaches to transition theory rely on the notion that language acquisition is highly dependent upon language practice and experience. Supporting the significance of practice and experience, Kolb, Gibb, and Robinson (2003) state that "the organization of brain circuitry is constantly changing as a function of experience" (p. 1). Research has shown that language experience and practice tunes the cortex – the outer layer of the brain. The size of corpus callosum is also associated with the experience one gains from the environment (Mårtensson et al., 2012). Concerning the importance of practice in transition theories of SLA, Ellis (1998) holds that both lexical recognition and production processes "are independently governed by the power law of practice" (p. 639), i.e., an increase in the number of practice trials is conducive to a decrease in the reaction time for a particular task (Newell & Rosenbloom, 1981).

On the other hand, Mitchell and Myles (2004) have dichotomized cognitive approaches to SLA into processing and emergentist approaches. Processing approaches take into account how L2 learners process linguistic information and how their ability to process L2 develops overtime. Emergentist, or constructionist, approaches to SLA, incompatible with the innate-based perspectives of SLA projected by Chomsky (1957), rely on a usage-based view of language development. That is, "many of the rule-like regularities that we see in language emerge from the mutual interactions of the billons of associations that are required during language usage" (Ellis, 2003, p. 44).

In the following sections, processing approaches to SLA will be presented. Then having delved into Pinenaman's (1998a, 1998b) processability theory (PT), to achieve a symbiosis between nature and nurture, emergentism will be dealt with.

PROCESSING APPROACHES TO SLA

Processing approaches to SLA have this feature in common that there are some mechanisms in the brain that deal with L2. Mitchell and Myles (2004) divide the processing approaches into information processing models and PT. Information processing models investigate how different memory stores deal with new second language information and how the information is restructured and automatized through repeated activation. Two common types of information processing models are McLaughlin's (1987) Information Processing Model and Anderson's (1982) Active Control of Thought (ACT) Model. PT, conversely, deals with the processing demands made by various aspects of the second language. That is, at any stage of SLA, learners can comprehend and produce only those linguistic forms that the present state of language processor can manage (Pienemann, 2008).

McLaughlin's Information Processing Model

The basic tenets of McLaughlin's information processing model state that humans are not able to attend to all the information embedded in a text, for "humans are limited-capacity processors" (McLaughlin, Rossman, & McLeod, 1983, p. 135). Thereupon,

McLaughlin (1987) calls on the necessity for restructuring and automatization. As McLaughlin asserts, the way human beings process information may be either controlled or automatic. Controlled processes are capacity-limited and temporary, while automatic processes are relatively permanent. For learning to happen, learners need to resort to controlled processing of L2. The controlled processing entails the activation of a number of nodes through association, and learning happens when there is a shift from controlled toward automatic processing. For this to happen, learners should give the process their full attention. Learning in this way is seen as the movement from controlled to automatic processing via practice. The continuity from the controlled to automatic processing of input results in a constant restructuring of the linguistic system of the second language.

Although McLaughlin's model is still in vogue, several scholars (e.g., Ellis, 1994) enumerate some of the drawbacks of this model. Ellis maintains that the notion of practice is constantly used in the model, yet no definition of practice is explicitly provided. Moreover, McLaughlin (1987) insists that some rules need to be learned before others, but he never accounts for the reason. Furthermore, McLaughlin's notion of restructuring does not explain which linguistic features should be restructured, nor does the model give the reason what makes learners restructure.

Anderson's Active Control of Thought (ACT) Model

Anderson's (1982) ACT model, from the one hand, suggests there are two major stages in the development of a cognitive skill, declarative and procedural stages. In the declarative stage, the knowledge is usually stored in words. In the procedural stage, however, knowing how to perform a task is encoded. On the other hand, Anderson declares that L2 learning (i.e., movement from the declarative to procedural knowledge) takes place in three stages: (1) the cognitive stage (the procedure described is learned, e.g., singular -*s* must be added to the verb preceded by a singular subject); (2) the associative stage (the way to perform the skill is practiced); and (3) the autonomous stage (the skill gets automatized).

Regarding SLA, Anderson theorizes what exactly happens in an EFL classroom setting is that students are exposed to a plethora of language rules and structures as the declarative knowledge, they put them into practice, and then they apply them to real-life settings that would make the declarative knowledge turn into the procedural knowledge. Nevertheless, the declarative-to-procedural concomitance is not later generalized by Anderson (1985), especially with respect to SLA. Apparently, there exist many rules unknown to learners, and there are many known rules that are not learned in formal settings, but learned through experience.

Based upon Mitchell and Myles' (2004) classification of processing approaches to SLA, two types of information processing models were briefly discussed in the preceding sections. In the following section, the PT, as proposed by Pienemann (1998a, 1998b), will be elaborated on.

Processability Theory

Pienemann's (1998b) PT assumes that there is a predictable sequence of stages for the acquisition of procedural skills (e.g., grammar) that are needed for language processing. Besides, none of these stages can be skipped because the cognitive processing of one stage is the prerequisite for the next stage.

According to Pienemann (1998a), in the first stage, or lemma (i.e., the core base of a lexicon), learners are equipped with mere lexical ingredients necessary to process language and move to the next stage. In the second stage, language learners utilize bound morphemes (i.e., a linguistic form that cannot be used on its own) in order to derive free morphemes (i.e., a linguistic form that can be used alone). Still, lack of meaningful dialogue prevails. In the third stage, the use of conjunctions empowers learners to come up with phrases, yet no syntactic production exists. It is in the fourth stage and, consequently, the fifth stage through which learners use syntactic-based phrases divulged with the lexical features in order to produce meaningful utterances.

PT is based on Kaplan and Bresnan's (1982) Lexical Functional Grammar (LFG). LFG considers language acquisition as a lexically-driven process; thus, it represents a lexical approach to grammar. In a lexically-driven process, lexical items do contain grammatical information (Fabri, 2008). For example, the lexical entry for *helped* is marked for past tense, and it entails an agent. In other words, the syntactic property of the verb is encoded in the lexicon. This lexical information is necessary for the formation of a sentence.

The central notion of LFG is the concept of feature unification, that is, the process of matching grammatical information in the sentence. For example, the sentence *Susan eat an apple is not grammatical because eat and Susan do not have the same person and number features. Pienemann (2008), in this regard, maintains that "every entry in the learner's mental lexicon needs to be annotated for the specific features of the target languages" (p. 19). For example, the entry *Susan* is assigned to the lexical category of noun and is annotated as a proper noun, and the feature number has the value of singular.

In fact, Pienemann's theory attempts to develop a theoretical framework in that the hierarchical order of the procedural skills is the same for each language. For example, an English L2 learner will first require the formation of the plural -*s* before learning how to form the verb in the third person singular present tense.

Another aspect of PT is *teachability hypothesis* (TH). Concerning TH, Mitchell and Myles (2004) mention that L2 learners pursue "a fairly rigid route in their acquisition of grammatical structures. That is, structures only become learnable when the previous steps on this acquisitional path have been acquired" (p. 116).

Nevertheless, to several scholars (e.g., Carroll, 1998; Hudson, 1993), Pienemann's (1998a, 1998b) developmental stages only give a partial view of acquisition because PT only deals with syntax and morphology. Although PT claims on providing researchers with information concerning developmental stages, it does not assert how long learners must stay at each single stage before they move forward to the next stage (Carroll, 1998). Besides, explanatory potential of PT is narrowly focused on the acquisition of speech processing procedures. Furthermore, it has no explanatory power regarding how learners construct their internal grammar and append novel pieces of language to their intricate interlanguage system (Gregg, 1999; Jordan, 2004).

In addition to the processing approaches, the other perspective on the cognitive approach to SLA, according to Mitchell and Myles' (2004) dichotomy, is emergentism that relies heavily on the usage-based view of language development.

EMERGENTIST APPROACHES TO SLA

Cognitive psychology does in no way reject the presence and dominance of behaviorism school of thought. In fact, cognitive psychology encompasses behaviorism as one of its components. One projection of behaviorism in the realm of cognitivism is emergentism. Emergentism is an approach to cognition that places emphasis on the interaction between the environment and the organism (Gregg, 2004).

Generally, two approaches to emergentism in SLA are worth mentioning: Ellis's (1998) empiricist emergentism and O'Grady's (2003, 2007) nativist emergentism. According to empiricist emergentism, L2 is acquired through usage by extracting regularities from the input and building stronger associations in the brain. Ellis (2003) maintains that "emergentists believe that many of the rule-like regularities that we see in language emerge from the mutual interactions of the billions of associations that are acquired during language usage" (p. 44). More importantly, what makes emergentism distinct from other types of SLA theories is that emergentists stress that language learning is similar to any other kind of learning which is the result of exposure to appropriate input that invokes network connections.

O'Grady's (2007) nativist emergentism, conversely, asserts that the properties of grammatical phenomena arise from the interaction of simpler and more basic non-linguistic factors including repetition and practice. In this regard, O'Grady (2003) contends that "no grammatical knowledge is inborn" (p. 44). He further remarks that language is the byproduct of the interaction between language acquisition device (LAD) and experience. Henceforth, incompatible with Chomsky's (1957) UG, O'Grady (2003) maintains that the emergence of language is not merely because of an innate LAD equipped with a set of finite grammatical principles, but it is based on the assumption that language naturally emerges from non-grammatical factors, such as repetition and interaction. In fact, the major dispute between empiricist emergentism and nativist emergentism "lies in the question of whether the input provides learners with enough information to support induction of the full language" (O'Grady, Lee, & Kwak, 2009, p. 73).

Cognitive approaches to SLA go beyond what happens inside people's head; in fact, cognitivists concentrate on the observable behavior and association. According to Evans and Green (2006), it is true that "cognitivism offers exciting glimpses into hitherto hidden aspects of the human mind" (p. 6). However, majority of cognitive approaches to SLA attempt to "make knowledge meaningful and help learners organize and relate new information to existing knowledge in memory" (Ertmer & Newby, 2013, p. 54).

PEDAGOGICAL IMPLICATIONS OF COGNITIVE APPROACHES TO SLA

As an interdisciplinary perspective on language and language learning, cognitive approaches to SLA are stringently contrasted with Chomsky's UG. Cognitive approaches ignore the rule-governed behavior of language acquisition and place emphasis on the associative learning ingrained through usage-based instruction (O'Grady, 2003).

In outlining the features of usage-based instruction, Ellis and Wulff (2015) enumerate the following themes: (1) constructions (i.e., language learning is the result of adding new information to the learners' developing linguistic system); (2) associative learning (i.e., construction is achieved when the form and meaning are associated); (3) exemplar-based learning (i.e., what has been learned earlier has been compared with an exemplar of a construction); (4) emergent relations and patterns (i.e., the emergence of complex language representations is the result of simpler emergent patters); and (5) rational cognitive processing (i.e., the association between form and meaning allows language users to be rational in the sense of having a mental model).

As Gettys and Lech (2013) maintain, an instructional unit derived from the tenets of usage-based approach to SLA is 100% theme-driven; it is resided in language samples that students learn to use and is taught inductively through the process of learning from examples. Along the same vein, when students learn to construct, "the learning course is seen as a process of adding up new constructions to the learner's developing linguistic system" (p. 59).

Accordingly, constructions of new forms contribute to the formation of grammatical knowledge in the mind. Thereupon, when a rich reservoir of examples of constructions is consolidated in long term memory, abstract knowledge of schema is developed. Schema is the building blocks of memory which build a relationship between different aspects of real world, including objects, actions, and concepts. Henceforth, having constructed a receptacle of grammatical knowledge in the mind, learners can fill their schema with new lexical items. The given idea which is primarily represented in the work of Piaget (1952) contends "a person's language development is primarily determined by the development of one's cognition. In other words, language is secondary to thought and serves to express thought" (Ji-Xian, 2001, p. 238).

One of the important implications of Piaget's adaptation for language teaching is that teachers need to adapt themselves to the learner's development level. Wood, Smith, and Grossniklaus (2001), in this regard, maintain that language instructional materials are necessary to be compatible with the learners' developmental level.

Accordingly, it is highly suggested that language teachers employ concrete and visual aids, use familiar examples to facilitate assimilation and accommodation of new information, and present problems that require mental analyses.

In fact, usage-based instruction is based on the motif that SLA happens while learners engage in interaction (Robinson & Ellis, 2008). Accordingly, Gettys and Lech (2013) assert that "language is not as a collection of rules but ... a by-product of communicative processes" (p. 58). Thus, learners should learn to extract regularities by practicing and generalizing what have been abstracted.

In the usage-based approaches to language learning, according to Gettys and Lech, there is "a radical departure from the grammar-driven curriculum: grammar does not serve as an organizing principle of the course and grammatical considerations are not taken into account in designing the course" (pp. 58–59). In a sense, proponents of usage-based instruction, including behaviorists (e.g., Skinner, 1957), constructionists (e.g., Goldberg, 2006), emergentists (e.g., O'Grady, 2003; Ellis, 2003), are consistent with the claim that "acquisition of grammar is the piecemeal learning of many thousands of constructions" (Ellis, 2002, p. 144). Besides, usage-based models and cognitive perspectives on SLA stress that human beings learn language while "processing input and producing language during *interaction* in social contexts where individually desired non-linguistic outcomes ... are goals to be achieved" (Robinson & Ellis, 2008, p. 490).

Moreover, in teaching vocabulary, "learners will understand and remember items that are thematically or meaningfully related more easily" (Verspoor & Tyler, 2009, p. 169). Hence, developers of instructional materials can design strategies for learners to minimize the burden of vocabulary acquisition. Hong (2010), in this regard, declares that the provision of gloss reduces students' burden of looking up the meaning of words in a dictionary, avoids the interruption of reading flow, and prevents learners of making wrong inference for the unfamiliar words in a particular context.

Poll (2011) introduces three themes in emergentism that has implications for language intervention. They are (1) language input (i.e., learning happens when learners are presented with sufficient input); (2) active engagement of learner with the input (i.e., language learning takes place as the result of active language processing); and (3) introduction of materials conducive to form-meaning mapping (i.e., learners should try to communicate and create natural contexts for the production of language). In sum, according to Poll, emergentism builds on contextual aids to learning and on potentially innate language learning mechanisms that increase the likelihood for learners to map language form to meaning.

Regarding the importance of input frequency in SLA, the focus of many cognitive approaches to SLA, O'Grady et al. (2009) argue that "what counts is not how many times learners hear a particular form – it is how many times they encounter mappings between a form and its meaning" (p. 71). As to O'Grady et al., *the*, for instance, is the most frequent word in the English language; nevertheless, it is acquired relatively late. Therefore, besides input frequency as an effective factor in learning lexical items, word saliency, the perceived importance of a word in a context, plays a crucial role in the acquisition of vocabulary (Brown, 1993). As Reinders (2012) states, the more salient the lexical items, the easier and earlier they will be acquired. Concerning the frequency and saliency of the input, EFL teachers need to bear in mind that the syntactic complexity of the text has effects on text comprehension (Barry & Lazarte, 1995); thus, texts with large proportion of complex sentences increase the burden of processing and memory load on learners that can have negative impacts on the amount and depth of the acquisition of unfamiliar lexical items (Watts, 2008, p. 13).

Finding natural sequence of acquisition is also of great importance for syllabus designers and instructors. If they know when and what grammatical features, for instance, should precede other grammatical forms, L2 learners learn grammatical items more efficiently. This gives an endorsement to what Pienemann (1998b) contends that "teachability is constrained by processability" (p. 250). That is, at each stage of SLA, human beings can only process (i.e., produce and comprehend) only those L2 forms that the current language processor can handle. For this reason, curriculum developers and instructors need to be aware of the order of structures to teach.

It should be mentioned that Pienemann's TH stresses that, in formal language instruction, developmental stages must be observed; "instruction will be most beneficial if it focuses on structures from the next stage" (Pienemann, 1998a, p. 250). Elsewhere, Pienemann (1995) claims, "it is important to know what is learnable at what point in time" (p. 4). In fact, on the importance of TH, Pienemann (1995, 1998a, 1998b) declares that teachers need to know about acquisition stages. In other words, "acquisition stages provide specific information on what learners can and cannot learn at different points in time" (Mansouri & Duffy, 2005, p. 82). According to Mansouri and Duffy, "acquisition stages enable teachers to determine the developmental readiness of individual learners to learn specific structures of the target language" (p. 82).

FINAL REMARKS

Although over the last two decades, a variety of approaches to SLA have appeared, "you never know which ones will catch the eye to become tomorrow's realities" (Lantolf, 1996, p. 739). The apparent meagerness of behaviorist explanations of SLA and the mere abstractness of UG steered researchers to look for an alternative theoretical framework. Thus, attempts are made to achieve a symbiosis between nature and nurture. MacWhinney's (1999) competition model, for instance, contends that language acquisition emerges as the result of both nature (biological) and nurture (environmental) processes.

The symbiotic attempts to consider both biology and environment in the formation of L2 imply that the notion of nature-nurture dichotomy should be abandoned if we agree that SLA is the byproduct of an interaction of the two. It is evident that attempts to exclude either nature or nurture in the study of SLA lead to equivocal evidence that boosts the notion of contradiction. Ellis (1994) reminds that "most theories of SLA are neither comprehensive nor truly modular. Rather they tackle a particular area or adopt a particular perspective (often derived from a parent discipline – cognitive psychology, social psychology, sociolinguistics, linguistics, neurolinguistics, education) "(p. 681). Therefore, the emergence of oppositional views, as to Beretta (1991), is a problem since SLA theories try to offer mutual exclusive explanations of the same facts. Overall, the emergence of new SLA theories has not been successful "in replacing their predecessors, but continue to coexist with them uncomfortably" (Spolsky, 1990, p. 609).

Revisiting is, therefore, necessary to juxtapose the findings of nature- and nature-based perspectives on SLA to pave the way toward comprehensiveness in theory construction in SLA. In sum, looking chronologically into the history of cognitive approaches to SLA, it can be claimed that more scholars are inclined to enjoy some qualities of both behaviorism and cognitivism.

REFERENCES

Anderson, J. R. (1982). Acquisition of cognitive skill. *Psychological Review, 8*(4), 369–406.
Anderson, J. R. (1985). *Cognitive psychology and its implications.* New York, NY: Freeman.
Barry, S., & Lazarte, A. (1995). Embedded clause effects on recall: Does high prior knowledge of content domain overcome syntactic complexity in students of Spanish? *Modern Language Journal, 79*(4), 491–504.
Beretta, A. (1991). Theory construction in SLA: Complementarity and opposition. *Studies in Second Language Acquisition, 13*, 493–511. doi:10.1017/S027226 3100 010305
Brown, C. (1993). Factors affecting the acquisition of vocabulary: Frequency and saliency of words. In T. Huckin, M. Haynes, & J. Coady (Eds.), *Second language reading and vocabulary learning* (2nd ed., pp. 263–286). Norwood, NJ: Ablex.
Brown, H. D. (2007). *Principle of learning and teaching.* New York, NY: Pearson Education.
Carroll, S. (1998). On processability theory and second language acquisition. *Bilingualism: Language and Cognition, 1*(1), 23–24. doi:10.1017/S1366728 998000030
Chomsky, N. (1957*). Syntactic structures.* Paris: Mouton.
Cummins, R. (1983). *The nature of psychological explanation.* Cambridge. MA: The MIT Press.
Ellis, N. (1998). Emergentism, connectionism and language learning. *Language Learning, 48*(4), 631–664. doi:10.1111/0023-8333.00063
Ellis, N. (1999). Cognitive approaches to SLA. *Annual Review of Applied Linguistics, 19*, 22–42. doi:10.1017/S0267190599190020
Ellis, N. (2002). Frequency effects in language processing. *Studies in Second Language Acquisition, 24*(2), 143–188. doi:10.1017/S0272263102002024
Ellis, N. (2003). Constructions, chunking and connectionism. In C. J. Doughty & M. H. Long (Eds.), *The handbook of second language acquisition* (pp. 43–63). London: Blackwell Publishing Ltd.
Ellis, N., & Wulff, S. (2015). Usage-based approaches to SLA. In B. VanPatten & J. Williams (Eds.), *Theories in second language acquisition* (pp. 75–93). London: Routledge.
Ellis, R. (1985). Sources of variability in interlanguage. *Applied Linguistics, 6*(2), 118–131. doi:10.1093/applin/6.2.118
Ellis, R. (1992). Learning to communicate in the classroom: A study of two learners' request. *Studies in Second Language Acquisition, 14*, 1–23. doi:10.1017/S02 72263100010445
Ellis, R. (1994). *The study of second language acquisition.* Oxford: OUP.
Ertmer, P. A., & Newby, T. J. (2013). *Performance improvement quarterly, 26*(2), 43–71.
Evans, V., & Green, M. (2006). *Cognitive linguistics: An introduction.* Edinburgh: Edinburgh University Press.

Fabri, R. (2008). Lexical functional grammar. In J. U. KeBler (Ed.), *Processability approaches to second language development and second language learning* (pp. 31–66). Newcastle: Cambridge Scholars Publishing.

Gettys, S., & Lech, I. (2013). *Cognitive perspective in SLA: Pedagogical implications for enhancing oral proficiency in foreign languages.* Retrieved from https://doaj.org/article/def0dcb500a24f6096a484edabca75e3

Goldberg, A. E. (2006). *Constructions at work: The nature of generalization in language.* Oxford: OUP.

Gregg, K. (1997). UG and SLA theory: The story so far. *Revista Canaria de Estudios Ingleses, 34*, 69–99.

Gregg, K. (1999). Review of M. Pienemann: Language processing and second language development: Processing theory. *The Clarion: EUROSLA, 5*(1), 10–17.

Gregg, K. (2004). The state of emergentism in second language acquisition. *Second Language Research, 19*(2), 95–128. doi:10.1191/0267658303sr213oa

Halliday, M. A. K. (1973). *Language in a social perspective: Explorations in the functions of language.* London: Edward Arnold.

Hong, X. (2010). Review of effects of glosses on incidental vocabulary learning and reading comprehension. *Chinese journal of Applied Linguistics, 33*(1), 56–73.

Hudson, T. (1993). Nothing does not equal zero: Problems with applying developmental sequence findings to assessment and pedagogy. *Studies in Second Language Acquisition, 75*(4), 461–493. doi:10.1017/S0272263100012389

Ji-Xian, P. (2001). A cognitive perspective on second language acquisition process. *Journal of Zhejiang University, 2*(2), 237–240. doi:10.1631/jzus.2001.0237

Jordan, G. (2004). *Theory construction in second language acquisition.* Amsterdam: John Benjamins.

Kaplan, R. M., & Bresnan, J. (1982). Lexical-functional grammar: A formal system for grammatical representation. In J. Bresnan (Ed.), *The mental representation of grammatical relations* (pp. 173–281). Cambridge, MA: The MIT Press.

Kolb, B., Gibb, R., & Robinson, T. E. (2003). *Brain plasticity and behavior.* Retrieved from http://www.communityworksinstitute.org/cwpublications/thebrain/thebrain.pdf

Lakoff, G. (1971). On generative semantics. In D. D. Steinberg & L. A. Jakobovits (Eds.), *Semantics* (pp. 232–296). Cambridge: CUP.

Lantolf, J. P. (1996). SLA theory building: Letting all the flowers bloom! *Language Learning, 46*(4), 713–749. doi:10.1111/j.1467-770.1996.tb01357.x

MacWhinney, B. (1999). The emergence of language. In B. MacWhinney (Ed.), *The emergence of language* (pp. ix–xvii). London: Lawrence Erlbaum Associates.

Mansouri, F., & Duffy, L. (2005). *The pedagogic effectiveness of developmental readiness in ESL grammar instruction.* Retrieved from http://www.dro.deakin.edu.au/eserv/DU:30003269/mansouri-pedagogiceffectiveness

Mårtensson, J., Eriksson, J., Bodammer, N. C., Lindgren, M., Johansson, M., Nyberg, L., & Lövdén, M. (2012). Growth of language-related brain areas after foreign language learning. *Neuroimage, 63*(1), 240–244. doi:10.1016/j.neuroimage.2012.06.043

McLaughlin, B. (1987). *Theories of second language learning.* London: Edward Arnold.

McLaughlin, B., Rossman, T., & McLeod, B. (1983). Second language learning: An information-processing perspective. *Language Learning, 33*(2), 135–158. doi:10.1111/j.1467.1983.tb00532.x

Mitchell, R., & Myles, F. (2004). *Second language learning theories* (2nd ed.). London: Hodder Arnold.

Nelson, K. (1991). The matter of time: Interdependence between language and thought in development. In S. A. Gelman & J. P. Byrnes (Eds.), *Perspectives on language and thought: Interrelations in development* (pp. 778–318). Cambridge: CUP.

Newell, A., & Rosenbloom, P. S. (1981). Mechanisms of skill acquisition and the law of practice. In J. R. Anderson (Ed.), *Cognitive skills and their acquisition* (pp. 1–55). Hillsdale, NJ: Erlbaum.

O'Grady, W. (2003). The radical middle: Nativism without universal grammar. In C. J. Doughty & M. H. Long (Eds.), *The handbook of second language acquisition* (pp. 43–63). Victoria: Blackwell Publishing Ltd.

O'Grady, W. (2007). *Does emergentism have a chance?* Paper presented to the 32nd Boston University Conference on language development, Boston, MA, USA.

O'Grady, W., Lee, M., & Kwak, H.-Y. (2009). Emergentism and second language acquisition. In W. C. Ritchie & T. K. Bhatia (Eds.), *The new handbook of second language acquisition* (pp. 69–55). London: Emerald.

O'Malley, J., & Chamot, A. (1990). *Learning strategies in second language acquisition.* Cambridge: CUP.

Owens, R. E. (1996). *Language development: An introduction* (4th ed.). Boston, MA: Allyn and Bacon.

Piaget, J. (1952). *The origins of intelligence in children.* New York, NY: International Universities Press. doi:10.1037/11494-000

Pienemann, M. (1995). *Second language acquisition: A first introduction.* Paper presented in National Language and Literacy Institute of Australia, University of Western Sydney, Penrith, Australia.

Pienemann, M. (1998a). *Language processing and second language acquisition: Processability theory.* Amsterdam: John Benjamins.

Pienemann, M. (1998b). *Language processing and L2 development.* Amsterdam: John Benjamins.

Pienemann, M. (2008). A brief introduction to processability theory. In J. U. Keßler (Ed.), *Processability approaches to second language development and second language learning* (pp. 9–30). Newcastle: Cambridge Scholars Publishing.

Pinker, S. (1994). *The language instinct: How the mind creates language.* New York, NY: William Morrow and Company.

Poll, G. H. (2011). Increasing odds: Applying emergentist theory in language intervention. *Lang Speech Hear Serv Sch, 42*(4), 580–591. doi:10.1044/0161-1461(2011/10-0041)

Reinders, H. (2012). Towards a definition of intake in second language acquisition. *Applied Research in English, 1*(2), 15–36.

Robinson, P., & Ellis, N. (2008). Conclusion: Cognitive linguistics, second language acquisition and L2 instruction-issues for research. In P. Robinson & N. C. Ellis (Eds.), *Handbook of cognitive linguistics and second language acquisition* (pp. 489–445). London: Routledge.

Skinner, B. F. (1957). *Verbal behavior.* Englewood Cliffs, NJ: Prentice-Hall.

Song, L. (2012). On the variability of interlanguage. *Theory and Practice in Language Studies, 2*(4), 778–783. doi:10.4304/tpls.2.4.778–783

Spolsky, B. (1990). Introduction to a colloquium: The scope and form of a theory of a second language learning. *TESOL Quarterly, 24,* 609–616. doi:10.2307/3587110

Tonneau, F. (2008). The concept of reinforcement: Explanatory or descriptive. *Behavior and Philosophy, 36,* 87–96.

Verspoor, M., & Tyler, A. (2009). Cognitive linguistics and second language learning. In W. C. Ritchie & T. K. Bhatia (Eds.), *The new handbook of second language acquisition* (pp. 159–177). London: Emerald.

Watts, M. L. (2008). Clause type and word saliency in second language incidental vocabulary acquisition. *Reading Matrix, 8*(1), 1–22.

Wendt, A. (1999). *Social theory of international politics.* Cambridge: CUP.

Wood, K. C., Smith, H., & Grossniklaus, D. (2001). *Piaget's stages of cognitive development.* Retrieved from http://epltt.coe.uga.edu

Parviz Maftoon
English Department College of Foreign Languages and Literature
Science and Research Branch
Islamic Azad University
Tehran, Iran

Nima Shakouri
English Department College of Foreign Languages and Literature
Science and Research Branch
Islamic Azad University
Tehran, Iran

HOSSEIN NASSAJI AND JUN TIAN

3. CONSTRUCTIVISM

INTRODUCTION

Constructivism is often broadly divided into two branches – cognitive and social with Jean Piaget and Lev Vygotsky as the key figures leading the two schools of thought. The major difference between the two schools of thought is their different views on the importance of social interaction on individual's cognitive development. To cognitive constructivists, individual cognitive development is perceived as a relatively solitary act (Russell, 1993). On the other hand, social constructivists advocate the important role social interaction plays in individual's cognitive development (Bruffee, 1986; Vygotsky, 1978, 1981a; Wertsch, 1985).

COGNITIVE CONSTRUCTIVISM

Cognitive constructivism emphasizes that children or learners develop their knowledge through their individual discovery of new information and reflection on their own previous knowledge. By doing so, they are able to transform knowledge in increasingly complex and sophisticated structures and making it their own (Slavin, 2003). Learners themselves are seen playing an important role in their individual cognitive development (Piaget, 1954, 1955, 1970).

According to Piaget, children construct their knowledge through being able to organize their knowledge into more complex structures by consistently and accurately recognizing different kinds of a certain object and then organizing them into higher groupings. For example, when they have observed many different kinds of birds, they will eventually know that they are a kind of animal. At the same time, children construct their knowledge of abstraction by consistently reflecting on their own actions to develop their awareness of the effective and justified actions. In summary, learning is a developmental process where self-regulation is emphasized in one's cognitive construction of knowledge.

SOCIAL CONSTRUCTIVISM

In recent years, more widely reviewed constructivist theories in the field of second language acquisition are the branch of social constructivism. Social-constructivist theories also referred to as sociocultural theories, view knowledge as socially accepted belief and see social interaction as influencing individual cognitive

© KONINKLIJKE BRILL NV, LEIDEN, 2018 | DOI:10.1163/9789004380882_003

development (Bruffee, 1986; Vygotsky, 1978, 1981a; Wertsch, 1985). According to social constructivists, "learning occurs among persons rather than between a person and things" (Bruffee, 1986, p. 787). These theories posit that people construct certain knowledge when they have achieved a general agreement about what they know in a community; with the consequence that knowledge changes or improves "as the community reconstructs itself" (Grabe & Kaplan, 1996, p. 380). In terms of language development, the theories argue that student-student interaction plays an important role in the development of individuals' linguistic knowledge.

Current social-constructivist theories owe much to the work of Lev S. Vygotsky, a mid-twentieth century Soviet social psychologist. An important theoretical concept of Vygotsky's social-constructivist theory is "inter- and intra-psychological processes". Vygotsky (1978) argues for a complex relationship between individual psychological development and social interaction. According to him, individual cognitive development cannot be achieved or furthered by isolated learning. Rather, he believes that people's intellectual development is closely related to the people they interact with and the way they interact. That is, learning occurs when more than one person is involved and when people are engaged in social interaction. To clearly explain this complicated relationship, Vygotsky (1981a) put forward a "general genetic law of cultural development":

Any function in the child's cultural development appears twice, or on two planes. First, it appears on the social plane, and then on the psychological plane.

First it appears between people as an interpsychological category, and then within the child as an intrapsychological category. This is equally true with regard to voluntary attention, logical memory, the formation of concepts, and the development of volition (p. 163).

Wertsch (1985) claims that the above-cited law highlights two important ideas in Vygotsky's theory. First, it explains individual and concrete group interactions play a crucial role in individual cognitive development. Second, it reveals the "inherent connection" between two modes of functioning: interpsychological (in communication) and intrapsychological (in thinking), in which social interactions act as the intermediary for individual cognitive development (p. 61). Lantolf and Appel (1994) further suggest that the transition from the inter- to the intra-psychological plane "marks the beginning of the child's control over his or her own behavior – that is, self-regulation" (p. 11). This process should be applicable to adult second language learners as well.

As far as language learning classes are concerned, the relationship between inter- and intrapsychological processes suggests that L2 classes should incorporate student-student interaction activities because peer interaction provides students with occasions to participate in concrete social interaction, trying to solve problems together by using the target language. Language now is "simultaneously a means of communication and a tool for thinking" (Swain & Lapkin, 1998, p. 320). In this external social activity, students have a chance to work with peers on the language itself. When students transfer the L2 knowledge developed in the social interaction to their internal psychological plane, they are likely to construct knowledge of the language, consciously or subconsciously.

There are a number of key constructs closely connected with the sociocultural theory of learning, all of which emphasize the social nature of learning and the role of social interaction in promoting language development. These include zone of proximal development, scaffolding, regulation, and internalization. In what follows we will discuss each.

Zone of Proximal Development

One of the most influential concepts of Vygotskian theory is the Zone of Proximal Development (ZPD). In explaining the relationship between instruction and development, Vygotsky (1978) introduces this concept of the ZPD to examine "those functions that have not yet matured but are in the process of maturation, functions that will mature tomorrow but are currently in an embryonic state" (p. 86). The ZPD is defined as "the distance between the actual developmental level as determined by independent problem solving and the level of potential development as determined through problem solving under adult guidance or in collaboration with more capable peers" (p. 86). Vygotsky contends that students' actual developmental level will reach their potential developmental level when they interact with more capable people or cooperate with their peers within the zone of proximal development (1978). He further argues that instruction itself is not development. Only when instruction is in students' zone of proximal development does it become effective because it would trigger the functions, which are in the process of maturation (Vygotsky, 1934, cited in Wertsch, 1985). According to Vygotsky, the shift from other-regulation, or intermental activity, to self-regulation, or intramental activity, takes place in the ZPD, which is determined by the learner's current level of development together with the form of instruction received (Wertsch, 1985). When this learning process is internalized, the learner's independent development is achieved.

Scaffolding

Another key concept is the notion of scaffolding. *Scaffolding* refers to the supportive environment created through the guidance and feedback learners receive during collaboration (Donato, 1994). When learners collaborate with others, they master what they have not been able to master independently. This happens particularly when learners interact with a more capable person. In such cases, the less capable participant's language skills can be expanded and elevated to a higher level of competence. A point to note is that scaffolding is support that is not random, but rather is negotiated within the learner's ZPD. It is a guided support jointly "constructed on the basis of the learner's need" (Nassaji & Swain, 2000, p. 36). The importance of negotiated help over random help within the ZPD was explored by Nassaji and Swain (2000) in an experimental study in which ESL students were provided with different kinds of help from a tutor when learning English articles. The results revealed that scaffolding within the learner's ZPD in a collaborative fashion helped the learner to acquire the target language forms more effectively than help that was provided randomly and provided in a non-collaborative fashion. There are a number of other studies in the field of L2 acquisition that have examined the role of interaction in promoting scaffolding and have found evidence that scaffolding occurs in student-teacher interaction when the teacher adjusts feedback to suit learners' language level (e.g., Aljaafreh & Lantolf, 1994; Ohta, 2001) or when learners interact to solve linguistic problems during collaborative pair work (e.g., Lapkin, Swain, & Smith, 2002; Storch, 1998, 2001).

Regulation

The third concept developed from a Vygotskian framework is the notion of regulation. According to Vygotsky learning is not only a social process, but it is also a process of moving from object-regulation to other-regulation to self-regulation. Object regulation is a stage where the learner's behaviour is controlled by objects in their environment. For example, at early stages of learning an L2, learners may be able to respond to only the stimuli that are available in here-and-now contexts. As they progress, they can respond to more abstract entities. Other-regulation refers to situations when the learner has gained some control over the object, but still needs the help or guidance of others. Self-regulation occurs when the learner becomes skilled and able to act autonomously.

The notion of regulation highlights two important ideas in sociocultural theory. First, it explains that new knowledge begins in interaction and becomes internalized and consolidated through interaction and collaboration. Second, it reveals the inherent connection between inter-psychological and intra-psychological (in thinking) functioning (Wertsch, 1985). In other words, it explains the transition from the inter-mental ability that is initially used in interaction to intra-mental ability (such as intentional thinking) that takes place inside the learner. This transition is evident when someone begins to act independently, showing control over his or her own behavior (Appel & Lantolf, 1994; Donato, 1994). Lantolf and Appel (1994) suggested that the transition from the inter-mental (inter-psychological) to the intra-mental (intra-psychological) plane "marks the beginning of the child's control over his or her own behavior – that is, self-regulation" (p. 11). This process should be applicable to adult L2 learners as well, in which the learner has appropriated and consolidated the new skills and knowledge. A number of researchers have explored these mechanisms and have found evidence that collaborative interaction helps learners progress from lower to higher order mental functions (see Lantolf, 2000 for a review of these studies).

Internalization

Another theoretical concept is "internalization". According to Vygotsky (1981a), internalization is not a simple transfer of external social development to a higher individual mental plane, although social function mediates the function of the intramental plane. Vygotsky emphasizes that internalization as a process is only achieved when people are able to "create" on their internal planes what has been performed in external social reality. That is, while internalization transforms social function to internal psychological function, it also changes the structure and functions of the process (Vygotsky, 1981b).

Vygotsky uses an example of a child's internalization of non-verbal pointing to illustrate this internalization process. When a child tries to grasp an object, the adult may interpret his attention as a directing sign and thus passes the object to the child. Wertsch (1985) explains that a child's mental functioning has begun to change from an unsuccessful non-communicative grasping movement to a successful communicative indication when s/he begins to master and use an indicatory gesture to direct an adult's attention to an object. His or her consciousness has developed on the plane of mental development functioning. In the future, the child may use this gesture in forthcoming demands, suggesting "additional development on the intrapsychological plane" and "subsequent progress on the interpsychological plane" (p. 65). This example illustrates the process of internalization and the inherent connection between inter- and intrapsychological functioning.

When L2 learners try to express themselves in a spoken or written form during peer interaction activities, if they can successfully express their intended meanings, an internal plane of consciousness may be formed and thus the knowledge of the language may be internalized. If they fail to express themselves effectively, the language forms may not be internalized. The external reality helps them to clarify their points until they can consciously produce an acceptable expression and make themselves understood. This acceptable expression may not exist in the language learner's intramental plane until it is created in their internal cognitive development through this peer-to-peer external interaction. In such a process, the knowledge that is internalized may become part of their internal plane, and is then available for use in their revised utterances and future language performance.

IMPLICATIONS FOR LANGUAGE TEACHING AND LEARNING

The concepts discussed above have important implications for second language teaching and learning. For example, the notion of the ZPD highlights the central role of collaboration in mediating learning and cognitive development. When learners collaborate within the ZPD, the act of collaboration pushes learners towards higher levels of development, enabling them to learn what they are capable of learning (Nassaji & Swain, 2000). At every stage of the learning process, peers who negotiate within their ZPD are likely to reach a more sophisticated developmental level within their potential ability (Nassaji & Cumming, 2000). Collaborative learning activities create a social context for students to interact with one another and receive feedback. This is captured in the notion of scaffolding. When interacting with less experienced peers, students may use their existing linguistic knowledge to give suggestions and thus consolidate their known knowledge, a process occurring on the intrapsychological plane and leading to independent development as well. This broadened ZPD to include novice-novice or learner-learner interactions to the traditional expert-novice interaction has become more accepted through investigated sociocultural explanations of L2 learners' conversations in their language learning process (Lightbown & Spada, 2006). In interaction, students, within the ZPD, also use what they already possess to develop what they have not mastered independently (Nassaji & Cumming, 2000). They may develop new expressions and ways of thinking with their peers' help, furthering their intramental development and internalization.

In summary, the social-constructivist theory provides strong support for the implementation of student-student collaborative activities in L2 classes: working groups or peer groups provide an external social environment for language learners to interact in. In Oxford's (1997) words, "Learning occurs while people participate in the sociocultural activities of their learning community, transforming (i.e., constructing) their understanding and responsibilities as they participate" (p. 448). This social interaction is a necessary precondition for language learners' individual psycholinguistic development through internalization of new information. In other words, introducing collaborative activities into L2 classrooms helps direct students towards their zone of proximal development, enabling them to learn in advance of development. At every stage of their learning process, peers negotiate within their ZPD, and they are likely to develop proper and/or more sophisticated expressions that are currently beyond their actual developmental level, but within their potential developmental level (Nassaji & Cumming, 2000). These better or more advanced expressions developed in collaboration will eventually be mastered by language learners and used in their subsequent language production. During this process, the target language is used not only to convey meanings, but also to develop meanings. The language itself is developing as well.

APPLICATION AND RESEARCH EVIDENCE

Little research has examined on the application of the cognitive constructivism in second language acquisition. The reason perhaps is that language acquisition is viewed more as a result of social interaction and therefore researchers have tended to apply more social constructivism. As noted earlier, social-constructivist theory views knowledge as socially accepted belief (Bruffee, 1986; Nassaji & Wells, 2000; Vygotsky, 1978, 1981a; Wertsch, 1985). In terms of language development, the theory posits that peer interaction plays an important role in the development individuals' linguistic knowledge. Thus, one of the areas in which this theory has been very influencing is in understanding the role of collaborative learning.

Collaborative learning is a vast area with many branches and studies in each. Due to the limitation of scope, we focus on studies in two areas: learning involving oral output (collaborative dialogue) and written output (collaborative writing).

Collaborative Dialogue

The importance of the role of oral interaction in L2 learning, as well as opportunities for collaborative negotiation has been emphasised in L2 learning. As noted before, according to this view, higher-order mental activities are all socially mediated operations. This mediation takes place through the use of various forms of physical and symbolic tools and artefacts, which allow us to establish a connection between ourselves and the world around us. In this view, an important tool of mediation is social interaction. An example of collaborative learning is collaborative output.

Collaborative output refers to activities that are designed to push learners to produce language collaboratively and also reflect on and negotiate the accuracy of their language production. Such activities are beneficial to L2 learners because when output is produced collaboratively, learners are not only pushed to use the target structure, but they will also get help from their peers when trying to make their meaning precise (Kowal & Swain, 1994; Swain & Lapkin, 2002; Swain, 2005). Swain and Lapkin (2002) noted that through collaborative negotiation, not only meaning is co-constructed but the language itself is developed as well. Swain further argued that such co-construction of language "allows performance to outstrip competence; it's where language use and language learning can co-occur" (Swain, 1997, p. 115).

There are a variety of collaborative output tasks for L2 classrooms that elicit output and also promote discussion about language forms (see Nassaji & Fotos, 2010; Nassaji, 2015). One such task that has received much attention in current research is the dictogloss (Wajnryb, 1990). A dictogloss is a kind of collaborative task that encourages learners to work together to reconstruct a text after it is presented to them orally (Wajnryb, 1990). In this task, the teacher reads a short text at a normal pace twice and asks the students to work in small groups (usually groups of two) and reproduce the text as close as possible to the original text. When the text is read the first time, students are asked to listen and try to comprehend the meaning of the texts. The second time, they will be asked to take notes by jotting down key words and concepts that they think will help them to reconstruct the text. Then they work together and use their resources to reconstruct the text as close as possible to the initial version. The text for the dictogloss can be an authentic text or a text the teacher constructs. It would be very helpful if the text that is chosen for dictogloss contains several instances of a particular grammatical form the task is going to focus on. Suppose that you as the teacher intent to teach or practice the use of relative clauses, you may choose a text in which this structure has occurred several times.

The aim of a dictogloss task is not only to push learners to produce output collaboratively, but also to promote negotiation of form and meaning. According to

Wajnryb (1990), there are a number of advantages for dictogloss. The first is that it promotes verbal interaction in a realistic communicative context. To complete the dictogloss, learners need to communicate with each other and help each other to reconstruct the passage. The second advantage is that it raises consciousness of a specific aspect of language use. In a dictogloss participants need to reconstruct the text as accurately as possible. To do this requires them to be engaged in extensive discussion about the lexical and grammatical forms. Since the dictogloss is a collaborative task, it encourages learners to pool their knowledge together and thus learn from each other. Because it is an output task, it enables learners to find out what they know and what they don't know. In other words, "the learners' own language indicates as awareness of something about their own, or their interlocutor's use of language" (Swain, 1998, p. 68). Swain and Lapkin (1995) suggested that output prompts learners to become conscious of their linguistics problems, and hence brings "to their attention something they need to discover about their L2" (p. 373). The discussion part of the dictogloss also encourages learners to reflect on their own language output.

Collaborative output tasks can also be designed in the form of jigsaw tasks. Jigsaw tasks are a kind of two-way information gap task in which students hold different portions of the information related to a task. Students should then share and exchange the different pieces of information to complete the task. According to Pica, Kanagy, and Falodun (1993), for a jigsaw task to be effective, it should have the following characteristics: it should be goal oriented and it should generate negotiation of meaning. For a jigsaw task to be an effective output task, it should also be able to push learners to reproduce a particular linguistic target embedded in the tasks. Jigsaw tasks are often designed in the form of segmented texts which students have to put together to create the original text. Students working in pairs will receive two versions of the text. The two versions can be prepared differently from the original passage. They either contain sentences which are the same as the ones in the original passage or differ from it, but a form with low salience in the original passage appears in a different form or order in the students' versions. The students then discuss their versions as they attempt to choose the accurate form and the target items.

A number of studies have investigated the use and effectiveness of dictogloss and jigsaw tasks and have shown positive effects of such tasks on promoting attention to form and L2 development. Kowal and Swain (1994), for example, examined whether collaborative negotiation tasks such as dictogloss can promote learners' language awareness. They collected data from intermediate and advanced learners of French who worked collaboratively to reconstruct a reading text. Their results showed that when students worked together to reconstruct the text, they noticed gaps in their language knowledge, their attention was drawn to the link between form and meaning, and they obtained feedback from their peers. Swain and Lapkin (2001) compared the effects of dictogloss with jigsaw tasks with two groups of French immersion students. The focus was on how co-construction of meaning collaboratively while doing the tasks promoted noticing aspects of the target language grammar. The researchers did not find any significant differences between the two types of tasks in terms of the overall degree of attention to form they generated, but they did find that the dictogloss led to more accurate reproduction of target forms than the jigsaw task. LaPierre (1994) studied the use of the dictogloss in Grade 8 French immersion classrooms. She also found a positive relationship between the linguistic forms that were correctly supplied during dictogloss interaction and learners' subsequent production of those forms. Nabei (1996) conducted a similar study with four adult ESL learners and found similar results. She found many instances where the activity promoted opportunities for attention to form, scaffolding, and corrective feedback. Pica, Kang, and Sauro (2006) investigated the effectiveness of jigsaw tasks with six pairs of intermediate-level English L2 learners. Their results showed evidence for the effectiveness of such tasks for drawing learners' attention to form and also for helping learners to recall the form and functions of target items. In a recent classroom-based study, Nassaji and Tian (2010) examined the effectiveness of a reconstruction cloze task and a reconstruction editing task for learning English phrasal verbs. Their results showed that completing the tasks collaboratively led to a greater accuracy of task completion than completing them individually. However, collaborative tasks did not lead to significantly greater gains of vocabulary knowledge. There are also other studies that have examined and provided evidence for the role of collaborative negotiation in L2 learning (e.g., García Mayo, 2002; Leeser, 2004; Nassaji, 2010, 2011; Storch, 1997, 2007). These studies have also shown beneficial effects for output tasks to create opportunities of focus on grammar as well as social interaction.

Collaborative Writing

Collaborative writing is a relatively new writing approach in language classes and is gaining interest among L2 instructors and researchers alike (Nixon, 2007) because it invites students to collaborate and discuss writing throughout the whole process of writing. In addition, unlike peer review, where students provide feedback on each other's drafts and only one student – the writer – has the ownership of the text, collaborative writing activities make both students responsible for the text they co-produce.

To explore and understand the effect of these processes, L2 researchers have often utilised one form of a constructivist theory such as the sociocultural theory. Studies in this area have usually investigated the roles of individual writing and collaborative writing (Storch, 1999, 2005; Nixon, 2007). Using a sociocultural theory to L2 collaborative writing, Storch (1999), for example, investigated the effect of collaboration on grammatical accuracy when eleven intermediate to advanced ESL students completed three tasks (a cloze task, a text-reconstruction task, and a short composition task) individually and collaboratively. It was found that students produced more grammatically accurate, but shorter and less complex, writings when working collaboratively than when working individually.

Storch (2005) compared collaborative and individual writing when 23 ESL students, nine pairs and five individuals, wrote a short paragraph. It was found that the collaborative writing products were shorter than individual writing products, but better in terms of task fulfilment, grammatical accuracy, and complexity. However, the differences were not statistically significant. The analysis of the verbal interactions of the 18 students working collaboratively showed that students spent most time on the writing phase rather than on the planning or revising phases, and more time in generating ideas, and engaging in language-related episodes (LREs) than in discussing structure or interpreting the graph. In the follow-up interviews, 16 of the 18 students had a positive attitude towards collaborative writing. Students favoured collaborative writing because it provided them with an opportunity to learn different ideas, different ways to express their ideas, and opportunities to improve their accuracy and vocabulary. Some students also described collaborative writing as a fun activity. However, some students expressed concerns that they, as language learners themselves, were not linguistically competent, that criticizing their partner could result in hurt feelings, and that writing was supposed to be individual.

Nixon (2007) investigated the quality of writing among 24 advanced Thai EFL students who completed one argumentative essay collaboratively and another one independently. The tasks and the writing conditions were counterbalanced. Similar to the findings in Storch (2005), no statistical difference was found between the collaborative writing and individual tasks. Nixon attributed this finding to the restricted time given to the collaborative condition. Students' interactions were segmented into LREs, including lexis, grammar and mechanics, and OREs (organizational related episodes), including paragraphs and rhetorical structure. It was found that LREs had the potential for scaffolding and that most of the LREs were initiated by explanation/confirmation requests and suggestions.

Storch (2002) investigated dynamic patterns of pair work when ten pairs of intermediate ESL students were involved in three tasks (a short composition, an editing task, and a text reconstruction task) in a 13-week longitudinal study. The analysis of the interactions found four patterns representing the role relationships of the students: collaborative, dominant/dominant, dominant/passive, and expert/ novice. The findings also showed that the collaborative pattern predominated in the data and that the different patterns remained stable regardless of the task or passage of time. When the relationship between dyadic patterns and L2 development was analysed based on the three writing tasks students completed together and an individual writing at the end of study, the findings suggested that the collaborative pairs showed more evidence of language development than the non-collaborative pairs. However, instances of transfer of incorrect knowledge were also identified.

Finally, in a recent study, Tian (2011) investigated the effects of peer review and collaborative writing on writing in Chinese-as-a-foreign language. Three writing conditions (peer review, collaborative writing, and individual writing) and three narrative writings plus questionnaires, videorecorded screen activities, and videorecorded interactions were used. Students' writing performance was examined with regard to fluency, complexity, and accuracy; their interaction content in the revision stage of the two collaborative writing activities (peer review and co-writing) and their perceptions of all three writing activities were also investigated. The research found no statistically significant differences in measures of fluency and complexity. However, peer review and collaborative writing resulted in significantly more accurate writing than individual writing. The analysis of students' verbal interactions in the two collaborative activities indicated significantly more on-task episodes and also significantly more language- and content-related episodes in peer review than in collaborative writing while significantly more idea-related episodes and text-reading episodes in collaborative writing than in peer review. Concerning students' perceptions, although there was a tendency that students preferred co-writing to peer review and peer review to individual writing, in general they held competing attitudes toward the three activities and believed each of the three had their own strengths. Overall, the findings of this study suggest that collaborative and individual writings each has their own merits in the development of L2 writing skills.

Overall, the limited research on collaborative writing calls for additional studies to further investigate this field. Additional studies should also consider different writing genres, different language proficiency levels, and different target languages. In Storch's studies, students were asked to write a short paragraph commentary of writing or of a graph report, and in Nixon's study, students worked on argumentative essays. In all studies on collaborative writing, students were at an intermediate or higher language proficiency level. Thus, it is necessary to look into how low-intermediate students interact when they work on less cognitively challenging tasks, such as writing a picture narrative (Tian, 2011). Moreover, Storch's studies were conducted in an ESL setting and Nixon's in an EFL setting. More research is needed to look into writing in languages other than English.

CONCLUSION

In this chapter, we have discussed the notion of constructivism and its application to second language learning. We discussed two types of constructivism: cognitive and social. Cognitive constructivism emphasizes that learning takes place through individual discovery of new information and reflection. Social constructivism emphasizes the role of social and collaborative interaction. When it comes to language learning, these theories suggest the need for creating opportunities for collaborative learning, reflection and social interaction. Therefore, we also discussed how such opportunities can be created in L2 classroom. Collaborative learning is a vast topic. Due to the limitation of scope, we focused on two lines of research in this area: oral collaborative output and collaborative writing. In each area, we examined a number of studies highlighting the importance of social interaction and the importance of the application of social constructivism in understanding their role in second language development.

REFERENCES

Aljaafreh, A., & Lantolf, J. (1994). Negative feedback as regulation and second language learning in the zone of proximal development. *Modern Language Journal, 78*, 465–83.

Appel, G., & Lantolf, J. (1994). Speaking as mediation: A study of L1 and L2 text recall tasks. *Modern Language Journal, 78*, 437–52.

Bruffee, K. A. (1984). Social construction, language, and the authority of knowledge: A bibliographical essay. *College English, 48*, 773–790.

De Guerrero, M. C. M., & Villamil, O. S. (1994). Social-cognitive dimensions of interaction in L2 peer revision. *The Modern Language Journal, 78*, 484–496.

De Guerrero, M. C. M., & Villamil, O. S. (2000). Activating the ZPD: Mutual scaffolding in L2 peer revision. *The Modern Language Journal, 84*, 51–68.

Donato, R. (1994). Collective scaffolding in second language learning. In J. P. Lantolf & A. Gabriela (Eds.), *Vygotskian approaches to second language research* (pp. 33–59). Norwood, NJ: Ablex.

García Mayo, M. P. (2002). The effectiveness of two form-focused tasks in advanced EFL pedagogy. *International Journal of Applied Linguistics, 12*, 156–75.

Grabe, W., & Kaplan, R. B. (1996). *Theory and practice of writing.* New York, NY: Addison Wesley Longmans Ltd.

Kowal, M., & Swain, M. (1994). Using collaborative language production tasks to promote students' language awareness. *Language Awareness, 3*, 73–93.

Lantolf, J. P. (2000). *Sociocultural theory and second language learning.* Oxford: Oxford University Press.

Lantolf, J. P., & Appel, G. (Eds.). (1994). *Vygotskian approaches to second language research.* Norwood, NJ: Ablex.

LaPierre, D. (1994). *Language output in a cooperative learning setting: Determining its effects on second language learning* (Unpublished MA thesis). University of Toronto, Toronto, ON, Canada.

Lapkin, S., Swain, M., & Smith, M. (2002). Reformulation and the learning of French pronominal verbs in a Canadian French immersion context. *Modern Language Journal, 86*, 485–507.

Leeser, M. (2004). Learning proficienty and focus on form during collaborative dialogue. *Langauge Teaching Research, 8*, 55–81.

Lightbown, P. M., & Spada, N. (2006). *How languages are learned.* London: Oxford University Press.

Moll, L. C. (1989). Teaching second language students: A Vygotskian perspective. In D. M. Johnson, & D. H. Roen (Eds.), *Richness in writing: Empowering ESL students* (pp. 55–69). White Plains, NY: Longman.

Nabei, T. (1996). Dictogloss: Is it an effective language learning task? *Working papers in Educational Linguistics, 12*, 59–74.

Nassaji, H. (2007). Reactive focus on form through negotiation on learners' written errors. In S. Fotos & H. Nassaji (Eds.), *Form focused instruction and teacher education: Studies in honour of rod ellis* (pp. 117–129). Oxford: Oxford University Press.

Nassaji, H. (2011). Correcting students' written grammatical errors: The effects of negotiated versus nonnegotiated feedback. *Studies in Second Language Learning and Teaching, 1*, 315–334.

Nassaji, H. (2015). *Interactional feedback dimension in instructed second language learning.* London: Bloomsbury Publishing.

Nassaji, H., & Cumming, A. (2000). What's in a ZPD? A case study of a young ESL student and teacher interacting through dialogue journals. *Language Teaching Research, 4*, 95–121.

Nassaji, H., & Fotos, S. (2010). *Teaching grammar in second language classrooms: Integrating form-focused instruction in communicative context.* London: Routledge.

Nassaji, H., & Swain, M. (2000). A Vygotskian perspective on corrective feedback in L2: The effect of random versus negotiated help on the learning of English articles. *Language Awareness, 9*, 34–51.

Nassaji, H., & Tian, J. (2010). Collaborative and individual output tasks and their effects on learning English phrasal verbs. *Language Teaching Research, 14*, 397–419.

Nassaji, H., & Wells, G. (2000). What's the use of 'triadic dialogue'?: An investigation of teacher-student interaction. *Applied Linguistics, 21*, 376–406.

Nixon, R. M. (2007). *Collaborative and independent writing among adult Thai EFL learners: Verbal interactions, compositions, and attitudes* (Unpublished PhD dissertation). University of Toronto, Toronto, ON, Canada.

Nyikos, M., & Hashimoto, R. (1997). Constructivist theory applied to collaboration: In search of ZPD. *Modern Language Journal, 81*, 506–517.

Ohta, A. S. (2001). *Second language acquisition processes in the classroom: Learning Japanese.* Mahwah, NJ: Lawrence Erlbaum.

Oxford, R. L. (1997). Cooperative learning, collaborative learning, and interaction: Three communicative stands in the language classroom. *The Modern Language Journal, 81*, 443–456.

Piaget, J. (1954). *The principles of genetic epistemology.* New York, NY: Basic Books.

Piaget, J. (1955). *The language and thought of the child.* New York, NY: Meridian.

Piaget, J. (1970). *The science of education and the psychology of the child.* New York, NY: Basic Books.

Pica, T., Kanagy, R., & Falodun, J. (1993). Choosing and using communication tasks for second language instruction. In G. Crookes & S. Gass (Eds.), *Tasks and language learning: Integrating theory and practice* (pp. 9–34). Clevedon: Multilingual Matters.

Pica, T., Kang, H., & Sauro, S. (2006). Information gap tasks: Their multiple roles and contrbutions to interaction research methodology. *Studies in Second Language Acquisition, 28*, 301–38.

Russell, D. R. (1993). Vygotsky, Dewey, and externalism: Beyond the student/discipline dichotomy. *Journal of Advanced Composition, 13*, 173–197.

Slavin, R. (2003). *Educational psychology: Theory and practice.* Boston, MA: Allyn and Bacon.

Storch, N. (1997). The editing talk of adult ESL learners. *Language Awareness, 6*, 221–32.

Storch, N. (1998). A classroom-based study: Insights from a collaborative text reconstruction task. *ELT Journal, 52*, 291–300.

Storch, N. (1999). Are two heads better than one? Pair work and grammatical accuracy. *System, 27*, 363–374.

Storch, N. (2001). How collaborative is pair work? ESL tertiary students composing in pairs. *Language Teaching Research, 5*, 29–53.

Storch, N. (2002). Patterns of interaction in ESL pair work. *Language Learning, 52*, 119–158.

Storch, N. (2005). Collaborative writing: Product, process and students' reflections. *Journal of Second Language Writing, 14*, 153–173.

Storch, N. (2007). Investigating the merits of pair work on a text editing task in ESL classes. *Language Teaching Research, 2*, 143–59.

Swain, M. (1997). The output hypothesis, focus on form, and second language learning. In V. Berry, B. Adamson, & W. T. Littlewood (Eds.), *Applying linguistics* (pp. 107–122). Hong Kong: English Language Centre, University of Hong Kong.

Swain, M. (1998). Focus on form through conscious reflection. In C. Doughty & J. Williams (Eds.), *Focus on form in classroom second language acquisition* (pp. 64–81). Cambridge: Cambridge University Press.

Swain, M. (2005). The output hypothesis: Theory and research. In E. Hinkel (Ed.), *Handbook on research in second language teaching and learning* (pp. 471–83). Mahwah, NJ: Lawrence Erlbaum Associates.

Swain, M., & Lapkin, S. (1995). Problems in output and the cognitive processes they generate: A step towards second language learning. *Applied Linguistics, 16*, 371–91.

Swain, M., & Lapkin, S. (1998). Interaction and second language learning: Two adolescent French immersion students working together. *Modern Language Journal, 82*, 320–337.

Swain, M., & Lapkin, S. (2001). Focus on form through collaborative dialogue: Exploring task effects. In M. Bygate, P. Skehan, & M. Swain (Eds.), *Researching pedagogic tasks: Second language learning, teaching and testing* (pp. 99–118). Harlow: Longman.

Swain, M., & Lapkin, S. (2002). Talking it through: Two French immersion learners' response to reformulation. *International Journal of Educational Research, 37*, 285–304.

Tian, J. (2011). *The effects of peer editing versus co-writing on writing in Chinese-as-a-foreign language* (Unpublished PhD dissertation). University of Victoria, Victoria, BC, Canada.

Villamil, O. S., & De Guerrero, M. C. M. (1996). Peer revision in the L2 classroom: Social-cognitive activities, mediating strategies, and aspects of social behavior. *Journal of Second Language Writing, 5*, 51–75.

Villamil, O. S., & De Guerrero, M. C. M. (1998). Assessing the impact of peer revision on L2 writing. *Applied Linguistics, 19,* 491–514.

Vygotsky, L. S. (1978). *Mind in society: The development of higher psychological processes.* Cambridge, MA: Harvard University Press.

Vygotsky, L. S. (1981a). The genesis of higher mental functions. In J. V. Wertsch (Ed.), *The concept of activity in soviet psychology.* Armonk, NY: M. E. Sharpe.

Vygotsky, L. S. (1981b). The instrumental method in psychology In J. V. Wertsch (Ed.), *The concept of activity in soviet psychology.* Armonk, NY: M. E. Sharpe.

Wajnryb, R. (1990). *Grammar dictation.* Oxford: Oxford University Press.

Wertsch, J. V. (1985). *Vygotsky and the social formation of mind.* Cambridge, MA: Harvard University Press.

Hossein Nassaji
University of Victoria
Canada

Jun Tian
University of Victoria
Canada

MICHAEL R. W. DAWSON

4. CONNECTIONISM

INTRODUCTION

Classical cognitive science assumes that cognition in general, and language processing in particular, involves the rule-governed manipulation of symbols (Chomsky, 1966; Fodor, 1975; Pylyshyn, 1984; von Neumann, 1958). Philosophically, classical cognitive science is closely aligned with nativism (Descartes, 1637/1960); practically, it is inspired by the operations of the digital computer which has for decades demonstrated how digital information processing can be used to model a variety of cognitive phenomena (Feigenbaum & Feldman, 1995; Newell & Simon, 1972).

Classical cognitive science has a long history of successes, and is the dominant school of thought in modern cognitive science (Dawson, 2013). However, it also has a long history of both theoretical and practical criticisms (Dreyfus, 1972, 1992). One consequence of these criticisms is that very different conceptions of cognition have also arisen to compete with classical cognitive science. One of these is connectionism (Aizawa, 1992; Bechtel & Abrahamsen, 2002; Dawson, 2004; Medler, 1998). The purpose of this chapter is to introduce some of the basic properties of connectionist cognitive science.

NEURAL INSPIRATION

Classical cognitive science is inspired by the operations of the digital computer, but classical cognitive science is inspired by a different information processor: the human brain. While electronic computers use a small number of fast components, the brain consists of a large number of very slow components (i.e. neurons). As a result, the brain must be a parallel processing device that "will tend to pick up as many logical (or informational) items as possible simultaneously, and process them simultaneously" (von Neumann, 1958, p. 51).

The basic medium of connectionism is a type of model called an artificial neural network, or a parallel distributed processing (PDP) network (McClelland & Rumelhart, 1986; Rumelhart & McClelland, 1986). Artificial neural networks consist of a number of simple processors that perform basic calculations and communicate the results to other processors by sending signals through weighted connections. The processors operate in parallel, permitting fast computing even when the

© KONINKLIJKE BRILL NV, LEIDEN, 2018 | DOI:10.1163/9789004380882_004

components involved are slow. Networks exploit implicit, distributed, and redundant representations. As a result, the behavior of artificial neural networks degrades gracefully when presented noisy inputs, and such models are damage resistant. These advantages accrue because artificial neural networks are intentionally biologically plausible or neuronally inspired.

Classical cognitive science develops models that are purely symbolic, and which can be described as asserting propositions or performing logic. In contrast, connectionist cognitive science develops models that are subsymbolic (Smolensky, 1988), and which can be described as statistical pattern recognizers. Networks use representations (Dawson, 2004; Horgan & Tienson, 1996), but these representations do not have the syntactic structure of those found in classical models (Waskan & Bechtel, 1997). Let us take a moment to describe in a bit more detail the basic properties of artificial neural networks.

ELEMENTS OF ARTIFICIAL NEURAL NETWORKS

An artificial neural network is a computer simulation of a 'brain-like' system of interconnected processing units. In general, such a network can be viewed as a multiple-layer system that generates a desired response to an input stimulus. A network's stimulus or input pattern is provided by the environment, and is encoded as a pattern of activity (i.e. a vector of numbers) in a set of input units. The response of the system, its output pattern, is represented as a pattern of activity in the network's output units. In modern connectionism, there will be one or more intervening layers of processors in the network, called hidden units. Hidden units detect higher-order features in the input pattern that allow the network to make a correct or appropriate response for a complex information processing problem.

The behavior of a processor in an artificial neural network, which is analogous to a neuron, can be characterized as follows: First, the processor computes the total signal (its net input) being sent to it by other processors in the network. Second, the unit uses an activation function to convert its net input into internal activity (usually a continuous number between 0 and 1) on the basis of this computed signal. Third, the unit converts its internal activity into an output signal, and sends this signal on to other processors. A network uses parallel processing because many, if not all, of its processing units will perform their operations simultaneously.

The signal sent by one processor to another is a number that is transmitted through a weighted connection, which is analogous to a synapse. The connection serves as a communication channel that amplifies or attenuates signals being sent through it, because these signals are multiplied by the weight associated with the connection. The weight is a number that defines the nature and strength of the connection. For example, inhibitory connections have negative weights, and excitatory connections have positive weights. Strong connections have strong weights (i.e., the absolute value of the weight is large), while weak connections have near-zero weights.

LEARNING AND NEURAL NETWORKS

The pattern of connectivity in a PDP network (i.e., the network's entire set of connection weights) defines how signals flow between the processors. As a result, a network's connection weights are analogous to a program in a conventional computer (Smolensky, 1988). However, a network's 'program' is not of the same type that defines a classical model. Networks do not employ either explicit symbols or rules. Instead, a network's program is a set of causal or associative links from signaling processors to receiving processors. The activity that is produced in the receiving units is literally caused by having an input pattern of activity modulated by an array of connection weights between units. In this sense, connectionist models seem markedly associationist in nature (Bechtel, 1985).

How does one assign connection weights to a network? While classical cognitive science is philosophically linked to Cartesian nativism, connectionist cognitive science is philosophically inspired by British empiricism (Locke, 1706/1977). As a result, connectionists assume that a network's connection weights are determined by what it experiences. The connection weights of a network are not innate; instead, they are learned.

In some systems, called self-organizing networks, unsupervised learning is used to determine connection weights (Carpenter & Grossberg, 1992; Grossberg, 1980, 1987, 1988; Kohonen, 1977, 1984). With unsupervised learning, networks are only provided input patterns, and are not provided any feedback about how they are to respond. This is analogous to what is called text learning by researchers who study language acquisition (Gold, 1967; Pinker, 1979). In unsupervised learning, each presented pattern causes activity in output units; this activity is often further refined by a winner-take-all competition in which one output unit wins the competition to be paired with the current input pattern. Once the output unit is selected via internal network dynamics, its connection weights (and possibly the weights of neighboring output units) are updated via a learning rule. As a result, unsupervised learning causes these networks to organize their weights in such a way that they reflect statistical regularities in the input patterns.

It is much more typical in cognitive science to teach networks to respond using a method called supervised learning, which is analogous to informant learning in the language acquisition literature (Gold, 1967; Pinker, 1979). Supervised learning is used to train a network to generate a desired response to every stimulus pattern in a training set. During supervised learning a network is presented an input pattern, and produces a response to it. The response of the network is compared to the desired response, usually by calculating the amount of error associated with each output unit. Error provides feedback to the network about its performance. This feedback is used to modify weights in such a way that the next time this pattern is presented to the network, the amount of error that it produces will be smaller.

A variety of learning rules, including the delta rule (Rosenblatt, 1958, 1962; Stone, 1986; Widrow, 1962; Widrow & Hoff, 1960) and the generalized delta rule

(Rumelhart, Hinton, & Williams, 1986), are supervised learning rules that work by correcting network mistakes. Each of these learning rules requires the construction of a training set, which is a collection of input patterns to present a network, as well as the desired output pattern for the network to generate to each input pattern. Supervised learning proceeds with the repeated presentation of individual stimuli in the training set. After each presentation, network errors are computed and are then used to modify connection weights. Ideally, learning from enough presentations of a training set will reduce the amount of error produced to an acceptable level, and it can then be said that the network has learned the desired input-output mapping.

WHAT CAN NETWORKS LEARN TO DO?

Supervised learning is used to train networks to generate desired responses to a set of input patterns. What kinds of responses can artificial neural networks learn to generate?

Artificial neural networks are most typically trained to perform pattern recognition (Pao, 1989; Ripley, 1996). Pattern recognition involves assigning each input pattern to a discrete category (Harnad, 1987). Artificial neural networks categorize patterns by generating output unit responses that can be interpreted as being "on" or "off". In other words, a network's output units are trained to generate a binary response to each input; the set of binary responses is the digital 'name' of the class to which the input pattern has been assigned. In the domain of language, networks that have been trained to 'read aloud' by mapping an orthographic representation of words into a phonological representation of how they should be pronounced (Plaut, McClelland, Seidenberg, & Patterson, 1996; Sejnowski & Rosenberg, 1988) provide interesting examples of pattern recognition.

A pattern recognition system that is capable of generating any pattern recognition mapping is exceptionally powerful, and is called an arbitrary pattern classifier. A modern connectionist network that has only two layers of hidden units between its input and output units has been proven to be an arbitrary pattern classifier (Lippmann, 1987, 1989). In other words, modern artificial neural networks have the power to solve any pattern recognition problem!

The activation functions of modern artificial neural networks are usually continuous. Therefore, they can be used to generate analog responses; they are not required to be trained to generate digital 'on' or 'off' responses (as is the case for pattern recognition). If one applies an analog interpretation to output unit activity, then networks can learn to perform a second kind of input-output mapping task, function approximation. In function approximation, the input units represent the values of variables passed into a function (i.e. the values of the set $x_1, x_2, x_3, ...x_N$). The output is a single (analog) value y that is the result of computing some function of those variables (i.e. $y = f(x_1, x_2, x_3, ...x_N)$). Many artificial neural networks have been trained to approximate functions (Girosi & Poggio, 1990; Hartman, Keeler, & Kowalski, 1989; Moody & Darken, 1989; Poggio & Girosi, 1990; Renals, 1989).

For instance, network responses can be interpreted as representing the probability that a pattern belongs to a class, or the likelihood of reward if a particular behavioral choice is made (Dawson, Dupuis, Spetch, & Kelly, 2009; Dawson, Kelly, Spetch, & Dupuis, 2010).

The most powerful system for approximating functions is called a universal function approximator. Consider taking any continuous function, and examining a region of this function from a particular starting point (one set of input values) to a particular ending point (a different set of input values). A universal function approximator is capable of approximating the shape of the function between these bounds to an arbitrary degree of accuracy. A number of proofs have shown that a modern artificial neural network with only a single layer of hidden units between its input and output units is capable of universal function approximation (Cotter, 1990; Cybenko, 1989; Funahashi, 1989; Hartman et al., 1989; Hornik, Stinchcombe, & White, 1989). "If we have the right connections from the input units to a large enough set of hidden units, we can always find a representation that will perform any mapping from input to output" (Rumelhart, Hinton, & Williams, 1986a, p. 319).

HOW CAN NETWORKS CONTRIBUTE TO COGNITIVE SCIENCE?

The previous section indicates that artificial neural networks are extremely powerful models, powerful enough to rival the theories of classical cognitive science. Not surprisingly, one can find connectionist models in every research domain that has also been explored by classical cognitive scientists. Even critics of connectionism admit that "the study of connectionist machines has led to a number of striking and unanticipated findings; it's surprising how much computing can be done with a uniform network of simple interconnected elements" (Fodor & Pylyshyn, 1988, p. 6).

That connectionist models can produce unanticipated results is a direct result of their empiricist nature. Unlike their classical counterparts, connectionist researchers do not require a fully specified theory of how a task is accomplished before modelling begins (Hillis, 1988). Instead, they can let a learning rule discover how to mediate a desired input-output mapping. Connectionist learning rules serve as powerful methods for developing new algorithms of interest to cognitive science. Hillis (1988, p. 176) has noted that artificial neural networks allow "for the possibility of constructing intelligence without first understanding it".

However, one problem with connectionist cognitive science is that the algorithms that learning rules discover are extremely difficult to retrieve from inside a trained network (Dawson, 1998, 2004, 2009; Dawson & Shamanski, 1994; McCloskey, 1991; Mozer & Smolensky, 1989; Seidenberg, 1993). This is because these algorithms involve distributed, parallel interactions amongst highly nonlinear elements. "One thing that connectionist networks have in common with brains is that if you open them up and peer inside, all you can see is a big pile of goo" (Mozer & Smolensky, 1989, p. 3).

In the early days of modern connectionist cognitive science, this was not a concern. This was a period of what has been called "gee whiz" connectionism (Dawson, 2009), in which connectionists modelled phenomena that were typically described in terms of rule-governed symbol manipulation. In the mid-1980s it was sufficiently interesting to show that such phenomena might be accounted for by parallel distributed processing systems that did not propose explicit rules or symbols. However, as connectionism matured, it was necessary for its researchers to spell out the details of the alternative algorithms embodied in their networks (Dawson, 2004). If these algorithms could not be extracted from networks, then "connectionist networks should not be viewed as theories of human cognitive functions, or as simulations of theories, or even as demonstrations of specific theoretical points" (McCloskey, 1991, p. 387). In response to such criticisms, connectionist cognitive scientists have developed a number of techniques for recovering algorithms from their networks (Berkeley, Dawson, Medler, Schopflocher, & Hornsby, 1995; Dawson, 2004, 2005; Gallant, 1993; Hanson & Burr, 1990; Hinton, 1986; Moorhead, Haig, & Clement, 1989; Omlin & Giles, 1996). Modern connectionists contribute to cognitive science by training networks to perform some task of interest, and then by analyzing the internal structure of a trained network in order to discover new approaches to solving cognitive problems (Dawson, 2013).

IS CONNECTIONISM BEHAVIORISM?

When cognitive psychology arose in the 1950s, it did so as a reaction against psychological behaviorism (Miller, 2003). The study of language was a key area in which this reaction was evident. It was argued that behaviorist theories of language (Skinner, 1957) were simply not powerful enough to capture the recursive, clausal structure of natural human language (Chomsky, 1959b). In computer science, a formal description of any class of languages (human or otherwise) relates its complexity to the complexity of a computing device that could process it (Hopcroft & Ullman, 1979; Révész, 1983). This has resulted in a classification of grammars known as the Chomsky hierarchy (Chomsky, 1959a). In the Chomsky hierarchy, the simplest grammars can be accommodated by simple devices called finite state automata. The most complex grammars used to describe human language can only be dealt with by the most powerful class of information processor, a universal machine like the universal Turing machine. With respect to the language debate between behaviorism and cognitivism, it was long ago proven that standard behaviorist or associationist theories only have the power of finite state automata, were unable to deal with the recursive structure of natural language, and therefore were inadequate when compared to cognitivist theories that appealed to universal machines (Bever, Fodor, & Garrett, 1968).

If an artificial neural network is merely a system that is trained to generate desired responses to various stimuli, then is it not merely a behaviorist model that is likely of little interest to modern cognitive science? Clearly some artificial neural networks are decidedly behaviorist in nature. For instance, the perceptron is a simple network that has input and output units, but has no hidden units at all (Rosenblatt, 1958, 1962). As a result, there are many input-output mappings that perceptrons are simply not powerful enough to learn (Minsky & Papert, 1969). Perceptrons can model many interesting phenomena in the animal learning literature (Dawson, 2008). However, a perceptron is certainly not powerful enough to deal with the recursive structure of human language!

Modern classical arguments against connectionist cognitive science (Fodor & Pylyshyn, 1988) cover much of the same ground as arguments against behaviorist and associationist accounts of language. That is, classical cognitive scientists argue that artificial neural networks do not have the computational power to capture the recursive regularities in human language.

What these arguments fail to recognize, though, is that modern artificial neural networks that use hidden units – called multilayered perceptrons – are far more powerful than the simple perceptrons of the 1950s. We saw earlier that multilayered networks have the power to be arbitrary pattern classifiers or to be universal function approximators, which suggests that they too belong to the class 'universal machine', the same class of models that serves as the foundation to classical cognitive science (Newell, 1980).

That multilayer perceptrons have the same computational power as a universal Turing machine was established long ago (McCulloch & Pitts, 1943). McCulloch and Pitts proved that a network of McCulloch-Pitts neurons could be used to build the machine head of a universal Turing machine; universal power was then achieved by providing this system an external memory. "To psychology, however defined, specification of the net would contribute all that could be achieved in that field" (McCulloch & Pitts, 1943, p. 131). More modern results have used the analog nature of modern processors to internalize the memory, indicating that an artificial neural network can simulate the entire Turing machine (Siegelmann, 1999; Siegelmann & Sontag, 1991, 1995).

In short, artificial neural networks may seem as though they are simply behaviorist devices. However, it has been established that modern multilayer perceptrons belong to the class of universal machines, and are therefore powerful enough to of interest to the study of cognition in general, and to the study of language in particular.

FURTHER READING

The goal of this chapter has simply been to introduce some of the elements of connectionism. Not surprisingly, a more technical grasp of this approach to modeling cognition and language requires a great deal more reading. Fortunately, a variety of books are available to provide a more detailed introduction to artificial neural networks; many of these works also provide software to be used to explore connectionism (Anderson, 1995; Bechtel & Abrahamsen, 2002; Dawson, 2004, 2005; Enquist & Ghirlanda, 2005; Freeman, 1994; Gluck & Myers, 2001;

McClelland & Rumelhart, 1988; Quinlan, 1991; Ripley, 1996). There are also collections of historically important papers, as well as more historical perspectives on the rise of connectionism in cognitive science (Anderson, Pellionisz, & Rosenfeld, 1990; Anderson & Rosenfeld, 1988, 1998). A reader would also do well to explore the seminal books that launched the modern connectionist revolution (Hinton & Anderson, 1981; McClelland & Rumelhart, 1986; Rumelhart & McClelland, 1986). Readers interested in the use of connectionism in the study of language also have some interesting resources available to them (Daniloff, 2002; Dijkstra & Smedt, 1996; Levy, 1995; Mammone, 1993; Pinker & Mehler, 1988; Selouani, 2011; Sharkey, 1992; Touretzky, 1991; Ward, 1994).

REFERENCES

Aizawa, K. (1992). Connectionism and artificial intelligence: History and philosphical interpretation. *Jornal of Experimental and Theoretical Artificial Intelligence, 4*, 295–313.

Anderson, J. A. (1995). *An introduction to neural networks.* Cambridge, MA: MIT Press.

Anderson, J. A., Pellionisz, A., & Rosenfeld, E. (1990). *Neurocomputing 2: Directions for research.* Cambridge, MA: MIT Press.

Anderson, J. A., & Rosenfeld, E. (1988). *Neurocomputing: Foundations of research.* Cambridge, MA: MIT Press.

Anderson, J. A., & Rosenfeld, E. (1998). *Talking nets: An oral history of neural networks.* Cambridge, MA: MIT Press.

Bechtel, W. (1985). Contemporary connectionism: Are the new parallel distributed processing models cognitive or associationist? *Behaviorism, 13*, 53–61.

Bechtel, W., & Abrahamsen, A. A. (2002). *Connectionism and the mind: Parallel processing, dynamics, and evolution in networks* (2nd ed.). Malden, MA: Blackwell.

Berkeley, I. S. N., Dawson, M. R. W., Medler, D. A., Schopflocher, D. P., & Hornsby, L. (1995). Density plots of hidden value unit activations reveal interpretable bands. *Connection Science, 7*, 167–186.

Bever, T. G., Fodor, J. A., & Garrett, M. (1968). A formal limitation of associationism. In T. R. Dixon & D. L. Horton (Eds.), *Verbal behavior and general behavior theory* (pp. 582–585). Englewood Cliffs, NJ: Prentice-Hall.

Carpenter, G. A., & Grossberg, S. (1992). *Neural networks for vision and image processing.* Cambridge, MA: MIT Press.

Chomsky, N. (1959a). On certain formal properties of grammars. *Information and Control, 2*, 137–167.

Chomsky, N. (1959b). A review of B. F. skinner's verbal behavior. *Language, 35*, 26–58.

Chomsky, N. (1966). *Cartesian linguistics: A chapter in the history of rationalist thought* (1st ed.). New York, NY: Harper & Row.

Cotter, N. E. (1990). The Stone-Weierstrass theorem and its application to neural networks. *Ieee Transactions on Neural Networks, 1*, 290–295.

Cybenko, G. (1989). Approximation by superpositions of a sigmoidal function. *Mathematics of Control, Signals, and Systems, 2*, 303–314.

Daniloff, R. (2002). *Connectionist approaches to clinical problems in speech and language.* Mahwah, N.J.: Lawrence Erlbaum Associates.

Dawson, M. R. W. (1998). *Understanding cognitive science.* Oxford: Blackwell.

Dawson, M. R. W. (2004). *Minds and machines: Connectionism and psychological modeling.* Malden, MA: Blackwell.

Dawson, M. R. W. (2005). *Connectionism: A hands-on approach* (1st ed.). Oxford & Malden, MA: Blackwell.

Dawson, M. R. W. (2008). Connectionism and classical conditioning. *Comparative Cognition and Behavior Reviews, 3*, 1–115.

Dawson, M. R. W. (2009). Computation, cognition – and connectionism. In D. Dedrick & L. Trick (Eds.), *Cognition, computation, and pylyshyn* (pp. 175–199). Cambridge, MA: MIT Press.

Dawson, M. R. W. (2013). *Mind, body, world: Foundations of cognitive science*. Edmonton: Athabasca University Press.

Dawson, M. R. W., Dupuis, B., Spetch, M. L., & Kelly, D. M. (2009). Simple artificial networks that match probability and exploit and explore when confronting a multiarmed bandit. *Ieee Transactions on Neural Networks, 20*(8), 1368–1371.

Dawson, M. R. W., Kelly, D. M., Spetch, M. L., & Dupuis, B. (2010). Using perceptrons to explore the reorientation task. *Cognition, 114*(2), 207–226.

Dawson, M. R. W., & Shamanski, K. S. (1994). Connectionism, confusion and cognitive science. *Journal of Intelligent Systems, 4*, 215–262.

Descartes, R. (1637/1960). *Discourse on method and meditations*. Indianapolis, IN: Bobbs-Merrill.

Dijkstra, T., & Smedt, K. (1996). *Computational psycholinguistics: AI and connectionist models of human language processing*. London & Bristol, PA: Taylor & Francis.

Dreyfus, H. L. (1972). *What computers can't do: A critique of artificial reason* (1st ed.). New York, NY: Harper & Row.

Dreyfus, H. L. (1992). *What computers still can't do*. Cambridge, MA: MIT Press.

Enquist, M., & Ghirlanda, S. (2005). *Neural networks and animal behavior*. Princeton, NJ: Princeton University Press.

Feigenbaum, E. A., & Feldman, J. (1995). *Computers and thought*. Cambridge, MA: MIT Press.

Fodor, J. A. (1975). *The language of thought*. Cambridge, MA: Harvard University Press.

Fodor, J. A., & Pylyshyn, Z. W. (1988). Connectionism and cognitive architecture. *Cognition, 28*, 3–71.

Freeman, J. A. (1994). *Simulating neural networks with mathematica*. Reading, MA: Addison-Wesley.

Funahashi, K. (1989). On the approximate realization of continuous mappings by neural networks. *Neural networks, 2*, 183–192.

Gallant, S. I. (1993). *Neural network learning and expert systems*. Cambridge, MA: MIT Press.

Girosi, F., & Poggio, T. (1990). Networks and the best approximation property. *Biological Cybernetics, 63*, 169–176.

Gluck, M. A., & Myers, C. (2001). *Gateway to memory: An introduction to neural network modeling of the hippocampus and learning*. Cambridge, MA: MIT Press.

Gold, E. M. (1967). Language identification in the limit. *Information and Control, 10*, 447–474.

Grossberg, S. (1980). How does the brain build a cognitive code? *Psychological Review, 87*, 1–51.

Grossberg, S. (1987). Competitive learning: From interactive activation to adaptive resonance. *Cognitive Science, 11*, 23–63.

Grossberg, S. (1988). *Neural networks and natural intelligence*. Cambridge, MA: MIT Press.

Hanson, S. J., & Burr, D. J. (1990). What connectionist models learn: Learning and representation in connectionist networks. *Behavioral and Brain Sciences, 13*, 471–518.

Harnad, S. (1987). *Categorical perception*. Cambridge: Cambridge University Press.

Hartman, E., Keeler, J. D., & Kowalski, J. M. (1989). Layered neural networks with Gaussian hidden units as universal approximation. *Neural Computation, 2*, 210–215.

Hillis, W. D. (1988). Intelligence as emergent behavior, or, the songs of Eden. In S. R. Graubard (Ed.), *The artificial intelligence debate* (pp. 175–189). Cambridge, MA: MIT Press.

Hinton, G. E. (1986). *Learning distributed representations of concepts*. Paper presented at the 8th Annual Meeting of the Cognitive Science Society, Ann Arbor, MI.

Hinton, G. E., & Anderson, J. A. (1981). *Parallel models of associative memory*. Hillsdale, NJ: Lawrence Erlbaum Associates.

Hopcroft, J. E., & Ullman, J. D. (1979). *Introduction to automata theory, languages, and computation*. Reading, MA: Addison-Wesley.

Horgan, T., & Tienson, J. (1996). *Connectionism and the philosophy of psychology*. Cambridge, MA: MIT Press.

Hornik, M., Stinchcombe, M., & White, H. (1989). Multilayer feedforward networks are universal approximators. *Neural Networks, 2*, 359–366.

Kohonen, T. (1977). *Associative memory: A system-theoretical approach*. New York, NY: Springer-Verlag.

Kohonen, T. (1984). *Self-organization and associative memory*. New York, NY: Springer-Verlag.

Levy, J. P. (1995). *Connectionist models of memory and language*. London & Bristol, PA: UCL Press.

Lippmann, R. P. (1987, April). An introduction to computing with neural nets. *IEEE ASSP Magazine*, 4–22.

Lippmann, R. P. (1989, November). Pattern classification using neural networks. *IEEE Communications Magazine*, 47–64.

Locke, J. (1706/1977). *An essay concerning human understanding*. London: J.M. Dent & Sons.

Mammone, R. J. (1993). *Artificial neural networks for speech and vision*. London & New York, NY: Chapman & Hall.

McClelland, J. L., & Rumelhart, D. E. (1986). *Parallel distributed processing* (Vol. 2). Cambridge, MA: MIT Press.

McClelland, J. L., & Rumelhart, D. E. (1988). *Explorations in parallel distributed processing*. Cambridge, MA: MIT Press.

McCloskey, M. (1991). Networks and theories: The place of connectionism in cognitive science. *Psychological Science, 2*, 387–395.

McCulloch, W. S., & Pitts, W. (1943). A logical calculus of the ideas immanent in nervous activity. *Bulletin of Mathematical Biophysics, 5*, 115–133.

Medler, D. A. (1998). A brief history of connectionism. *Neural Computing Surveys, 1*, 18–72.

Miller, G. A. (2003). The cognitive revolution: A historical perspective. *Trends in Cognitive Sciences, 7*(3), 141–144.

Minsky, M. L., & Papert, S. (1969). *Perceptrons: An introduction to computational geometry* (1st ed.). Cambridge, MA: MIT Press.

Moody, J., & Darken, C. J. (1989). Fast learning in networks of locally-tuned processing units. *Neural Computation, 1*, 281–294.

Moorhead, I. R., Haig, N. D., & Clement, R. A. (1989). An investigation of trained neural networks from a neurophysiological perspective. *Perception, 18*, 793–803.

Mozer, M. C., & Smolensky, P. (1989). Using relevance to reduce network size automatically. *Connection Science, 1*, 3–16.

Newell, A. (1980). Physical symbol systems. *Cognitive Science, 4*, 135–183.

Newell, A., & Simon, H. A. (1972). *Human problem solving*. Englewood Cliffs, NJ: Prentice-Hall.

Omlin, C. W., & Giles, C. L. (1996). Extraction of rules from discrete-time recurrent neural networks. *Neural Networks, 9*, 41–52.

Pao, Y.-H. (1989). *Adaptive pattern recognition and neural networks*. Reading, MA: Addison-Wesley.

Pinker, S. (1979). Formal models of language learning. *Cognition, 7*, 217–283.

Pinker, S., & Mehler, J. (1988). *Connections and symbols*. Cambridge, MA: MIT Press.

Plaut, D. C., McClelland, J. L., Seidenberg, M. S., & Patterson, K. (1996). Understanding normal and impaired word reading: Computational principles in quasi-regular domains. *Psychological Review, 103*, 56–115.

Poggio, T., & Girosi, F. (1990). Regularization algorithms for learning that are equivalent to multilayer networks. *Science, 247*, 978–982.

Pylyshyn, Z. W. (1984). *Computation and cognition*. Cambridge, MA: MIT Press.

Quinlan, P. (1991). *Connectionism and psychology*. Chicago, IL: University of Chicago Press.

Renals, S. (1989). Radial basis function network for speech pattern classification. *Electronics Letters, 25*, 437–439.

Révész, G. E. (1983). *Introduction to formal languages*. New York, NY: McGraw-Hill.

Ripley, B. D. (1996). *Pattern recognition and neural networks*. Cambridge: Cambridge University Press.

Rosenblatt, F. (1958). The perceptron: A probabilistic model for information storage and organization in the brain. *Psychological Review, 65*(6), 386–408.

Rosenblatt, F. (1962). *Principles of neurodynamics*. Washington, DC: Spartan Books.

Rumelhart, D. E., Hinton, G. E., & Williams, R. J. (1986). Learning representations by back-propagating errors. *Nature, 323*, 533–536.

Rumelhart, D. E., & McClelland, J. L. (1986). *Parallel distributed processing* (Vol. 1). Cambridge, MA: MIT Press.

Seidenberg, M. (1993). Connectionist models and cognitive theory. *Psychological Science, 4,* 228–235.

Sejnowski, T. J., & Rosenberg, C. R. (1988). NETtalk: A parallel network that learns to read aloud. In J. A. Anderson & E. Rosenfeld (Eds.), *Neurocomputing: Foundations of research* (pp. 663–672). Cambridge, MA: MIT Press.

Selouani, S. (2011). *Speech processing and soft computing.* New York, NY: Springer.

Sharkey, N. E. (1992). *Connectionist natural language processing.* Dordrecht & Boston, MA: Kluwer Academic Publishers.

Siegelmann, H. T. (1999). *Neural networks and analog computation: Beyond the turing limit.* Boston, MA: Birkhauser.

Siegelmann, H. T., & Sontag, E. D. (1991). Turing computability with neural nets. *Applied Mathematics Letters, 4,* 77–80.

Siegelmann, H. T., & Sontag, E. D. (1995). On the computational power of neural nets. *Journal of Computer and System Sciences, 50,* 132–150.

Skinner, B. F. (1957). *Verbal behavior.* New York, NY: Appleton-Century-Crofts.

Smolensky, P. (1988). On the proper treatment of connectionism. *Behavioral and Brain Sciences, 11,* 1–74.

Stone, G. O. (1986). An analysis of the delta rule and the learning of statistical associations. In D. E. Rumelhart & J. McClelland (Eds.), *Parallel distributed processing* (Vol. 1, pp. 444–459). Cambridge, MA: MIT Press.

Touretzky, D. S. (1991). *Connectionist approaches to language learning.* Boston, MA: Kluwer Academic Publishers.

von Neumann, J. (1958). *The computer and the brain.* New Haven, CT: Yale University Press.

Ward, N. (1994). *A connectionist language generator.* Norwood, NJ: Ablex.

Waskan, J., & Bechtel, W. (1997). Directions in connectionist research: Tractable computations without syntactically structured representations. *Metaphilosophy, 28*(1–2), 31–62.

Widrow, B. (1962). Generalization and information storage in networks of ADALINE "neurons". In M. C. Yovits, G. T. Jacobi, & G. D. Goldsteing (Eds.), *Self-organizing systems 1962* (pp. 435–461). Washington, DC: Spartan Books.

Widrow, B., & Hoff, M. E. (1960). *Adaptive switching circuits.* Institute of Radio Enginners, Wester Electronic Show and Convention, Convention Record, Part 4, pp. 96–104.

Michael R. W. Dawson
Department of Psychology
University of Alberta
Canada

SHAWN LOEWEN AND JENNIFER MAJORANA

5. INTERACTIONISM

THE INTERACTION APPROACH IN SLA

The interactionist framework proposes that conversational communication is a primary context for second language (L2) acquisition. From this perspective, the ordinariness of everyday conversation between language learners and their teachers or peers should not be underestimated in terms of its importance in L2 development. The Interaction Hypothesis (Long, 1996) emphasizes the role of input, negotiation for meaning, noticing, and output in L2 acquisition. As Long states, "negotiation for meaning, and especially negotiation work that triggers interactional adjustments by the native speaker (NS) or more competent interlocutor, facilitates acquisition because it connects input, internal learner capacities, particularly selective attention, and output in productive ways" (1996, pp. 451–452). In addition, many interactionist researchers have investigated the effectiveness of corrective feedback that teachers provide in response to students' non-target-like utterances during meaning-focused interaction. Together, these constructs comprise the primary focus of interactionist theory and research.

One of the most important factors in L2 acquisition is input, which is the language that is available to the learner (Gass, 1997). Input can be conceptualized in terms of positive and negative evidence. Positive evidence provides information about what is linguistically possible in the language, and it consists of all the language that learners hear and see around them (Gass, 2003; Leeman, 2003; Bruton, 2000). In contrast, negative evidence is information about what is not possible (i.e., is ungrammatical) in the target language (Ellis, 2006). Researchers historically have been divided on the issue of whether positive evidence alone is sufficient for L2 acquisition. Krashen's (1985) Input Hypothesis argued that positive evidence, in the form of comprehensible input, is the driving force of acquisition, and that the teacher's role is to make input comprehensible. In this framework, negative evidence plays a minimal role in L2 acquisition, contributing only to explicit knowledge, which according to Krashen cannot become proceduralized, or result in improved communicative competence. Other researchers stress the importance of both negative and positive evidence, asserting that positive evidence alone is insufficient, in part because negative evidence is required to help learners avoid ungrammatical forms (Long, 2007). Furthermore, some studies have shown that negative evidence produces greater gains in learning than positive evidence (e.g. Strapp, Helmick, Tonkovich, & Bleakney, 2011). The interactionist approach argues that through

© KONINKLIJKE BRILL NV, LEIDEN, 2018 | DOI:10.1163/9789004380882_005

linguistically modified input, learners receive both positive and negative evidence, creating optimal conditions for L2 acquisition.

Evidence is only useful, however, if it is perceived by the learner; perception is required before input can become intake, which in turn can be integrated into the learner's cognitive system. Consequently, the constructs of attention, noticing and awareness have informed and complemented the interactionist framework of SLA. Schmidt (1990, 1993) argued that second language learners must *notice*, or focus their attention on, an aspect of the language in order to learn it. In other words, the placement of the L2 learner's conscious awareness is a considerable factor in second language acquisition. Noticing can also be conceptualized as the learner encoding language into short-term memory, paving the way for later encoding into long-term memory (Robinson, 1995).

The measurability of noticing presents some difficulty, however. How can researchers determine what has or have not been noticed, besides observing its assumed effect on the learners' interlanguage? Some approaches to measure noticing include asking participants to underline, take notes, or to think out loud, all in an attempt to determine what learners focus their attention on. However, such techniques may interfere with learners' cognitive processes. One less intrusive measure of noticing that has been employed recently is eye tracking technology, which allows researchers to gather information about what learners focus on while they read (e.g. Godfroid, Boers, & Housen, 2013). It is also possible to take learners' responses to corrective feedback, known as uptake, as an indication of noticing, and while there is some evidence regarding the relationship between uptake and other measures of noticing (e.g., Egi, 2010), it is important to remember that uptake is a verbal, not a cognitive, phenomenon.

The opportunity to produce output in the context of interaction, in addition to receiving input, is another important component of the interactionist framework. The Output Hypothesis (Swain, 1985, 2000) was the first to formally theorize the insufficiency of input alone for SLA, based on Swain's observations about the failure of French immersion students in Canada to acquire grammar at expected levels even after years of exposure. Swain hypothesized that output, or production, draws learners' attention to gaps in their interlanguage, which "triggers cognitive processes that might generate new linguistic knowledge or consolidate their existing knowledge" (Swain, 2000, p. 201). She points out that comprehension of input does not require syntactic analysis; L2 learners can often understand the gist of their interlocutor's meaning without processing all of the morphosyntactic features of the input. However, to produce output, learners must not only convey the semantic meaning, but also encode the correct morphosyntactic features. Consequently, pushed output that results in syntactic processing can lead to precision, cohesiveness, and appropriateness (i.e. pragmatic awareness) in an L2 learners' production (Swain, 1985). In addition, output can lead to increased language automaticity. Furthermore, producing output also gives learners the opportunity to test their hypotheses about their interlanguage (Mackey, Gass, & McDonough, 2000) and receive feedback from other speakers about the grammaticality of those hypotheses. For example, learners might produce a specific grammatical form in order to confirm their knowledge of that form. If the form is incorrect, learners may experience a breakdown in communication or receive correction from their interlocutor.

As a result, in the interactionist framework, errors that lead to repetition, segmentation, and rephrasing – the process of negotiating for meaning – are viewed as beneficial to language acquisition, because this "work" draws attention to form-meaning relationships and gaps in interlanguage (Mackey, 2007; Mackey, Abbuhl, & Gass, 2012). When an error is made in the context of interaction, the flow of information is interrupted, and both interlocutors have the opportunity to modify their utterances in order to continue. These modifications, known as negotiated interaction, are exactly what makes input comprehensible to the L2 learner, and what helps L2 learners' interlanguage progress toward more target-like forms (Long, 1996). If learners produce an utterance that is not understood by their interlocutor, there may be negotiation of meaning through which the miscommunication is resolved. The listener may produce a clarification request, such as *What do you mean?*, or a confirmation check, such as *Do you mean X?*, in an attempt to understand the speaker. The speaker also might try to avert a communication breakdown by producing a comprehension check, such as *Do you understand what I mean?*. These negotiations can lead to feedback and repair of meaning.

Feedback may also be provided even if there is no breakdown in communication, if interlocutors simply wish to focus on accurate linguistic production. Such oral corrective feedback has been found to be important for L2 development (Lyster & Saito, 2010; Mackey & Goo, 2007; Russell & Spada, 2006; Li, 2010), in large part because it provides negative evidence about the learner's utterance, indicating that it is incorrect in some way. Corrective feedback can be provided several ways. One of the most common types of feedback in L2 classrooms, a recast, consists of a linguistic reformulation of a student's incorrect utterance that still maintains the meaning of the utterance (Loewen & Philp, 2006). In Example 1, the teacher corrects the student's preposition and pluralization errors, but keeps the learner's message intact. The recast provides negative evidence by indicating that an error has been made, but it also provides positive evidence because it gives the correct form to the student. Consequently, recasts have been referred to as a type of input-providing feedback.

Example 1: Recast

Student: maybe everyday have a lot of people die by the cigarette
Teacher: die from cigarettes
Student: die from cigarettes, so maybe …

Another type of corrective feedback has been referred to as a prompt or elicitation, wherein the teacher attempts to elicit the correct form, rather than providing it for the learner. In the example below, the student initially uses the incorrect gender for the French noun *maison*. Instead of providing the correct form through a recast, the teacher draws attention to the error, and elicits the correct form from the learner. Such output-prompting types of feedback provide negative evidence, rather than positive, with the goal of involving the learner in greater cognitive processing in order to come up with the correct form.

Example 2: Prompt (from Lyster, 2004, p. 405)

Teacher: *Il vit où un animal domestique? Où est-ce que ça vit?*
          Where does a pet live? Where does it live?
Student: *Dans un maison.*
          In a (masc.) house.
Teacher: *Dans? Attention.*
          In? Careful.
Student: *Dans une maison.*
          In a (fem.) house.

A third type of corrective feedback is metalinguistic feedback, which generally involves the teacher indicating that an error has been made and providing metalinguistic information about the nature of the error. In Example 3, the learner makes an error in using the past tense, which the teacher points out directly.

Example 3: Metalinguistic feedback

Student: He kiss her.
Teacher: Kiss – you need past tense.
Student: He kissed her.

In addition to providing positive and/or negative evidence, corrective feedback also affords learners opportunities to modify their output in response to corrective feedback, something that can contribute to L2 development (Goo & Mackey, 2013; Swain, 2000). Learners have the chance to respond to corrective feedback if they indeed notice it. Uptake is considered successful if learners produce the correct linguistic form (as in Example 1), or it may be unsuccessful, as in Example 4 where the learner simply repeats the incorrect form during the communicative task. Although uptake cannot be equated with acquisition, successful uptake may be an indication that the learner has noticed the corrective feedback (see Ellis & Sheen, 2006).

Example 4: Unsuccessful uptake

Student: what kind of the company?
Teacher: what?
Student: what kind of the company?
Teacher: oh, a drug company

Characteristics of the feedback itself, such as length, timing, and intensity of feedback for a specific feature, may influence its effectiveness (Sheen, 2006;

Loewen, 2012). In particular, the role of explicitness has been controversial. As the interactionist position accepts that second language learners must notice a feature of the language in order to acquire it, then a concern for research into corrective feedback is how explicit corrective feedback must be to be noticed without interrupting communication (Russell & Spada, 2006). Explicit feedback is overt and therefore more noticeable, but it may interrupt the communicative purpose of a conversation, such as a teacher making metalinguistic comment about a grammatical or lexical feature. In contrast, recasts fit nicely into the flow of conversation; however, they may sometimes be too implicit, with the result that the learner does not notice that he or she has been corrected. Studies have produced conflicting results regarding the most effective types of feedback, suggesting that it might be best for teachers to incorporate a variety of feedback techniques in their classroom interactions (Mackey & Goo, 2007; Russell & Spada, 2006).

This discussion of the core constructs of the interactionist approach – input, negotiation for meaning, corrective feedback, output, and noticing – warrants a word about contextual characteristics of interaction, and the effects that these can have on interaction. It may be the case that some contextual features are better for interaction than others. If so, it is beneficial for L2 instructors to consider which contexts provide the richest opportunities for language learning as they develop tasks and pedagogical tools.

Contextual characteristics can be related to the interlocutors, the tasks, and the interaction modality. In terms of interlocutors, corrective feedback most often comes from teachers who may or may not be native speakers of the L2. As such, in the majority of corrective feedback studies it is the teacher or researcher who provides the feedback (Li, 2010; Russell & Spada, 2006). However, because of the importance of task-based group work, peer feedback, in which learners respond to each other, has also been researched. Several studies have found peer feedback to be beneficial for L2 learning (e.g. Adams, 2007), but studies have also shown that unless learners are trained and encouraged to provide feedback, they tend not correct each other (e.g., Sato, 2013). In light of this, teachers should consider strategic learner pairing, and take thoughtful responsibility for emphasizing collaboration in the classroom in order to optimize the positive impacts of peer corrective feedback.

The proficiency and first language (L1) of learners can also affect interaction. Specifically, different patterns of interaction emerge when learners of different or similar proficiency levels are paired. Several studies (e.g. Leeser, 2004), have found that high proficiency students are more likely than low proficiency ones to negotiate for meaning when they are communicating with someone of their own proficiency level, while working with a partner of a lower proficiency improved learner performance. Higher proficiency learners are more likely to negotiate when interacting with lower proficiency students; however, it is not clear that the lower proficiency students are always able to benefit from that negotiation. Additionally, there is more negotiation if the learners have different L1s (Watanabe & Swain, 2007). Student proficiency level is bound to vary within even a single class; teachers can use this to their advantage by grouping students of different proficiencies and L1s to promote more constructive interaction.

Individual learner factors, such as language aptitude and working memory (Li, 2013), as well as age (Swain & Lapkin, 1989) and motivation (Russell & Spada, 2006) also impact the way learners negotiate for meaning and perceive corrective feedback. First, learners with greater working memories appear to be able to benefit more from corrective feedback during interaction, perhaps because they are better able to hold both their incorrect utterance as well as the correct form in their working memory at the same time. This ability enables them to make the linguistic comparisons that are important for feedback to be effective. Second, although both younger and older L2 learners are able to engage in interaction, some research suggests that older learners are better able to take advantage of the acquisitional benefits that interaction can afford (Oliver, Philp, & Mackey, 2008). Finally, more motivated learners may engage in more interaction. Specifically, learners that have considerable investment in their identities as L2 learners interact more in the classroom than do learners who view the L2 class as just another academic subject (Tomita & Spada, 2013).

Characteristics of the task can also influence the interaction (Gass, Mackey, & Ross-Feldman, 2005). Tasks can have several different options. They can be open or closed, which refers to the outcome of the task: Is there only one outcome, or are there multiple? For example, in an opinion gap task, each individual can simply express their opinion, which leaves the outcome open; however, in a consensus task, learners must come to an agreement. Such closed tasks tend to result in more communication and interaction because learners must work together to come to an agreement. Another characteristic of interactive tasks is how the information is distributed among the participants. If information is shared, then there is less incentive to interact. However, if learners must exchange information, as in a jigsaw task, in order to complete the task, then more interaction may occur.

Another important component of L2 classroom interaction is the linguistic forms that result in negotiation and feedback. Grammar, pronunciation, and vocabulary are the most common targets for feedback in the classroom (Ellis, Basturkmen, & Loewen, 2001; Lyster & Ranta, 1997). However, feedback on vocabulary and pronunciation seems to be more easily perceived by learners, when compared to feedback on morphosyntax (Mackey et al., 2000). Accordingly, feedback also seems to have a greater effect on the acquisition of vocabulary than grammar, although studies have shown that interaction can benefit the acquisition of vocabulary (de la Fuente, 2002), pronunciation (Saito & Lyster, 2012a, 2012b), and grammar (Mackey & Goo, 2007). Nevertheless, instructors may need to make grammatical feedback more explicit for learners to benefit from it.

With the increasing use of technology in the classroom, interactionist researchers are examining the effects of modality on interaction. In particular, computer-meditated communication (CMC) which has been defined as "a real-time synchronous conversation that takes place over the computer via the Internet" (Baralt & Gurzynski-Weiss, 2011, p. 206) has received recent attention. Researchers suggest that CMC promotes different kinds of communication strategies between learners than face-to-face (FTF) interaction does, so the two modalities should be used for different pedagogical purposes (Kim, 2014a). For example, learners may attend less to corrective feedback in CMC than FTF interaction (Kim, 2014b) or exhibit fewer uptakes (Smith, 2005). On the other hand, there is some evidence of comparable noticing patterns between CMC and FTF interaction (Gurzynski-Weiss & Baralt, 2014). One reason for CMC's burgeoning popularity may lie in the hope that it could help reduce communication apprehension or foreign language anxiety (Kern, 1995). Some effects in anxiety reduction have been observed in text-chat (Satar & Özdener, 2008) but a direct correlation is not necessarily supported by empirical evidence (Baralt & Gurzynski-Weiss, 2011; Arnold, 2007).

In summary, there are many factors that may influence interaction in the classroom. Nevertheless, current research suggests that interaction is a positive influence on L2 acquisition. As learners are exposed to input, engage in the negotiation for meaning, and produce output, they are involved in processes that are vital for learner development. First, they can receive comprehensible input, a necessary condition for SLA. Furthermore, they can experience heightened noticing of ungrammatical forms or gaps in interlanguage through negotiation of meaning and corrective feedback. Finally, learners are pushed to map syntactic forms onto semantic messages and to test linguistic hypotheses. As one recent meta-analysis of interaction studies concludes, interaction plays "a strong facilitative role in the learning of lexical and grammatical target items" (Mackey & Goo, 2007, p. 438). Consequently, L2 teachers and learners should seek to incorporate interaction into the L2 classroom whenever possible.

REFERENCES

Adams, R. (2007). Do second language learners benefit from interacting with each other? In A. Mackey (Ed.), *Conversational interaction in second language acquisition* (pp. 29–52). Oxford: Oxford University Press.

Arnold, N. (2007). Reducing foreign language communication apprehension with computer-mediated communication: A preliminary study. *System, 35*(4), 469–486.

Baralt, M., & Gurzynski-Weiss, L. (2011). Comparing learners' state anxiety during task-based interaction in computer-mediated and face-to-face communication. *Language Teaching Research, 15*(2), 201–29.

Bruton, A. (2000). What exactly are positive and negative evidence in SLA? *RELC Journal, 31*(2), 120–133.

de la Fuente, M. J. (2002). The roles of input and output in the receptive and productive acquisition of words. *Studies in Second Language Acquisition, 24*(1), 81–112.

Egi, T. (2010). Uptake, modified output, and learner perceptions of recasts: Learner responses as language awareness. *The Modern Language Journal, 94*, 1–21.

Ellis, R. (2006). Researching the effects of form-focussed instruction on L2 acquisition. *AILA Review, 19*, 18–41.

Ellis, R., Basturkmen, H., & Loewen, S. (2001). Learner uptake in communicative ESL lessons. *Language Learning, 51*(2), 281–318.

Ellis, R., & Sheen, Y. (2006). Re-examining the role of recasts in SLA. *Studies in Second Language Acquisition, 28*(4), 575–600.

Gass, S. (1997). *Input and interaction in SLA*. Mahwah, NJ: Erlbaum.

Gass, S. (2003). Input and interaction. In C. Doughty & M. Long (Eds.), *The handbook of second language acquisition* (pp. 224–255). Malden, MA: Blackwell.

Gass, S., Mackey, A., & Ross-Feldman, L. (2005). Task-based interactions in classroom and laboratory setting. *Language Learning, 55*, 575–611.

Godfroid, A., Boers, F., & Housen, A. (2013). An eye for words: Gauging the role of attention in incidental L2 vocabulary acquisition by means of eye-tracking. *Studies in Second Language Acquisition, 35*, 483–517.

Goo, J., & Mackey, A. (2013). The case against the case against recasts. *Studies in Second Language Acquisition, 35*, 127–165.

Gurzynski-Weiss, L., & Baralt, M. (2014). Exploring learner perception and use of task-based interactional feedback in FTF. *Studies in Second Language Acquisition, 36*, 1–37.

Kern, R. (1995). Restructuring classroom interaction with networked computers: Effects on quantity and characteristics of language production. *The Modern Language Journal, 79*, 457–476.

Kim, H. Y. (2014a). Learning opportunities in synchronous computer-mediated communication and face-to-face interaction. *Computer Assisted Language Learning, 27*(1), 26–43.

Kim, H. Y. (2014b). Revisiting synchronous computer-mediated communication: Learner perception and the meaning of corrective feedback. *English Language Teaching, 7*(9), 64–73.

Krashen, S. (1981). *Principles and practice in SLA*. Englewood, NJ: Prentice-Hall International.

Krashen, S. (1985). *The input hypothesis: Issues and implications*. New York, NY: Longman.

Leeman, J. (2003). Recasts and second language development: Beyond negative evidence. *Studies in Second Language Acquisition, 25*(1), 37–63.

Leeser, M. (2004). Learner proficiency and focus on form during collaborative dialogue. *Language Teaching Research, 8*, 55–81.

Li, S. (2010). The effectiveness of corrective feedback in SLA: A meta-analysis. *Language Learning 60*(2), 309–365.

Li, S. (2013). The interactions between the effects of implicit and explicit feedback and individual differences in language analytic ability and working memory. *The Modern Language Journal, 97*(3), 634–654.

Long, M. (1996). The role of the linguistic environment in SLA. In W. Ritchie & T. Bhatia (Eds.), *Handbook of second language acquisition* (pp. 413–468). San Diego, CA: Academic Press.

Long, M. (2007). *Problems in SLA*. Mahwah, NJ: Erlbaum.

Loewen, S. (2012). The role of feedback. In A. Mackey & S. M. Gass (Eds.), *The Routledge handbook of second language acquisition* (pp. 24–40). New York, NY: Routledge.

Loewen, S., & Philp, J. (2006). Recasts in the adult English L2 classroom: Characteristics, explicitness, and effectiveness. *The Modern Language Journal, 90*(4), 536–556.

Lyster, R. (2004). Differential effects of prompts and recasts in form-focused instruction. *Studies in Second Language Acquisition, 26*(3), 399–432.

Lyster, R., & Ranta, L. (1997). Corrective feedback and learner uptake: Negotiation of form in communicative classrooms. *Studies in Second Language Acquisition, 19*(1), 37–66.

Lyster, R., & Saito, K. (2010). Oral feedback in classroom SLA: A meta-analysis. *Studies in Second Language Acquisition, 32*, 265–302.

Mackey, A. (2007). Introduction. In A. Mackey (Ed.), *Conversational interaction in second language acquisition* (pp. 1–26). Oxford: Oxford University Press.

Mackey, A., Abbuhl, R., & Gass, S. M. (2012). Interactionist approach. In A. Mackey & S. M. Gass (Eds.), *The Routledge handbook of second language acquisition* (pp. 7–23). New York, NY: Routledge.

Mackey, A., Gass, S., & McDonough, K. (2000). How do learners perceive interactional feedback? *Second Language Learning, 22*(4), 471–97.

Mackey, A., & Goo, J. (2007). Interaction research in SLA: A meta-analysis and research synthesis. In A. Mackey (Ed.), *Conversational interaction in second language acquisition* (pp. 407–452). Oxford: Oxford University Press.

Oliver, R., Philp, J., & Mackey, A. (2008). The impact of teacher input, guidance and feedback on ESL children's task-based interactions. In J. Philp, R. Oliver, & A. Mackey (Eds.), *Second language acquisition and the younger learner: Child's play?* (pp. 131–147). Amsterdam: John Benjamins.

Robinson, P. (1995). Attention, memory, and the "noticing" hypothesis. *Language Learning, 45*(2), 283–331.

Russell, J., & Spada, N. (2006). The effectiveness of corrective feedback for the acquisition of L2 grammar: A meta-analysis of the research. In J. M. Norris & L. Ortega (Eds.), *Synthesizing research on language learning and teaching* (pp. 133–164). Amsterdam: John Benjamins.

Satar, H. M., & Özdener, N. (2008). The effects of synchronous CMC on speaking proficiency and anxiety: Text versus voice chat. *The Modern Language Journal, 92*(4), 595–613.

Saito, K., & Lyster, R. (2012a). Effects of form-focused instruction and corrective feedback on L2 pronunciation development of /ɹ/ by Japanese learners of English. *Language Learning, 62*(2), 595–633.

Saito, K., & Lyster, R. (2012b). Investigating the pedagogical potential of recasts for L2 vowel acquisition. *TESOL Quarterly, 46*(2), 387–398.

Sato, M. (2013). Beliefs about peer interaction and peer corrective feedback: Efficacy of classroom intervention. *The Modern Language Journal, 97*(3), 611–633.

Schmidt, R. (1990). The role of consciousness in second language learning. *Applied Linguistics, 11,* 129–158.

Schmidt, R. (1993). Awareness and SLA. *Annual Review of Applied Linguistics, 13,* 206–225.

Sheen, Y. (2006). Exploring the relationship between characteristics of recasts and learner uptake. *Language Teaching Research, 10*(4), 361–392.

Smith, B. (2005). The relationship between negotiated interaction, learner uptake, and lexical acquisition in task-based computer-mediated communication. *TESOL Quarterly, 39*(1), 33–58.

Strapp, C. M., Helmick, A. L., Tonkovich, H. M., & Bleakney, D. M. (2011). Effects of negative and positive evidence on adult word learning. *Language Learning, 61*(2), 506–532.

Swain, M. (1985). Communicative competence: Some roles of comprehensible input and comprehensible output in its development. In S. Gass & C. Madden (Eds.), *Input in second language acquisition* (pp. 235–253). Rowley, MA: Newbury House.

Swain, M. (2000). French immersion research in Canada: Recent contributions to SLA and applied linguistics. *Annual Review of Applied Linguistics, 90,* 199–212.

Swain, M., & Lapkin, S. (1989). Canadian immersion and adult second language teaching: What's the connection? *The Modern Language Journal, 73*(2), 150–159.

Tomita, Y., & Spada, N. (2013). Form-focused instruction and learner investment in L2 communication. *The Modern Language Journal, 97,* 591–610.

Watanabe, Y., & Swain, M. (2007). Effects of proficiency differences and patterns of pair interaction on second language learning: Collaborative dialogue between adult ESL learners. *Language Teaching Research, 11*(2), 121–142.

Shawn Loewen
Michigan State University
East Lansing, Michigan, USA

Jennifer Majorana
Saginaw Valley State University
Michigan, USA

GRAHAM V. CROOKES

6. CRITICAL THEORIES OF SLA AND THEIR APPLICATIONS TO REFLECTIVE AND EFFECTIVE TEACHING

INTRODUCTION

For second language teachers (though not necessarily for SLA researchers), the *raison d'etre* for the existence of the field of Second Language Acquisition is to inform second language teaching; to put it more sharply, it is to encourage the best, and thus necessarily the most creative second language teaching. The relationship, and the possibility of SLA informing SLT, has been the topic of persistent discussion, to which I have contributed in the past (e.g. Crookes, 1997, 1998). In the present contribution, I look at a developing subarea of SLA theory, "critical SLA", and relate it to a corresponding area of SL teaching, "critical L2 pedagogy", which is also a manifestation of creativity, or an example of creative language teaching.

ASPECTS OF THEORY OF SLA

The relationship between theory and practice is not direct; it also depends on what one means by theory. For our field, some years ago Stern (1983, pp. 25–26) provided a simple tripartite analysis of this matter. According to Stern, we have, first, a wide sense of the term, referring to "the systematic study of the thought" related to language teaching. Second, we have "language teaching 'methods', 'philosophies', or 'schools of thought', ... based on different linguistic and psychological assumptions, often emphasizing different objectives". Finally third, we have scientific theories possibly in the form of "a logically connected set of hypotheses" which have an explanatory function concerning their domain of reference. It is also worth noting three-part taxonomy of theories in general, dividing them into substantive, middle-range, and grand theory (LeCompte & Preissle, 1993, pp. 134–135). The first is "interrelated propositions or concepts which create explanations for the existence of phenomena lodged in particular aspects of populations, settings, or times. They are restricted to features of populations, settings, and times that can be identified concretely ... Theories developed to explaining formal learning and teaching in school settings ... are substantive in nature". Middle-range theory (a term coined by Merton, 1967) refers to "relationships which hold under specified conditions irrespective of time and place" (Kaplan & Manners, 1972, p. 13, cited in ibid.).

Finally there is grand theory, "comprehensive … explanations of large and complex categories of phenomena": Darwin's theory of evolution, Marx's theory of society, and Newton's theory of motion. In considering theories, it should be borne in mind that most are accompanied by or associated with specific philosophies of science (i.e., they represent the right, and not the wrong way, to theorize, according to a particular view) and they usually represent an a priori selection of what is relevant to what is to be theorized; that is, they embody or draw upon a metatheory of the domain in question.

Despite much discussion of the relationship between SLA and SLT, there is little in print concerning precisely how one might get from the former to the latter. In one of the few references to the matter Doughty and Long (2003) separate the two and indicate that a theory of SLT is likely to take the form of a set of principles, some of which (but by no means all of which) are informed by SLA theory. Others of them may well be chosen on the basis of values, I believe (cf. Crookes, 2009), or on the basis of other domains of theory beyond SLA. In my most recent remarks on the topic of the relationship between theory and practice, I have made use of the long-standing term 'praxis' whose existence implies that the separation of theory and practice (and thus of the fields of SLA and SLT) is partly language-created (Crookes, 2013b; cf. Pennycook, 2001, p. 3), using two terms where one would be better. 'Praxis' refers to practice that is theoretically-grounded and has the potential to revise and improve theory. Thus ideally, in SLT, we should be aiming at praxis, not ivory-tower theory nor unreflective, uninformed practice. And certainly language teachers can hope for theories of SLA that would support good, perhaps "creative" teaching.

In the past, mainstream SLA, for those who thought it should inform SLT was subject to criticism on a variety of grounds, one of which was that, in search of theoretical strength and purity, it responded to a philosophy of science that called for universal generalizations. And in pursuit of those same universals, it thereby rendered it almost unable to speak to the specific contexts of second language teachers. (Though this is a bit of an oversimplification, and there are legitimate positions on both sides of this argument.) However, SLA (or the area of study which includes studies of second language learning, now perhaps less attached to the old acronym) has expanded to include perspectives on scientific practice that are not at all committed to universal generalization. Attention to the specific and the local is far more common in the last 10 to 20 years than it was earlier. It might be said that at one level this is a return to the roots of early SLA, manifested in the many early case studies that got the field going (Hatch, 1977; cf. Duff, 2007).

These days, when we research or attempt to learn about approaches to understanding specific cases of second language learning, we are more likely to have in mind a person, or perhaps categories of people, who learn in particular contexts; and for many specialists, the individuals themselves will not be the abstracted information-processing cognitive systems that used to be implied by mainstream SLA theory, but individuals who are far more embodied, located in space, time, history and culture. More technically, this is a move away from what has been called the "unencumbered" individual of liberal sociopolitical and psychological theory, towards a conception of the second language learning individual who has gender, class, and race, at least. Associated with this shift, or indeed going ahead of it, an additional shift in SLA theory is indicated by the interest in "identity". Whereas previously personal identity was assumed to be fairly fixed now identity *change* is seen as closely involved in SL learning. A broad range of approaches to SLA that go beyond the limited conceptions of the late 20th century are now available (e.g., Atkinson, 2011).

Not only do we now have non-mainstream SLA (or to put it better, we have a more sophisticated range of philosophical and theoretical options in SLA), we have in fact always had non-mainstream versions of the social sciences that feed into or support SLA. SLA draws on theories of language and theories of learning, and implicitly also on theories of education, of educational institutions, and of psychology and sociology. It also, as the point above about the individual implies, draws on philosophy and political theory, where necessary. Despite the early influence of Schumann, theories of learning in mainstream SLA reflected mainstream psychology; however, increasingly we have (again) social theories of learning (see below). And where we had mainly structural theories of learning, naturally we can refer to the acquisition of language understood as functions or functional. But in this chapter I want to get a little further beyond the mainstream than that. In particular, I intend to examine or search for theories of L2 learning that favor those individuals who are *not* in the mainstream. That is to say, both theories of the person as well as learning need to be explored. And then a connection to creative language teaching will be made.

THE IDEA OF THE CRITICAL

All ideas should be subject to careful scrutiny. This is one of the roles of philosophy, and in western philosophy, this idea is particularly associated with Kant (cf. Djaballah, 2011). Limiting the matter, for the moment, to ideas about society, one can talk of a theory of society, and one can imagine a critique of that. This allows us to imagine or call for a critical theory of society. Any society, or social theory, can be critiqued from a variety of viewpoints, presumably from specific values positions. In the 20th century, following radical critiques of society, in which social critics and critical social theorists debated the shortcomings of the developing and powerful nation-states of Europe in particular, the term "critical theory", was developed as a short-hand for a theory of society which prioritized radically democratic values: equality, freedom, social justice. All of these had been prioritized by social theorists of "the left", from social democrats, through socialists, communists, anarchists, and libertarians, whether secular or religious (which is to say, there were also Christian democrats, not to mention Arab socialists; religious values have often been radical values).

Critique informed by radical social theory was also directed at the cultural and scientific outputs of most societies, or we can say "mainstream" societies.

Analysts of science and of the social sciences gradually started to show, or attempt to show, that the natural sciences, despite their inbuilt self-correcting tendencies, nevertheless sometimes favoured the establishment, and promoted ideas in society which supported the powerful against the weak. These early critiques of the natural sciences were in due course followed up by critiques of the social sciences. In addition, radical or at least non-mainstream scientists tried to construct alternative visions of the social sciences; critical social science. Most of these efforts were forward looking, but legitimate efforts were also made to recuperate science, or the knowledge, of cultures other than those dominant during the 20th century. "Indigenous knowledge" and "non-western science" were identified for the West and their values promoted, instead of being denied and denigrated as had previously been the case.

Consequently, and arriving at the end of the 20th century or the beginning of the 21st, we have programmatic accounts of critical social science, critical applied linguistics, critical second language teaching, and potentially (the subject of the next section) critical second language acquisition.

TOWARDS CRITICAL THEORIES OF SLA

Do we have critical theories of SLA? Given the lack of attention to critical matters in mainstream SLA, an initial answer might be "no", but perhaps they are present, just not fully recognized. One problem is the term SLA itself. Perhaps wrongly, it still seems to be interpreted (by my students, at least) as implying individualist and cognitively-oriented theories of L2 learning. If we understand it to mean all theories of L2 learning, that might be better, as it would be less likely to eliminate research on L2 learning that, while not using the term SLA, nevertheless addresses cases of L2 learning, including those where critical matters have been brought in (examples?)

And then, the term "theories" also has both narrow and broad understandings. If it means formalized and specifically causal-process theories, then there is little on offer. If it means something closer to "substantive" theories (as defined above by LeCompte & Preissle) – understandings of processes involved in specific examples of L2 learning, such as those that have emerged from many classroom studies or ethnographies of L2 learning such as those collected in Norton and Toohey (2004) – then we are on safer ground. Even then, as Block (2014) points out, the older conventional understandings of "the critical" which identify "social class" as the main basis of oppression *and* as a central factor or aspect of an L2 learning study, are rarely to be found.

Towards a Critical Theory of the Person for SLA

There are, in addition, interesting places to start. Let me point out first that there are critical versions of most of the social sciences that feed into applied linguistics.

That said, we can begin by noting the existence of the least well known of these, critical psychology. This was developed in Germany in the late 1960s by Holzkamp, as a theoretical project indicating the limitations of mainstream psychology, putting forward alternative concepts (e.g., Fox, Prilleltensky, & Austin, 2009). Its concept of the person is important:

In his historical analysis of the human psyche, Holzkamp pointed out that on account of the societal form of human life, we, in comparison with other creatures, can always create a changing relationship to the world which we inhabit. Humans do not live immediately within a natural environment, where meanings dictate the activities of living beings, but rather in a mediated social world, where meanings reflect possibilities of action and allow for a consciousness of the world. It is this unique relationship that creates our awareness of being a subject. Regardless of how determined given conditions in life may be, the individual subject always deals with them in a relationship of possibilities. We humans are subjects who can always act (Schraube, 2000, p. 49).

Holzkamp is taking up a conception of the person, of the psyche, of the psychological, which is not that given by mainstream society. With it we can ask: 'what is learned when a student acquires a second language in a critical sense', and the answer would be, an ability to function with critical understanding and engage in anti-oppressive action in their second language and culture. This would be a form of radical acculturation and thus of identity shift (Watts, Williams, & Jagers, 2003).

A "theory of the person" may be an unfamiliar phrase, but stated as "theories of identity" or of "the self", it appears increasingly from the mid-1990s in applied linguistics and within explorations of L2 learning. These days identity as an aspect of L2 learning is seen as not fixed, nor merely associated with membership in a socially determined, structural features of society such as class, or race, or gender. This fluid and multiple understanding of identity are often referred to as "post-structuralist" (cf. Norton, 2014). According to critical pedagogy specialist Morgan (1998, p. 12) "language 'conditions' our expectations and desires and communicates what might be possible in terms of ourselves – our identity – and the 'realities' we might develop". Importantly, for the oppressed, "An individual's identity in L2 contexts is mediated by the reactions of others to that individual's social and cultural position, which, in turn, can influence that individual's motivation to learn" (Ricento, 2005, p. 899). Where are we, then, in terms of a theory of the person appropriate to critical SL learning? It seems that we must have a conception of the person which may be close to that arising from a pragmatist, community-oriented, and possibly performance-oriented theory of society; the individual is in society, and the individual and society have a mutually-constituting relationship (involving discourse processes), *and* society is characterized by difference, diversity and conflict. Communities socialize individuals, but the individual only exists (and performs his/her many roles) in relation to the many communities s/he is simultaneously a member of. The person is not only located, or positioned, in these multiple webs of power, but also acts within them, on them, and is acted upon by them, with varying degrees of agency not only to result in benefit for her/himself and associates but also on occasion to alter the way these structures themselves are constituted.

Critical Theories of Learning

Besides a theory of the person (who is learning) we also obviously need a critical theory of learning. A possible source for this, for critical SLA, is sociocognitive theories of learning. This work started in Soviet Russia, as psychological theorizing intended to be located within understandings of human learning consistent with the social theory of Marx, popular in that time and place (e.g., Vygotsky, 1926/1997). These theories emphasize cultural elements, broadly speaking "tools", by which learners engage what is to be learned, and facilitate or hinder that learning. Vygotskyan theory provides a view of learning as inherently social, as occurring particularly between individuals with greater and lesser amounts of knowledge, and taking place through dialogue.

Activity Theory

One recent development of sociocognitive theory is "activity theory". This developed (explains Thorne, 2005, p. 395) through Leont'ev's ... formulation that emphasized the genesis and mediation of mind through *sensuous human activity* ... Activity in this sense refers to social relations and rules of conduct that are governed by cultural, political, and economic institutions ... Leont'ev and subsequent activity theorists elaborated this shift by more formally operationalizing the roles of communities, the rules that structure them, and "the continuously negotiated distribution of tasks, powers, and responsibilities among the participants of an activity system" (Cole & Engeström, 1993, p. 7).

Swedish psychologist Engeström developed the idea of mediation to include social and institutional rules, division of labor, and community as theoretically-crucial components. In addition, he specified a transformative orientation or tendency. He accepts the idea that humans learn in order to act, often to act so as to improve matters, and he wishes his theories to include this possibility. This pre-specification of what is to be considered in activity theory indicates the way it represents, at one level, a metatheory (Nardi, 1996). Thorne (2004, p. 63) has explained this work for our field, and writes: "The goal of activity theory is to define and analyze a given activity system to diagnose possible problems, and to provide a framework for implementing innovations".

Activity theory has been challenged to take up a critical orientation. Thorne (2005, p. 396) identified its weakness in its "assumption ... that scientific concepts and formal schooling have a positive valence for all populations ... This idealized perspective is in direct contradiction to the research of reproduction theorists and critical pedagogues ...". But "[p]ractitioners of ... activity theory are attempting to address [this] ... by focusing greater attention on power and agency in their analyses, particularly by including concerns voiced in the critical sociology of knowledge literature (ibid.)" In that case, the future-oriented, innovation-oriented nature of activity theory along with its emphasis on what the learning environment does, and does not provide, and how its cultural rules impinge on the learner, might be useful for critical SLA.

But equally important is for outcomes of a local action to enhance an individual's capacity to perform relevant and competent identities. This is one aspiration that activity theory shares with critical pedagogy – not only to cultivate developing expertise at the level of communicative performance, but also to support ones continued development as a person. As Lantolf and Pavlenko (2001, p. 145) suggested from an activity theoretical perspective, SLA is "about much more than the acquisition of forms: it is about developing, or failing to develop, new ways of mediating ourselves and our relationships" (Thorne, 2005, p. 401).

In a recent (non-SLA) study of learning Sawchuk (2006) interviewed Canadian working-class laborers, to explore the implications of class-consciousness for learning. These individuals are contemptuous about what can be learned in mainstream (middle-class) schools. Sawchuk's research is intended to support the development of social forms of learning more appropriate and supportive of working-class culture that those of formal (middle-class) school. From a critical perspective, by and large, oppressed groups fail to learn in culturally-inappropriate educational institutions, and this applies to working class, black, women, and so on. However, again as Block (2014) has pointed out, matters such as social class have yet to appear systematically in studies of L2 learning.

Sociocultural Theory

Besides activity theory, more directly Vygotskyan work under the general heading of sociocultural theory is present in studies of SL learning. As with activity theory, it too has been criticized for its lack of attention to inequities associated with class and race, not to mention gender and other sites of oppression. An attempt to generate a more general theory of learning that is sensitive to sites of oppression is Panofsky's work (2003). Drawing on earlier work in this area, she presents five categories of cultural elements which mediate learning. Being part of culture, they are likely to be present under favorable circumstances, and absent or distorted under unfavorable circumstances. They thus provide the possibility of explaining, in a systematic way, the diversity of learning associated with oppressive and discriminatory circumstances versus favorable and resource-rich circumstances.

- *Cultural activities* such as producing goods, raising and educating children, making and enforcing policies and laws, providing medical care. It is through these activities that humans survive and develop themselves. They are basic to the ways in which individuals interact with objects, people, and even oneself.

65

- *Cultural values, schemas, meanings, concepts*. People collectively endow things with meaning. Youth, old age, man, woman, bodily features, wealth, nature, and time mean different things in different societies.
- *Physical artifacts* such as tools, books, paper, pottery, eating utensils, clocks, clothing, buildings, furniture, toys, games, weapons and technology which are collectively constructed.
- *Psychological phenomena* such as emotions, perception, motivation, logical reasoning, intelligence, memory, mental illness, imagination, language, and personality are collectively constructed and distributed.
- *Agency*. Humans actively construct and reconstruct cultural phenomena. This "agency" is directed at constructing cultural phenomena and it is also influenced by existing cultural activities, values, artifacts, and psychology (Panofsky, 2003).

Panofsky then surveys studies of learning and social class (and the extends to other sites of oppression, such as race and gender) against this system of categories and finds that they interact with social class within schools so as to result in differential treatment of students' attempts at learning (teacher response to errors, in-class productions, actual selection of curricular materials, ways of handling misbehavior, articulated expectations, etc). (This is of course consistent with many individual studies, some famous, such as early work in the sociology of education: Bernstein, 1961; Bowles & Gintis, 1976; and subsequent ethnographies of education: Heath, 1983; Willis, 1977). This interaction is strong and negative to such an extent, Panofsky argues that a different *consciousness* is produced when lower-class students experience the relational features of school. The cultural activity of school, as experienced by these students, involves a different set of physical artifacts, differential evocation of psychological phenomena, and differential development of agency, because school itself presents cultural values different to those of oppressed groups. In developed countries, school students themselves have experienced an extensive period of "symbolic violence", says Panovsky. This empirically-grounded survey and theorizing of the mediational aspects of culture explains many cases of failure to learn in mainstream schools; it also suggest that teachers working with oppressed groups have to consider a range of instructional strategies and other forms of action to deal with the basic dysfunctionality of school as it is generally experienced by students from non-mainstream, non-middle class (white, etc.) culture.

Social Learning Theory

Besides the sociocultural traditions, perhaps the most prominent current form of social learning theory to be applied in L2 contexts is that originated by Lave (e.g., Rogoff & Lave, 1984), a social anthropologist originally working on informal learning in everyday (non-school) settings, subsequently developed and popularized by Wenger (1998). It focuses on how "communities of practice" develop and how a learner "apprentices", i.e., socially learns through participating with a group of more skilled individuals. Its potential has been recognized by L2 specialists Zuengler and Miller (2006, pp. 42–43):

> Researchers who incorporate critical theory into their exploration of second language learning argue that one must account for relations of power in order to gain a fuller understanding of the practices and interactions in which learners participate – and thus of their learning processes. ... Critical theorists tend to view marginalized members of a community as having their access to learning blocked because they may be prevented from participating meaningfully in target-language social practices.

This point was made very clear by Pavlenko (2000) surveying numerous studies with data documenting this. However, surprisingly little work has taken this insight up (Block, 2014). In addition, there is more to be learned in critical SLA than just L2 competence, and we have certainly not got as far in using the concept of a community of practice as have some critical educators. What is to be learnt is not simply language, even as a set of practices, but must include conscientization: a different way of thinking about (and acting on) the world, mediated by language. For example, consider Duncan-Andrade and Morrell's (2008, pp. 11–12) account of projects they undertook with urban youth to foster learning, operating very explicitly out of a critical view of society (with an explicit focus on race) and a participatory curriculum which made use of the concept of a community of practice. Their efforts draw on the possibility of a *counter-cultural* community of practice.

We advocate for an urban education model that utilizes critical counter-cultural communities of practice (4Cs), developing a critical and engaged citizenry with a democratic sensibility that critiques and acts against all forms of inequality. In short, communities of practice can be defined as follows:

- Who: "groups of people who share a common concern or a passion for something they do and who interact regularly to learn how to do it better".
- What is it about: it's *a joint enterprise* as understood and continually renegotiated by its members.
- How does it function: *mutual engagement* that binds members together into a social entity.
- What capability does it produce: the *shared repertoire* of communal resources (routines, sensibilities, artifacts, vocabulary, styles, etc.) that members have developed over time.

A counter-cultural community of practice recognizes the existence of a dominant set of institutional norms and practices and intentionally sets itself up to counter those norms and practices. In urban classrooms, a countercultural community of practice responds directly to structural and material inequalities in the school and the larger community. The developing counter-cultural community of practice disenfranchisement despair and academic failure to be replaced with large quantities of community critical consciousness hope and academic achievement.

To develop these critical counter-cultural communities of practice in our own work with urban youth, we attempted to employ the five steps of the cycle of critical praxis [a classic action research formulation]: identify a problem, research the problem, develop a collective plan of action to address the problem, implement the collective plan of action, evaluate the action, assess its efficacy, and re-examine the state of the problem.

Developing a full-blown alternative community or at least a group of people in a school who think and act differently seems highly desirable base for critical forms of learning. And finally, though space does not allow for developing this matter here, we do also actually need critical theories of the (second) language to be learned, to have more complete theories of critical SLA.

APPLYING CRITICAL THEORIES OF SLA TO SUPPORT CREATIVE L2 TEACHING – GENERAL CONSIDERATIONS

Creative (language) teaching has been an aspiration discussed intermittently from time to time in our field (e.g., Argondizzo, 2013; Stanislawzcyk & Yavener, 1976), though without much agreement concerning how 'creative' or 'creativity' is to be understood. One recent example from within applied linguistics is L2 researcher Wei's (2011) uptake of Bhabha's (1994) use of the term 'creativity', adjacent to and collaborating with our other key term, 'critical'. In L2 learning and multilingual language use, creativity and criticality are linked. For Wei,

> Creativity can be defined as the ability to choose between following and flouting the rules and norms of behaviour, including the use of language. It is about pushing and breaking the boundaries between the old and the new, the conventional and the original, and the acceptable and the challenging. Criticality refers to the ability to use available evidence appropriately, systematically and insightfully to inform considered views of cultural, social and linguistic phenomena, to question and problematize received wisdom, and to express views adequately through reasoned responses to situations. (p. 1223)

The most obvious and transparent application of the theories discussed above in pursuit of creative language teaching involves taking up the conception of the learner that is to be found in them. This is an active individual, very much located in a diverse society, linked to various groups of others by race, class, gender, ethnicity, and participating in global flows of people; located in a range of institutions and contexts signified by an ecological perspective. This is also a person engaged in choice, not just rule-following, which problematizes and decides a new concerning behaviour in society.

What that means for teaching in the classroom is that we teachers (and students) stand a much better chance of being creative if we recognize these aspects of the individual. As discussed in many expositions of critical language pedagogy (e.g., Crookes, 2013a), the learner can be actively involved in the construction of curriculum, and (setting aside institutional constraints) we teachers can work with them to creatively construct new courses, course material, or new variants on established courses, using at least to some extent materials that the learners create. We can encourage learners to draw on their connections to those who use the target language, either locally or elsewhere, even including in some cases their own distant relations and friends; or these can be created using the technological resources that are easier to establish than before.

We also should identify and respond creatively to the past experiences of learners, who may have learnt negative lessons from their experiences of educational institutions so far. This means we should also draw from socially-sensitive studies of learning in the L2 classroom to recognize that a diverse classroom is not always a hospitable place for minorities; or indeed, is actively repressive of them (Panovsky, above). Our creative responses to that may range from smaller in-class initiatives, through at least to co-curricular responses (see Duncan-Andrade & Morrell, above). At one level, the classic literature of critical pedagogy notes this. In various places Freire refers, for example, to ways in which he helped peasants who had short and unsuccessful experiences with formal education realize that they *did* have knowledge and agency; and he placed this kind of activity or discussion near the beginning of a course. Somewhat similarly, Shor (1987) reports starting his L1 freshman composition classes with activities that invite his mainly working-class (white, US) students to articulate their hatred of school, in some effort to then get beyond it into a more critical and useful classroom experience. The critical L2 teacher should at least be involved in naming the problem (that whites, males, and the able-bodied, not to mention the more proficient L2 learners in the class) take over and displace other learners with less cultural capital (cf. Crookes, 2003).

Our active and creative learner should be supported in taking creative action outside the classroom. For critical second language teachers, the hope is that language learning will lead to students' improved capacity for creative action in society to improve it.

CRITICAL L2 PEDAGOGY AS A MANIFESTATION OF CREATIVE LANGUAGE TEACHING

Although critical second language teaching has proceeded in advance of critical theories of second language learning, it is certainly consistent with them and might continue to develop further through engagement with critical SLA (not to mention though engagement also with critical theoretical understandings of the second language(s) to be learned). Indeed, returning for a moment to the term 'praxis' used earlier, the ideal relationship is cyclical and interactive, so that critical language pedagogy should not only be informed by, but should also inform, critical SLA. This is most likely to happen through the work of teacher-researchers (or perhaps scholar-teachers), who try out aspects of critical language pedagogy and report on successes or failures of their students to learn, thus developing or furthering critical (local) classroom theories of SLA.

A number of specialists have identified important or definitional aspects of critical language pedagogy. For example, Wallerstein (1983) mentions the importance of a listening phase on the part of the course designer or teacher, and the importance of paying attention to finding out about the learners' real lives and needs. This implies that this information will be used to create curriculum that responds to those needs, rather than uncreatively using preexisting, preset, commercial materials or state-mandated textbooks without supplementation or adaptation.

Dialogue is classically important in critical pedagogy, and this leads to what Wallerstein referred to as "education as a two-way process". Certainly, critical language pedagogy implies an interactive approach to learning within the classroom. The role of learner includes the idea that learners can also teach – they have material to bring into the classroom and course, and they are not the only person in the room who can take on the teacher role. So we expect to see a very active classroom, with a range of groupings, but certainly including small group work, and student-fronted presentations. The understanding of the learner as having material and resources to bring to the course implies that the students' first language is seen as a resource, and is not excluded from the classroom. (Thus at a basic level of classroom interaction, critical language pedagogy clearly shares much with the "strong" implementation of communicative language teaching, or with task-based language teaching, though it puts much more of the development of course content in the creative hands of the learners.)

Central to critical language pedagogy is the idea of critical thinking. Wallerstein (1983) again:

> Critical thinking in the classroom does not take place randomly; a teacher promotes inquiry by posing questions and providing information to lead the discussion into a larger social context. Students evaluate the forces that exert control on their lives. Layoffs, racism on the job, cultural discrimination, inflation, education, family – these forces limit their choices of how they live. Critical thinking begins when people make the connections between their individual lives and social conditions. It ends one step beyond perception – towards the *action* people take to regain control over social structures detrimental to their lives. (p. 16)

This use of available evidence to decide whether, or how, to push the boundaries also illustrates the bringing together of criticality with creativity.

Dialogue and critical thinking naturally come together in "discussion", a classroom activity that is likely to get disproportionate emphasis in critical second language teaching. Critical language teaching does not get this from critical theories of SLA, though it does derive it from critical theory of learning. That is because a critical theory of learning asks about the conditions that facilitate or even cause the development of critical understandings of the material to be learned, along with the development of critical consciousness; and it answers that these matters are particularly learned through critical dialogue. (This is as opposed to uncritical theories of learning which hypothesize a non-active, almost automatic or unconscious learner; or a theory of learning which doesn't operate at any social psychological level, a level, that is, in which motivation or the learners' attitude to the material to be learned is in any way causal.)

Another activity type characteristic of critical language pedagogy in the Freirean and subsequent tradition (exemplified particularly by Wallerstein) is the use of 'codes'. "Emotionally laden", a code is an projective device, a "concrete physical expression" of a critical theme manifesting as "a daily problem situation that is immediately recognizable to students" (ibid, pp. 19–20). This might be an extract of language (dialogue or text), or a drawing or photo, possibly created by the teacher, or by students, or the class working together. The code should not close off discussion and should be open to more than one interpretation. By stimulating language content and discussion, this creative element of lesson planning and in-class materials design allows students to bring as much language as possible to bear on the topic, while thinking (creatively) about its meaning and the problem it poses to them. Creative problem-solving on the part of the students would be the goal of this problem-posing on the part of the teacher.

CONCLUSION

My brief sketch of prototypical (but creative) critical language pedagogy practices serves to illustrate in a preliminary way both the demands and the possibilities for creative teaching that a critical language pedagogy and accompanying critical theories of SLA offer. Increasing number of publications offer extended realistic reports of creative critical language teachers in action and critical language teacher educators as well (many cited, reviewed, and summarized in Crookes, 2013a). I do not know to what extent (if at all) such language teachers consciously draw upon critical theories of L2 learning, though I am sure they would certainly easily be able to articulate their theoretical understandings of the second language learner, of language itself, and of the institutional and social contexts of second language learning and teaching. That is to say, they would have and be acting out of critical philosophies of language teaching, having integrated critical SLA and SLT perspectives in that. In short, they would have a critical praxis of second language education, which is what in my opinion critical SLA has most to offer.

REFERENCES

Argondizzo, C. (Ed.). (2013). *Creativity and innovation in language education*. Berlin: Peter Lang.

Atkinson, D. (Ed.). (2011). *Alternative approaches to second language acquisition*. New York, NY: Routledge.

Benesch, S. (2001). *Critical English for academic purposes*. Mahwah, NJ: Lawrence Erlbaum.

Bernstein, B. (1961). Social class and linguistic development: A theory of social learning. In A. H. Halsey, J. Floud, & C. A. Anderson (Eds.), *Education, economy and society* (pp. 288–314). New York, NY: Free Press.

Bhabba, H. (1994). *The location of culture*. London: Routledge.

Block, D. (2014). *Social class in applied linguistics*. New York, NY: Routledge.

Bowles, S., & Gintis, H. (1976). *Schooling in capitalist America*. New York, NY: Basic Books.

Cole, M., & Engeström, Y. (1993). A cultural-historical approach to distributed cognition. In G. Salomon (Ed.), *Distributed cognitions* (pp. 111–138). Cambridge: Cambridge University Press.

Crookes, G. V. (1997). What influences how and what second and foreign language teachers teach. *Modern Language Journal, 81*(1), 67–79.

Crookes, G. V. (1998). On the relationship between S/Fl teachers and S/Fl research. *TESOL Journal, 7*(3), 6–10.

Crookes, G. V. (2003). *A practicum in TESOL*. Cambridge: Cambridge University Press.

Crookes, G. V. (2009). *Values, philosophies, and beliefs in TESOL*. Cambridge: Cambridge University Press.

Crookes, G. V. (2013a). *Critial ELT in action*. New York, NY: Routledge.

Crookes, G. V. (2013b, October 15). *How should "from practice into theory" be understood, for philosophies of language teaching and critical language pedagogy*. Plenary presentation, KoreaTESOL Conference, Sookmyung Womens' University, Seoul, Korea. Retrieved from https://www.youtube.com/watch?v=8DXjFDuz3xA

Djaballah, M. (2011). *Kant, Foucault, and forms of experience*. New York, NY: Routledge.

Doughty, C. J., & Long, M. H. (2003). Optimal psycholinguistic environments for distance foreign language learning. *Language Learning and Technology, 7*(3), 50–80. Retrieved from http://www.llt.msu.edu/vol7num3/doughty/default.html

Duff, P. (2007). *Case study research in applied linguistics*. New York, NY. Routledge.

Duncan-Andrade, J. M., & Morrell, E. (2008). *The art of critical pedagogy*. New York, NY: Peter Lang.

Fox, D. R., Prilleltensky, I., & Austin, S. (Eds.). (2009). *Critical psychology: an introduction* (2nd ed.). New York, NY: Sage Publications.

Hatch, E. R. (1978). *Second language acquisition*. Rowley, MA: Newbury.

Heath, S. B. (1983). *Ways with words*. Cambridge: Cambridge University Press.

LeCompte, M. D., & Preissle, J. (1993). *Ethnography and qualitative design in educational research* (2nd ed.). San Diego, CA: Academic Press.

Morgan, B. (1988). *The ESL classroom*. Toronto: University of Toronto Press.

Nardi, B. A. (1996). Activity theory and human-computer interaction. In B. A. Nardi (Ed.), *Context and consciousness* (pp. 7–16). Cambridge, MA: MIT Press.

Norton, B. (2014). Identity and poststructuralist theory in SLA. In S. Mercer & M. Williams (Eds.), *Multiple perspectives on the self in SLA* (pp. 59–74). Bristol: Multilingual Matters.

Norton, B., & Toohey, K. (Eds.). (2004). *Critical pedagogies and language learning*. Cambridge: Cambridge University Press.

Panovsky, C. P. (2003). The relations of learning and student social class. In A. Kozulin, B. Gindis, V. S. Ageyev, & S. M. Miller (Eds.), *Vygotsky's educational theory in cultural context* (pp. 411–431). Cambridge: Cambridge University Press.

Pavlenko, A. (2000). Access to linguistic resources. *Estudios de Sociolingüinguistica, 1*(2), 85–105.

Ricento, T. (2005). Considerations of identity in L2 learning. In E. Hinkel (Ed.), *Handbook of research on second language teaching and learning* (pp. 895–910). New York, NY: Routledge.

Rogoff, B., & Lave, J. (Eds.). (1984). *Everyday cognition*. Cambridge, MA: Harvard University Press.

Sawchuk, P. H. (2006). Activity and power. In P. H. Sawchuk, N. Duarte, & M. El Hammoumi (Eds.), *Critical perspectives on activity* (pp. 238–268). Cambridge: Cambridge University Press.

Schraube, E. (2000). Reflecting on who we are in a technological world. In T. Sloan (Ed.), *Critical psychology* (pp. 46–54). London: Palgrave Macmillan.

Shor, I. (1987). *Critical teaching and everyday life.* Chicago, IL: University of Chicago Press.

Stanislawczyk, I. E., & Yavener, S. (1976). *Creativity in the language classroom.* Rowley, MA: Newbury House.

Graham V. Crookes
University of Hawai'i
Honolulu, USA

PART 2

SKILLS/SUBSKILLS

JOHN M. LEVIS AND SHANNON MCCROCKLIN

7. REFLECTIVE AND EFFECTIVE TEACHING OF PRONUNCIATION

WHY TEACH PRONUNCIATION?

Pronunciation is an inescapable part of spoken communication, and all speakers have an accent of some sort. It is impossible to speak a language without pronouncing it, and it is impossible to understand other speakers without negotiating their pronunciation. Most adult language learners need help with pronunciation in order to be more intelligible and to understand others. Yet activities that work to enhance global speaking ability, which prioritize fluency (such as communicative or task-based activities) may not improve pronunciation (which typically requires activities prioritizing accuracy) because fluency and accuracy in speech are often seen as competing goals. We believe that specific attention to, and instruction in, pronunciation can help learners not only improve their pronunciation, but also, if done well, complement fluency-oriented speaking and listening goals.

Knowing how to teach pronunciation is an essential skill for any language teacher. However, English language teachers often report feeling uncertain about or inadequate in teaching pronunciation (Breitkreutz, Derwing, & Rossiter, 2001; Burgess & Spencer, 2000; Foote, Holtby, & Derwing, 2012; Macdonald, 2002). Rarely do teachers say they feel inadequate teaching grammar or other language features or skills. But pronunciation is different. This is why it is especially important to consider what makes an effective pronunciation teacher.

WHAT MAKES AN EFFECTIVE PRONUNCIATION TEACHER?

When we talk about effective and reflective teaching of pronunciation, we are talking about teachers' practices in regard to students (effective teaching) and in regard to themselves (reflective teaching). Effective teaching depends on teachers understanding what makes learners more intelligible, why pronunciation is important to intelligibility, and how students' pronunciation skills can improve. Reflective teaching means that teachers look critically at their own teaching; they question and evaluate their own beliefs about pronunciation teaching and purposefully work to incorporate systematic reflection into their practice for more successful future teaching.

© KONINKLIJKE BRILL NV, LEIDEN, 2018 | DOI:10.1163/9789004380882_007

Although we could provide many characteristics of effective pronunciation teachers, this chapter looks at four characteristics that are particularly important. Effective pronunciation teachers understand the factors that affect pronunciation learning, assess their learners' needs, have an appropriate goal for teaching pronunciation, and employ varied techniques in a coherent framework for teaching pronunciation. Finally, the chapter describes suggestions to become a more reflective pronunciation teacher, including questions to consider before teaching pronunciation and suggestions for ways to incorporate reflection during teaching.

Understanding Factors That Affect Pronunciation Learning

An effective pronunciation teacher understands that pronunciation learning in a foreign or second language (we use L2 to refer to both of these learning contexts) occurs differently for different learners. In fact, few areas in language show such variation in ultimate attainment. Many factors seem to be connected to this variation. One of the most obvious is the influence of the first language (L1). L2 learners come into the new language with pronunciation patterns from their L1 already fixed in place. German speakers do not speak or hear English the way French speakers or Farsi speakers do. Further, the articulatory movements of their L1s are automatic, often leaving traces of their L1 (an accent) on their L2. Changing these articulatory patterns is challenging, not only for new sounds, but also for new patterns of speaking and voice quality distinctions.

In addition to the L1, age differences are critical in the success of pronunciation learning. Native accents for adult learners are rare, perhaps constituting evidence of a critical period in language learning (Scovel, 2000). Researchers have argued that once learners reach a certain age, the possibility of native-like abilities in the L2 either stops or steadily decreases (e.g., DeKeyser & Larson-Hall, 2005). Language learning still occurs, just not by the same mechanisms that operate in learning the L1. However, other research indicates that pronunciation evidence for the Critical Period Hypothesis is not as clear as once thought. For example, we know that some L2 learners become native-like in pronunciation and ability to use the L2 even when they start their learning well beyond the critical period (Coppieters, 1987; Ioup, Boustagui, Tigi, & Mouselle, 1994; Moyer, 2013).

Though they are a minority of L2 learners, these so-called exceptional learners (Moyer, 2014) have certain characteristics in common in their pronunciation learning. They approach pronunciation learning metacognitively, that is, they think about how to learn most effectively and test their ideas out. Further, they strongly identify with the new language, are socially outgoing in how they approach learning and use the language in as many ways as they can. In other words, they want to sound like natives, they approach language learning through interacting with others, and they seek out ways to use the language.

Assessing Pronunciation Needs

Another mark of an effective teacher is the ability to determine which errors are important for students. Pronunciation materials usually have many exercises that are simply not important for any given student. Applied to vowel and consonant sounds, this means that not only should a teacher be able to determine which problems are common in a class, but they should also be able to evaluate whether particular errors are worth the time they will take. More importantly, teachers need to assess suprasegmental needs. An effective teacher pays attention to those things that are likely to make a difference in communication while deemphasizing anything that is unlikely to make an immediate difference. Some errors are not worth time because their payoff is small, such as the "th" sounds of English. Although these sounds are well-known problems for almost all learners, they do not seem to cause great loss of intelligibility (Jenkins, 2000; Munro & Derwing, 2006).

Experienced teachers often have a good idea of what students need, especially with a class of students who all share the same L1. In addition, some teacher resource books (e.g., Avery & Ehrlich, 1992; Swan & Smith, 2001) list out typical errors according to L1. However, these general guidelines can only give an approximate diagnosis for a particular group of students. Errors vary not only according to a student's L1 but also according to proficiency level, linguistic environment and many individual factors that are hard to predict. As a result, it is important to make decisions about pronunciation according to the needs of actual students. The level of the students will also affect teacher decisions. For example, beginning students may benefit from being taught the prosody of functional routines such as greetings and introductions (Muller Levis & Levis, 2014) while more advanced students may need other practice, such as consonant or vowel sounds that affect intelligibility and have not improved naturally. Using a diagnostic test at the beginning of the semester can help identify not only the students' pronunciation level, but also common problems across students.

Choosing an Appropriate Goal for Teaching

Using language is a social activity, and pronunciation is the most public face of language. As a result, effective pronunciation teaching must also take the social face of pronunciation into account (Levis, 2015). Social affiliations and cultural interests may affect the pronunciation success of the learner (Gatbonton & Trofimovich, 2008; Marx, 2002). Further, as students work to change their accent they may find their identity challenged (Piller, 2002). Because of the links between accent and identity, some theorists are uncertain about the ethical ramifications of pushing students towards a native-like accent (Daniels, 1995; Porter & Garvin, 1989). It is important to note, however, that many students report wishing to sound like a native speaker (Andreasson, 1994; Derwing, 2003, Sobkowiak, 2005; Yamaguchi,

2002). Students' pronunciation goals, however, are likely to vary according to overall language learning purposes and goals. For example, students who want to study in an English-speaking country may have different goals than those who wish to remain in their home countries. Because of this, teachers should take the time to learn about their students' goals and help students explore ways pronunciation learning may affect their sense of identity (McCrocklin & Link, 2016).

Student goals should affect the models of pronunciation that are introduced in the class. Students wishing to use the language with other non-native speakers may be more interested in learning from non-native speaker models. Additionally, Murphy (2014) argues that intelligible nonnative speakers may be the best pronunciation models because learners may be better able to aspire to the achievement of such models. On the other hand, students that hope to study in a particular country may have a particular native model that they prefer as it is more useful to their goals. Providing appropriate models of English may also allow teachers to find speakers of the language that can make pronunciation lessons more interesting. Cutler (2014) found that teenaged and young adult immigrants in New York often pronounced English like hip-hop music singers. This accent, often stigmatized by mainstream American English speakers, provided an attractive identity to immigrant learners for whom this was the best fit for their social needs. Indeed, the disembodied voices of language learning recordings may not represent models that students want to imitate.

An effective pronunciation teacher also understands the differences between accent and intelligibility. Accent means the way that any speaker speaks a language. Intelligibility is a measure of how understandable a speaker is. This distinction makes a big difference in how we approach pronunciation. Traditionally, pronunciation teaching has tried to help learners achieve a native accent. This is called the Nativeness principle (Levis, 2005). As discussed above, a native accent is rare in L2 learning. If nativeness is the correct goal for learning, then pronunciation learning is doomed to failure in most cases. A different view of pronunciation teaching is based on the Intelligibility principle (Levis, 2005). In this approach, pronunciation teaching should target the features of speech that are most important in making communication successful.

The distinction between accent and intelligibility is important because someone can speak with a very strong accent yet be completely intelligible (Munro & Derwing, 1995). Helping students work toward intelligibility means paying attention to a number of facts. First, it means that not all pronunciation errors are equal in their effects on understanding. For instance, Munro and Derwing (2006) studied the effects of high-functional load (e.g., /l/-/n/ as in *light* pronounced as *night*) and low-functional load errors (e.g., /ð/-/d/ as in *then* pronounced as *den*). High functional load errors affected listeners' ability to understand more than low-functional load errors. Second, teachers need to recognize that suprasegmental features of language may lead to noticeable improvement more quickly than segmental features. Derwing, Munro, and Wiebe (1998) found that listeners judged the spontaneous speech of learners more favorably when they had been taught with suprasegmentals than when they had been taught with lessons using only vowels and consonants. Finally, teaching for intelligibility means that pronunciation is important not only for speaking, but also for listening. In other words, speakers must not only be understood by others, they must understand the speech of the people they are talking to. Teaching for accent means that the full burden of successful communication is on the nonnative speaker. Teaching for intelligibility recognizes that both parties must be intelligible to each other.

Knowing Teaching Techniques and Frameworks

Effective pronunciation teachers need an eclectic set of approaches to teaching and a framework for how to use the tools in their work. This means that they need a variety of techniques to help students learn the pronunciation of the L2 and need to understand how the techniques fit together in teaching. Research has shown that the most common techniques used in teaching pronunciation are "listen and repeat" and "read aloud" (Carey, Sweeting, & Mannell, 2015). This is like trying to build furniture with only a hammer and a screwdriver. While both hammers and screwdrivers are important, building furniture requires more tools. The same is true of pronunciation teaching. Many pronunciation teaching activities and ideas are available in professional books (e.g., Celce-Murcia, Brinton, & Goodwin, 2010), teacher activity collections (see Murphy & Baker, 2015), published articles (Goodwin, 2004; LeVelle & Levis, 2014), at conferences, and on the internet. And of course, teachers often create their own teaching activities that are excellent and effective.

Perhaps more important than individual teaching tools is an overall knowledge of how the tools work together. This means teachers need a framework. We recommend the communicative framework of Celce-Murcia, Brinton, and Goodwin (2010). This framework recognizes that L2 learners need to understand the pronunciation feature they are learning (metacognitive knowledge), perceive new sounds (perception), make new sounds in controlled contexts (controlled production), pronounce while trying to focus on meaning and the pronunciation feature (guided production), and develop automatic abilities to pronounce while communicating (communicative practice). Although these types of techniques are not all communicative, we follow Harmer (1982), who said that communicative teaching will also require activities that are not communicative. With pronunciation, different needs require different techniques.

- Explanation: Focus is on cognitive understanding of the pronunciation features and/or pronunciation system
  - Example techniques: Use of phonetic symbols, sagittal diagrams, and charts
- Perception: Focus is on hearing pronunciation distinctions
  - Example techniques: Discrimination, identification, and minimal pair sentence exercises

- Controlled: Focus is on mastery of pronunciation form
  - Example techniques: Repeating, reading aloud, and naming from pictures
- Guided: A dual focus on pronunciation and other elements of language
  - Example techniques: Information gap and picture narratives
- Communicative practice: Focus is on language use with no explicit attention to pronunciation
  - Example techniques: Using authentic materials, discussion, and role plays

In addition, teachers need tools that connect pronunciation to other areas of language. English is well-known for its unclear connections between the way words are spelled and the way they are pronounced. Although the English spelling system is very well-suited to a morphologically focused language (Chomsky, 1972), and its sounds are largely predictable if readers recognize the clues in the system (Dickerson, 2015), the immediate reaction to the spelling system from both native and nonnative speakers is that it is wildly inconsistent. This makes it all the more important for teachers to be aware of the ways that spelling can be used predictively as a guide for pronunciation.

Another connection that teachers should be aware of is how listening comprehension is connected to the ability to understand spoken pronunciation (Cauldwell, 2011), especially the pronunciation differences of stressed and unstressed words. Field (2008) compares these to the bricks (stressed words) and mortar (unstressed words) used in building a wall. When we look at a brick wall, we see the bricks, not the mortar. Yet it is the mortar that holds the bricks together. Likewise, when we listen to English, we more easily hear the stressed words (usually content words such as nouns, verbs, and adjectives) than we do the unstressed words (usually function words such as prepositions, pronouns, and auxiliaries). Yet the unstressed words specify the relationships between the stressed words, and being able to understand the unstressed words in normal speech leads to greater understanding and less guessing.

TEACHING REFLECTIVELY

Once teachers understand the basic skills of effectively teaching pronunciation, they can improve their teaching through reflective practice. Reflective teaching has spread in the last several decades, gaining widespread acceptance as a way for teachers to improve their classroom effectiveness (Zeichner & Liston, 2014). Yet resources for incorporating reflection are uneven in different educational areas. Resources are especially limited in regard to pronunciation teaching. This section provides a rationale for reflective pronunciation teaching, questions to evaluate a teacher's beliefs about pronunciation, methods for incorporating purposeful reflection into teaching, and an example of what reflective pronunciation teaching may look like.

Most teachers are inherently but not systematically reflective. If a lesson goes poorly, teachers ponder what went wrong, often for days. When a lesson goes well, teachers excitedly return to that lesson in the future, but they may not have thought carefully about why the lesson went so well. Incorporating the principles of reflective teaching means that teachers further commit to purposeful and consistent evaluation of their ideas, beliefs, experiences, and context, with a goal of improving their teaching over time (Zeichner & Liston, 2014, p. 14). By purposefully thinking about successful and less successful classroom experiences, and why certain results or reactions may have happened, teachers can evaluate the success of their approach while exploring other teaching approaches that may better help them reach their goals (Cruikshank & Applegate, 1981).

Reflective pronunciation teaching starts before teaching ever happens. It is important for teachers to think about their beliefs, and previous experiences with pronunciation teaching or learning, and what they hope to achieve by their pronunciation teaching. By answering each of the questions below (adapted from Farrell, 2007) and considering beliefs about pronunciation teaching, teachers will gain new insights about the ways they approach pronunciation teaching.

Questions for Reflection before Teaching Pronunciation:

- What experiences have I had learning pronunciation? What types of activities did my teacher use? How did I feel during those lessons?
- What is the most difficult aspect of learning the pronunciation of a foreign language?
- What are appropriate goals for pronunciation teaching?
- How do I see the teacher's role in the pronunciation classroom?
- How is pronunciation usually taught at my school?
- What are the advantages and challenges of teaching pronunciation where I usually teach?
- How would I evaluate my current pronunciation of English?
- Which aspects of pronunciation teaching am I most excited about?
- What are my biggest concerns about teaching pronunciation?

Reflecting during Teaching

As teachers enter the classroom and try various pronunciation teaching activities with students, it is important that teachers commit to continued reflection. To encourage systematic reflection during the course of teaching, we recommend three methods of reflection, as introduced by Farrell (2007): journals, recorded lessons or peer observations, and action research. Each of these methods has complementary advantages for teachers.

- Journals are useful for reflective teaching because they are a quick and easy way to keep track of feelings and thoughts about teaching over a long period of time. Journals that are kept regularly allow teachers to identify trends across

83

multiple lessons. An example journal page (see Appendix A) shows how teachers can turn reflective questions into narrative frames, or stories about the teaching. Researchers have discovered that these types of stories can be useful because they allow common practices and trends to be noticed (Macalister, 2012).

- Recorded lessons and peer observations are useful because they allow teachers to see themselves and what is happening during lessons. They allow reflection in a way that may be impossible during class while teachers are guiding lessons and monitoring class progress. Further, by asking a peer to observe, teachers can not only get another perspective on the teaching, but also can engage another individual in brainstorming and problem-solving for issues that may arise during the teaching. Farrell (2007) warns, however, that peer observations need to be 'non-judgmental', unlike supervisor observations in which the teacher is being evaluated for meeting pre-determined criteria. For teaching pronunciation, a peer observer should also have sympathy for the goal of teaching pronunciation. Observations are meant to help, not to force teachers to justify the teaching of pronunciation.

- Action research is useful for reflective teaching because it encourages teachers to make changes to their teaching (based on their teaching situation) and try new activities while being thoughtful of why they are teaching and what they want to achieve. Action research begins when a teacher notices a problem or issue in their teaching that they wish to address (Burns, 2010). Farrell (2007) suggests that after identifying a problem or issue, the teacher should collect data on the teaching to locate source of the issue, review articles or book chapters about the issue, look for suggested solutions, implement changes as part of the action plan, and monitor and reflect on success of the changes.

While each of these methods for reflection is useful for encouraging reflection, they are likely to be most useful when used in combination. The following example, a composite picture developed from a number of different teachers we have known, shows the potential for using reflective teaching (and specifically multiple methods) for improving pronunciation teaching.

Example

Bahar is a nonnative teacher. She teaches in an EFL context to students who share her L1. She believes pronunciation is an essential skill in learning to speak and listen, so she teaches an English pronunciation class to intermediate learners. At the beginning of each week, she introduces two pronunciation topics: a new sound (a segmental topic) and a suprasegmental topic, such as something about thought groups, phrase stress, or intonation. Students practice with the topics for the rest of the week. Practice includes controlled, guided and communicative exercises. At the beginning of the following week, Bahar introduces a new segmental and suprasegmental topic. Because Bahar journals about her classes after each lesson, she discovers a problem. On the first day of each week, she usually complains about student participation. Sometimes students are quiet and hesitant when called on and sometimes they do not seem to understand the topic and struggle to complete tasks.

Bahar decides to video-record the introductory lessons for three weeks and, while she reviews her recorded lessons, makes notes about activities, timing, and recorded student comments. She is shocked to realize that each week she spends only about five minutes on listening practice. She notices that students make comments that indicate they are struggling to hear what she wants them to learn. She realizes that she is usually nervous about the listening activities from her textbook because she often has to read them aloud but is uncertain about her own pronunciation.

For the next semester, she decides to revise her approach to the first day of the week, initiating an action research project by adding more listening work. She asks to have her class moved to a computer lab for the first day of the week. She finds resources online such as minimal pair listening practice (for an example see www. manythings.org/pp/) and recorded talks with transcripts (for examples of highly intelligible native and non-native speakers see www.ted.com). In her action research, on the first day of each week, Bahar introduces the segmental topic and the students practice their listening with the game-like minimal pair website. She also introduces a suprasegmental topic and students use sections of transcripts from recorded talks to mark where they hear the suprasegmental feature. Bahar continues to journal and records a couple of her class periods in the second semester. Her students now feel more comfortable when they practice pronouncing because they are more confident in their listening. Even though Bahar still serves as a pronunciation model for some activities each week, the use of outside resources relieves the pressure of having to be a perfect model.

In summary, Bahar's use of journaling helped her notice a problem that she might have otherwise missed. This led her to record her class and allowed her to observe that she gave her students insufficient time in listening to get ready for production practice. As a result, she implemented changes to her class and observed how the changes helped. Reflection involved, as Bahar's case shows, a daily or weekly element (journaling), a focused observation period (the video-recording), and a plan to change the approach to teaching to meet the students' needs (action research).

CONCLUSION

As mentioned earlier, oral communication includes, at the very least, both speaking and listening. It is important to remember that pronunciation is connected to and interacts with speaking and listening abilities. Students are developing at least two distinct types of skills in speaking a language. First, they are learning to speak the new language with ease and fluency. Second, they are learning to pronounce accurately, initially in very controlled ways, but eventually also in the stream of fluent speech. Speaking frequently and speaking to many people in the L2 helps the development of these speaking skills, and ultimately in being able to better attend to pronunciation. Additionally, learners are building their ability to understand the speech and pronunciation of others in social interaction. Speaking and pronunciation are both social in nature, and extensive improvement in both can only occur with regular social interaction (Levis & Moyer, 2014).

To summarize some of what we have discussed:

- One cannot speak without pronouncing.
- Everyone, native or nonnative, speaks with some kind of accent.
- Different factors influence L2 pronunciation, including age, aptitude, and the speaker's L1.
- Some pronunciation differences may make the speaker unintelligible to the listener, while others will not. Differences that affect intelligibility are the most important.
- Each learner and class will have unique needs that should be assessed.
- Pronunciation teaching will be most successful when it involves a variety of ways to practice.
- Pronunciation teachers can improve their practice through reflective practice.

Many teachers are reluctant to teach pronunciation, but non-native speaking teachers may be especially hesitant to jump into the teaching of pronunciation. They may feel that their own pronunciation is not good enough or assume that their students will learn pronunciation better from a native speaker. It is important to note that there is no evidence that learning pronunciation occurs as a direct result of only listening to desirable accents. Non-native teachers can be successful pronunciation teachers and can help inspire students by showing an example of successful language learning.

Teachers can help their students improve their pronunciation by understanding the factors that affect pronunciation achievement, such as the L1 and age, and by choosing appropriate models and goals for students in their classes (using student needs and preferences to choose appropriate pronunciation models and emphasizing intelligibility in production). Teachers should have a wide variety of techniques to address pronunciation. But teachers should also recognize that effective teaching demands reflective teaching, and that only through reflective teaching will they improve. Teachers should commit to purposeful reflective pronunciation teaching through the use of journals, peer and video recorded teaching, and mini-action research, in order to improve their teaching over time.

REFERENCES

Andreasson, A. (1994). Norm as a pedagogical paradigm. *World Englishes, 13*(3), 395–409.
Breitkreutz, J., Derwing, T. M., & Rossiter, M. J. (2001). Pronunciation teaching practices in Canada. *TESL Canada Journal, 19*(1), 51–61.

Burgess, J., & Spencer, S. (2000). Phonology and pronunciation in integrated language teaching and teacher education. *System, 28*(2), 191–215.

Burns, A. (2010). *Doing action research in English language teaching: A guide for practitioners*. New York, NY: Routledge.

Carey, M. D., Sweeting, A., & Mannell, R. (2015). An L1 point of reference approach to pronunciation modification: Learner-centered alternatives to 'listen and repeat'. *Journal of Academic Language and Learning, 9*(1), A18–A30.

Celce-Murcia, M., Brinton, D. M., & Goodwin, J. M. (2010). *Teaching pronunciation: A course book and reference guide*. Cambridge: Cambridge University Press.

Chomsky, N. (1972). Phonology and reading. In H. Levin (Ed.), *Basic processes in reading* (pp. 3–18). New York, NY: Harper & Row.

Coppieters, R. (1987). Competence differences between native and near-native speakers. *Language, 63*(3), 544–573.

Cruickshank, D., & Applegate, J. (1981). Reflective teaching as a strategy for teacher growth. *Educational Leadership, 38*, 553–554.

Crystal, D. (2012). *English as a global language* (2nd ed.). Cambridge: Cambridge University Press.

Cutler, C. (2014). Accentedness, "passing" and crossing. In J. Levis & A. Moyer (Eds.), *Social dynamics in second language accent* (pp. 145–169). Boston, MA: DeGruyter.

Daniels, H. (1995). Psycholinguistic, psycho-affective and procedural factors in the acquisition of authentic L2 phonology. *Speak Out!, 15*, 3–10.

DeKeyser, R., & Larson-Hall, J. (2005). What does the critical period really mean? In J. Kroll & A. De Groot (Eds.), *Handbook of bilingualism: Psycholinguistic approaches* (pp. 88–108). Oxford: Oxford University Press.

Derwing, T. M. (2003). What do ESL students say about their accents? *Canadian Modern Language Review, 59*(4), 547–567.

Derwing, T. M., Munro, M. J., & Wiebe, G. (1998). Evidence in favor of a broad framework for pronunciation instruction. *Language Learning, 48*(3), 393–410.

Dickerson, W. B. (2015). Using orthography to teach pronunciation. In M. Reed & J. Levis (Eds.), *The handbook of English pronunciation* (pp. 484–500). Boston, MA: Wiley.

Farrell, T. (2007). *Reflective language teaching: From research to practice*. New York, NY: Continuum.

Field, J. (2008). Bricks or mortar: Which parts of the input does a second language listener rely on? *TESOL Quarterly, 42*(3), 411–432.

Foote, J. A., Holtby, A. K., & Derwing, T. M. (2012). Survey of the teaching of pronunciation in adult ESL programs in Canada, 2010. *TESL Canada Journal, 29*(1), 1–22.

Gatbonton, E., & Trofimovich, P. (2008). The ethnic group affiliation and L2 proficiency link: Empirical evidence. *Language Awareness, 17*(3), 229–248.

Goodwin, J. (2004). The power of context in teaching pronunciation. In J. Frodesen & C. Holten (Eds.), *The power of context in language teaching and learning* (pp. 225–236). Boston, MA: Thomson/Heinle.

Harmer, J. (1982). What is communicative? *ELT Journal, 36*(3), 164–168.

Ioup, G., Boustagui, E., El Tigi, M., & Moselle, M. (1994). Reexamining the critical period hypothesis. *Studies in Second Language Acquisition, 16*(1), 73–98.

Jenkins, J. (2000). *The phonology of English as an international language*. Oxford: Oxford University Press.

LeVelle, K., & Levis, J. (2014). Understanding the impact of social factors on L2 pronunciation: Insights from learners. In J. Levis & A. Moyer (Eds.), *Social dynamics in second language accent* (pp. 97–118). Boston, MA: Degruyter.

Levis, J. M. (2005). Changing contexts and shifting paradigms in pronunciation teaching. *TESOL Quarterly, 39*(3), 369–377.

Levis, J. M. (2015). Learners' views of social issues in pronunciation learning. *Journal of Academic Language and Learning, 9*(1), A42–55.

Levis, J. M., & Moyer, A. (2014). *Social dynamics in second language* accent. Boston, MA: DeGruyter.

Macalister, J. (2012). Narrative frames and needs analysis. *System, 40*, 120–128.

Macdonald, S. (2002). Pronunciation – Views and practices of reluctant teachers. *Prospect, 17*(3), 3–18.

Marx, N. (2002). Never quite a 'native speaker': Accent and identity in the L2-and the L1. *Canadian Modern Language Review, 59*(2), 264–281.

McCrocklin, S., & Link, S. (2016). Accent, identity, and a fear of loss? ESL students' perspectives. *Canadian Modern Language Review, 72*(1), 122–149.

Moyer, A. (2013). *Foreign accent: The phenomenon of non-native speech.* New York, NY: Cambridge University Press.

Moyer, A. (2014). Exceptional outcomes in L2 phonology: The critical factors of learner engagement and self-regulation. *Applied Linguistics, 35*(4), 418–440.

Munro, M. J., & Derwing, T. M. (1995). Foreign accent, comprehensibility, and intelligibility in the speech of second language learners. *Language Learning, 45*(1), 73–97.

Munro, M. J., & Derwing, T. M. (2006). The functional load principle in ESL pronunciation instruction: An exploratory study. *System, 34*(4), 520–531.

Murphy, J. M. (2014). Intelligible, comprehensible, non-native models in ESL/EFL pronunciation teaching. *System, 42,* 258–269.

Murphy, J. M., & Baker, A. (2015). History of ESL pronunciation teaching. In M. Reed & J. Levis (Eds.), *The handbook of English pronunciation* (pp. 36–65). Boston, MA: Wiley.

Piller, I. (2002). Passing for a native speaker: Identity and success in second language learning. *Journal of Sociolinguistics, 6*(2), 179–208.

Porter, D., & Garvin, S. (1989). Attitudes to pronunciation in EFL. *Speak Out!, 5,* 8–15.

Scovel, T. (2000). A critical review of the critical period research. *Annual Review of Applied Linguistics, 20,* 213–223.

Sobkowiak, W. (2005). Why not LFC? In K. Dziubalska-Kołaczyk & J. Przedlacka (Eds.), *English pronunciation models: A changing scene* (pp. 131–150). Berlin: Peter Lang.

Yamaguchi, C. (2002). Towards international English in EFL classrooms in Japan. *The Internet TESL Journal, 8*(1). Retrieved from http://iteslj.org/Articles/Yamaguchi-Language.html

Zeichner, K., & Liston, D. (2014). *Reflective teaching: An introduction* (2nd ed.). New York, NY: Routledge.

John M. Levis
Iowa State University
Ames, Iowa
USA

Shannon McCrocklin
Southern Illinois University
Carbondale, Illinois
USA

APPENDIX A: EXAMPLE JOURNAL PAGE WITH NARRATIVE
FRAMES FOR REFLECTION

Journal of Pronunciation Lesson on (*Date*)

Today in class I taught

_____

_____

_____

using the activities,

_____

_____

_____

because (rationale)

_____

_____

_____

I thought the lesson was

_____

_____

_____

Student reactions were

_____

_____

_____

If I teach it again, I might change

_____

_____

_____

CONSTANCE WEAVER AND DOROTHY GILLMEISTER

8. REFLECTIVE AND EFFECTIVE
TEACHING OF GRAMMAR

INTRODUCTION

This chapter recounts the intellectual and experiential journey of two college professors, one in teaching a graduate TESOL class and the other in teaching English to middle and high school and then to university students in Korea. It chronicles our adventures in moving from theory and research into practice, then evaluating that practice and confirming our theoretical principles. Our experiences as well as theory and research support a constructivist, second language acquisition model of learning and teaching English as an additional language, and each of us, in our different environments, concluded that the primary role of the teacher in teaching English to speakers of other languages is to provide comprehensible input, and to make input comprehensible. Both, we believe, are essential in helping non-native speakers of English develop grammatical facility in this increasingly global language.

Because we insist upon coherence between theory and practice, our procedures and practices, our instructional designs – not a formal method or approach – are consistent with the model of second language teaching articulated by Richards and Rogers (2001, ch. 2), wherein methodology and design link theory and practice. A diagram from a 2001 article by Rodgers nearly, but not quite, captures what for decades has characterized our own teaching. Our own model is more complex, indicating that everything affects everything else:

In Figure 8.1, the double-ended arrows indicate the multiple and complex transactions between and among theory, research, and practice. For instance, just as theory and research affect instructional design and practice, so observation of and especially reflection upon teaching practices may affect both future instructional design and theory. Indeed, we contend that such reflection and revision are necessary hallmarks of an excellent teacher.

This chapter is divided into two sections, the first has been written by Constance Weaver and the second by Dorothy Gillmeister.

© KONINKLIJKE BRILL NV, LEIDEN, 2018 | DOI:10.1163/9789004380882_008

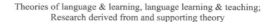

Theories of language & learning, language learning & teaching;
Research derived from and supporting theory

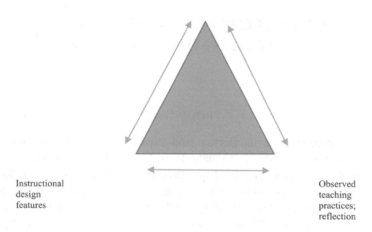

Instructional
design
features

Observed
teaching
practices;
reflection

*Figure 8.1. Weaver and Gillmeister's "everything affects
everything else" model of language teaching*

PART 1
THEORY, RESEARCH, AND PRACTICE: LEARNING GRAMMAR
THROUGH READING, TEACHING GRAMMAR DURING WRITING

Early in the 1990s, I, Connie Weaver, was unexpectedly told that our Linguistics department at Western Michigan University had developed a TESOL program that required my graduate course in psycholinguistics in reading. Well versed in reading theory and practice (Weaver, 1994 and later editions), I first reconsidered learning theories with which I was already familiar. One of these was the widely acclaimed theory of learning posited by Brian Cambourne of Australia in the 1970s and further expanded in his "Toward an Educationally Relevant Theory of Literacy Learning: Twenty Years of Inquiry" (1995). Cambourne's conditions for literacy learning and teaching are based upon observations of first language acquisition and what best promotes it; clearly, they are just as relevant to the acquisition of additional languages. Representing conditions for learning in general, Cambourne's most recent visual model, like our "everything affects everything else model", seeks to demonstrate the interrelationships between and among various factors that promote the acquisition of literacy (Cambourne, 2009).

In the early 1990s, though, all I had available to me was Cambourne's original characterizations of these language and literacy learning principles (Cambourne, 1988) (Figure 8.2). What seemed especially relevant then were the notion that we must (1) engage learners in meaningful encounters with language (akin to Stephen Krashen's concept of "comprehensible input", 1982); demonstrate how language works (which may have given rise to our belief that we must make other input comprehensible); and – especially important, we think – acknowledge the validity of the observation that language is not learned from one-shot teaching (a behavioral approach), but rather is learned gradually, with gross approximations of the target language gradually giving way to closer and closer approximations of the target language. This, Gillmeister and I both know, is especially true for the learning of grammar.

These conditions of learning, by the way, closely resemble principles underlying a communicative approach to language teaching (Rodgers, 2001, p. 2). Not familiar with those at the time, I was heavily influenced by Stephen Krashen's five conditions for second language acquisition (1982). Especially crucial, I thought, were the importance of minimizing fear of failure (the affective filter concept) and the importance of comprehensible input from which language acquisition would develop naturally.

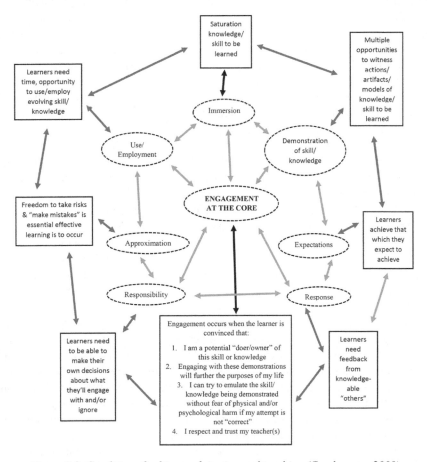

Figure 8.2. Conditions for literacy learning and teaching (Cambourne, 2009)

In planning for my graduate course in understanding and teaching reading as a psycholinguistic process, I was determined to foster the international students' own command of English through "methods", loosely speaking, that reflected these theories. Thus armed with theory, I sought research demonstrating its success.

At first, I delved into research I was already aware of, namely research in the South Pacific and Southeast Asia summarized by Warwick Elley.

Research on Second Language Acquisition in the South Pacific and Southeast Asia

What follows is mostly derived from what I later wrote (Weaver, 1996, pp. 50–51) about Warwick Elley's review of nine studies (1991).

In "Acquiring Literacy in a Second Language: The Effect of Book-Based Programs", Warwick Elley (1991) reviews nine studies of the acquisition of English as a second language, most of which were undertaken with children in the South Pacific and Southeast Asia. Most notable among these is his own earlier study (Elley & Mangubhai, 1983). Typically these studies compared the results of programs based on structured systematic instruction in English with "book flood" programs, which exposed children to large numbers of high-interest storybooks. In other words, the studies compared the effects of a direct instruction (behavioral) approach with an indirect instruction (constructivist) approach designed simply to provide children with comprehensible input.

The direct instruction approach typically was based upon the principles articulated by structural linguists (e.g., Bloomfield, 1942) and audiolingual methodology: practice on a carefully sequenced set of grammatical structures, through imitation, repetition, and reinforcement. In contrast, the book flood approaches reflected "natural" or whole language learning principles. They usually involved sustained silent reading of an extensive number of picture books. The Shared Book Experience (Holdaway, 1979) involved not only reading but discussing the books and doing related activities, or a combination of Sustained Silent Reading and the Shared Book Experience. In one instance, these two procedures were supplemented by a modified language experience approach involving children in reading material they had dictated.

For our focus on grammar, it is most important to note that students in the book flood programs in natural settings often did better on tests of grammatical structures than students who received direct instruction in them (Elley, 1991, p. 389). Overall, direct approaches to teaching grammar and vocabulary were usually less effective than exposure to massive amounts of natural texts, especially picture books and material dictated by the learners. This goes a long way toward confirming Krashen's hypotheses that a low affective filter and high amounts of comprehensible input are crucial for the acquisition of an additional language.

When I read Elley's review, I noted that those studies in which the experimental subjects not only read but also discussed their reading and perhaps did related activities were especially successful. This research and my immersion in whole language principles and practices (Weaver, 1990) led to my conviction that the teacher's role is not only to provide comprehensible input, but also to make input more comprehensible. Later, influenced by Terrell (1991), I specifically concluded that a modest amount of direct instruction, when students' writing shows readiness for it, could make grammatical constructions more comprehensible, even within basically a communicative approach.

Still later my interest led me to other research confirming Elley's conclusion that wide reading is a powerful force in the acquisition of grammar, for students of all ages (e.g. Krashen, 2004, 2011).

As Krashen (2013) suggests, though, it may be especially important that such reading be not only self-chosen but "compelling" for the reader.

When planning my graduate TESOL class, however, I found especially persuasive not only Elley's 1991 summary, but also some articles by a professor at the City University of New York.

Research on Teaching Reading and Writing to Pre-Entrance College Students

My teaching was greatly influenced by a whole language approach to ESL at the City University of New York, as implemented and described by Ann MacGowan-Gillhooly ("Fluency First: Reversing the Traditional ESL Sequence", 1991b, and "Fluency Before Correctness: A Whole Language Experiment in College ESL", 1991a). For students seeking admission to CUNY but not having sufficient skill in reading and writing English, MacGowan-Gilhooly developed courses that reversed the order of CUNY's traditional three courses that focused on correctness first. In contrast, the new courses focused first on fluency, next on clarity, and only last on correctness. It was hypothesized that such a sequence would enable more students to pass sooner the tests in reading and writing that were required for admission to regular university classes.

- I described these courses in some detail in Weaver (1996, pp. 52–54) because I strongly believe that these details will help others design more effective programs. Here are just a few important points: In ESL 10, the students read 1,000 pages of popular fiction, along with autiobiographical and biographical works – about 70 pages a week. Their writing included – but was not limited to – a writing project that had to total 10,000 words by the end of the term. Of course, students received assistance with clarity from peers and the teacher. "By semester's end, most [students] were reading and writing fluently and even more correctly than in the beginning, without having received any corrections or grammar instruction" (MacGowan-Gilhooly, 1991b, p. 80).
- ESL 20 focused on clarity in organizing and developing expository papers. Again, students read widely, and discussed their readings in small groups. Their semester-long project of 10,000 words involved writing about some aspect of the

United States. Various kinds of writing were included. By the end of the term, most students were writing clearly enough to pass the course.

- ESL 30, the last course in the sequence, focused on the elimination of the most serious and most frequently occurring errors, and looking just for these errors while editing.

MacGowan-Gillhooly notes (1991b):

Traditional approaches seemed to inhibit experimentation and exaggerate the importance of errors. Before the course [ESL 30], students could not apply rules they had learned in their writing; but after it, it seemed they could. Yet the only grammar instruction they had had was in the context of questions about their own writing as they revised it. (p. 84)

Clearly such observed results support the claims of the theorists I had taken to heart.

Weaver's Class and the Results of a Focus on Fluency, Including Some Modest Gains in Grammatical Fluency

In planning my psycholinguistics and reading class, I operated on the hunch that many international students' fluency in English might be inadequate for a graduate program in Teaching English as a Second Language. Typically the Asian students – the majority in the class – had studied English grammar, learned vocabulary by memorizing definitions, and translated texts word for word. Some were already teaching English in their home countries. Even so, most had not really learned to read or write in English – or to speak more than a few halting sentences.

Anticipating this, I engineered a "book flood" program of my own. I required the students to read about 75 pages of literature a week, typically fiction, because it often includes a wider range of both vocabulary and grammatical constructions than non-fiction. I encouraged the students to read self-chosen junior novels, or – if they were teaching English at elementary grade levels – to read several picture books. Most important, I insisted that they not use their dictionaries to look up meanings of many words, but instead read more globally for meaning; after all, I said, they'd never finish the reading if they tried to look up numerous words! In addition, the students were to respond to the reading by means of dialogue journal entries. These typically resembled book reports instead, but at least the students wrote. Happily, the students came to love this immersion in comprehensible fiction, even though the essence of the course involved reading professional articles on a psycholinguistic concept of the reading process, with implications for their own reading, as well as for their teaching of English.

At the end of the semester, one student wrote, "At the beginning of the semester, I could read only three or four pages at a time in English and write just a few sentences, but by the end I could read a hundred pages and write several pages". Other students who began the semester with limited command of English grammatical structures also made notable progress, especially with embedded clauses, movable modifiers, and a few other constructions (Weaver, 1996, p. 55).

Though few students were involved, our results were congruent with the principle of lowering students' affective filter, engaging them in massive amounts of comprehensible input, and accepting approximations of the target constructions in English. Note in particular that I did not correct students "errors" in writing or speaking, nor expect them to. With the students' final papers, I simply guided the writers in making revisions, while attending to grammar only as necessary for clarity, during the revision or editing process. If I had attended to errors routinely, I would have looked for patterns and addressed only one or two patterns with each student or a very small group of students at the point of need, as is common in teaching writing as a process to native speakers of English (Rosen, 1987; Weaver, 1994). The need for such teaching, as we help adolescent and adult ESL writers, is also expressed by Krashen (2013).

While there is a typical order of second language acquisition for some grammatical morphemes (like noun plural or past tense in English, with more advanced ESL learners, each individual's creative use of grammar in acquiring English is unique (Gass & Selinker, 2001, p. 49). This makes an editing approach to revising grammar especially important, with the teacher providing assistance by clarifying thesalient features of grammar – in other words, by making grammatical constructions and grammatical revision/editing comprehensible. Kroll and Schafer (1978) contrast a product (behavioral) approach to learners' "errors" with a process (constructivist) approach. Following are the final two points attributed to the constructivist view:

- Errors are a natural part of learning a language; they arise from learners' active strategies: overgeneralization, ignorance of rule restrictions, incomplete rule application, hypothesizing false concepts.
- We need to assist the learner in approximating the target language by supporting active learning strategies, while recognizing that not all errors will disappear.

The final point is attributed to J. R. Richards (1971), and accords with what I've observed through decades of experience in teaching writing. I now prefer to abandon the concept of "error" and instead refer to grammatical approximations in approaching standards of a mainstream English.

In their book *ESL/EFL Teaching: Principles for Success* (1998), Yvonne and David Freeman wrote that traditional methods of teaching grammar haven't worked well for English language learners, whether native or non-native speakers of English. "In many foreign countries, students study English for years but never progress beyond a basic knowledge of English grammar" (1998, p. xv). They suggest that to reverse this trend of failure, teachers need to base their practices on a new set of principles. These constructivist principles are not only explained and exemplified in their own work (1998, 2014 and other books), but also demonstrated in the lengthy chapter they generously wrote for the second edition of my *Reading Process and Practice* (1994) and thoroughly exemplified in the teaching of Roche and Gonzales, briefly sketched in the next section.

Teaching Grammar During the Writing Process

In chapter 1 of *Grammar to Enrich and Enhance Writing* (2008), I included the "Michigan Model" of the writing process, adding where in the writing process I think grammar can be taught. After guiding students in revising for content and organization, I recommend that teachers support students in revising for sentence structure, and teach needed grammatical constructions in that context. Finally, teachers need to guide and support students in the editing process, before proofreading. Figure 8.3 suggests teaching grammar only during the revision and editing phases of the writing process.

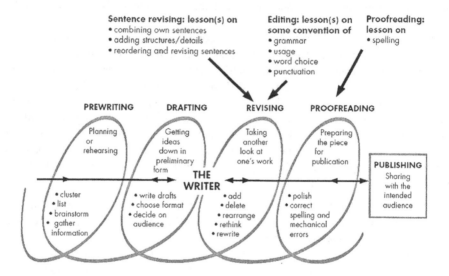

Figure 8.3. The basic recursive model of the writing process – the loops and the text within – was prepared for the Michigan Proficiency Examination Framework for Writing by the Michigan Council of Teachers of English 1993. In Weaver with Bush (2008), Weaver added suggestions on the teaching of grammar above the basic MCTE/MDE model

A few years ago when I heard Jason Roche and Yadira Gonzales present at a conference their outstanding practices in teaching Hispanic high school students, I asked them if they could write a chapter on how they teach editing, to complete a book I was writing on teaching grammar in the writing process. They readily agreed, and the result is that the last chapter of *Grammar to Enrich and Enhance Writing* is theirs: "The Transformative Classroom: Rethinking Grammar Instruction for English Language Learners". In short, they could not write about how they teach grammar without articulating their guiding constructivist theory and principles – the same as mine! – and discussing the entire unit that eventually led through various reading, speaking, and writing activities to a discussion of how they teach writing process. Theirs is truly an enriched language and literacy approach, making their focus on grammar only a minor, though important, part of what they did when they were still teaching high school.

Grammatical Revision and Editing in Roche & Gonzales' Classes

In their own words: When we begin to notice a global issue in the writing of many students – a group or the whole class – we develop a mini-lesson designed to meet that need. The following mini-lesson addresses the standard use of subordinate clauses.

Mini-Lesson on Subordinate Clauses[1]

1. Share a model: Using the front page of *The Fresno Bee* newspaper, we pull out a couple of obvious examples of subordinate clauses, write down the sentences and the different clauses on a three-column chart, and ask the students to discuss what they are noticing.
2. Name it: At this point, we like to name what it is the author is doing. In other words, we provide the students with the definitions for the concepts of independent and subordinate clauses. We also discuss the importance of complex sentences.
3. Create another model: We provide the students with examples of common subordinating conjunctions. Then as a class, we look for a few more examples from the newspaper (or whatever text has been chosen as a model), eliciting a little more participation from students. We add to the chart as they find more examples.

Time	Cause	Condition	Contrast
after, as	as, because	as if,	although
as soon as,	in order that,	assuming that,	even though,
before, since	since, so that	if, in case, unless	rather than,
till, untill		when, whether	though,
when, while			whereas, while

4. Releasing responsibility: Students keep working on the chart, in groups or with a partner. We wander from group to group, ensuring that students understand what is being asked of them and answering any questions that arise.
5. Applying to writing: Students (perhaps w ith a partner) look for examples in their drafts of sentences that use subordinate clauses and determine whether they are written correctly and punctuated conventionally. They might also look for simple sentences to combine into complex ones. Again, we wander through the room, guiding students who have questions or confusions.

Informal Editing Conversations

As our young writers work through a series of drafts on their way to a published piece, we take advantage of critical teaching moments during informal conversations. Here are the procedures we've developed:

1. We read the students' papers, jotting down on sticky notes strengths as well as areas that may need editing. We focus on one or two interlanguage patterns (patterns of those acquiring a new language) that dominate the writing. With a pencil, we mark the text that we want students to read aloud in a conference.
2. In the conference, we go over the entire paper, making positive comments about the writing. We praise the students for risks they've taken, their attempts at revision, and the overall ideas they have communicated. The focus is on content, and we make it a point to praise students for what they are doing well.
3. We ask the students to read an excerpt from their writing out loud (the part we've chosen beforehand that shows a grammatical mistake or an interlanguage feature). Usually, once students read their writing out loud, they notice the feature that needs to be changed and change it right then and there.
4. When students do not recognize the grammatical feature, we have them reread the sentence out loud again and ask, "Does this make sense? Does what you wrote here sound like language?"
5. If students are struggling, we ask, "Is there a way to rewrite this so that is makes sense?" Usually our students are quick to state how they would rewrite the sentence. But if they are still struggling, together we come up with a new way to edit the writing.

We then read the initial sentence and the new sentence and ask, "Does the new sentence you (or we) came up with make more sense? What do you notice?"

We select what we review with our students very carefully. Some students face a seemingly unsurmountable number of grammatical issues, but we review only one or two features of their writing during a conference. We want our students to continue to write, and we know some of the desired features will appear naturally as they acquire English over time. We also remind them how important reading is to their English language development and suggest more books for them to read independently. We want to empower our students, not raise their affective filter.

These conversations are fast and easy, but they are important because they are specifically related to the students' own writing. That is not to say that the same student will not continue to make the same kinds of "errors" – or use of the same interlanguage features – in the future. We may need to have the same kinds of conversations several times over the course of the year before a student begins to apply the rule correctly. In part, this demonstrates that learners must indeed form concepts for themselves.[2]

Though I haven't given details here, Roche and Gonzales' teaching of their ESL-student classes in California exemplified Rodgers' point that a "whole language" curriculum that includes broader engagement in language and literacy can increase learner awareness of how language works through literary study, process writing, authentic content, and learner collaboration (Rodgers, 2001, p. 6). Such programs can also include explicit teaching of grammar, especially during the writing process, along the lines of what Roche and Gonzales did. This is exactly the kind of program Gillmeister developed in her teaching at Yonsei University in Korea, a more challenging arena – but not before she had a more typical experience trying to teach English effectively in some Korean middle and secondary schools.

PART 2

ADDRESSING GRAMMAR WITHIN A LANGUAGE-RICH, LITERACY-RICH
APPROACH TO TEACHING EFL IN KOREA

In the mid-1990s, I, Dorothy Gillmeister, found myself in need of a new career and accepted the challenge of teaching English in South Korea. My introduction to Korea was as a teacher attached to the Gangwon-do Provincial Office of Education. I was hired directly from Canada as part of EPIK (English Program in Korea), a national initiative to introduce native speakers of English into elementary, middle, and high schools throughout Korea. At the time, I neither read nor spoke Korean. After a short orientation, I was sent to Jeongseon, an isolated town of about 12,000 people in the center of the province, the county seat of an area where agriculture and mining were the major sources of employment. It was a remote area, with no English-language newspapers or magazines, and no English television. I was based in a typical school comprising both middle- and high-school students, with three to five classes at each grade level. The average class size was 40 to 50 students. My assignment was to co-teach one lesson a week to every middle school class and every first-year high school class, following a challenging and rigid curriculum established by the Provincial Office of Education. My teaching partners were experienced Korean English teachers.

Although I had been trained as an elementary teacher in my youth, most of my work had been with adult learners; I had little idea of how to go about teaching such young students, with such a wide range of abilities. Luckily, I had a wonderful resource on tap: my sister, Lorraine Krause, who had received a "teacher of the year" award from the National Council of Teachers of English in the U.S., for the fantastic achievements of the students in her one-room K-6 country school. She became my model.

What I Initially Discovered about Teaching English in Korea

I found that opportunities to introduce innovation into the middle- and high-school curricula were drastically limited by the requirement that students cover a vast amount of material in a very short time, as well as the almost total absence of resource materials in the school or locally. The principal was unsupportive; he told me (through an interpreter) that he saw no point in the program, since the students would never need to speak English in their entire lives. (Though this may have been true for his generation, it was patently false in modern Korea.) My co-teachers varied in their interest and commitment to change.

I observed that the younger the students were, the more interested they were in learning English, and the more open they were to it. The senior students were uniformly of the opinion that English was both useless and impossible to learn. I was expected to change all this in 30 minutes a week.

Very quickly, I realized that the only contribution I could make in the limited timeframe was to introduce practices that would reduce fear and increase involvement in the material the students were learning. I created what became my mantra: "Don't be afraid of making a mistake: a mistake is just an opportunity to learn". I thanked students for their errors in class, and used them as teaching moments.

Whenever possible, I replaced solitary, seat-based exercises and repetitive recitations of the textbook with whole-group or small-group activities to increase how much each student could participate. As well as being pedagogically sound, it freed up a lot of class time that had been wasted.

Making what the students were learning more personal and relevant was another of my goals. For example, instead of having every student in turn read aloud an identical paragraph describing the identical drawing of a family photograph of some anonymous Western children, I had each student either draw a picture or bring in a photo of their own family and describe that to the class. I also encouraged their classmates to make comments and ask questions: "Is your brother older or younger than you?" "Is that Seorak-san park?" "Your sister is very pretty!"

Although I can't say I revolutionized the teaching of English grammar in Jeongseon, I can say that the students' (and teachers'!) curiosity about English and openness to trying to use it informally were considerably higher when I left than when I arrived.

The most important aspect of my year in Jeongseon, however, was not how much the students (and teachers) learned from me, but how much I learned from them: first, I realized that Korean high school graduates had rarely, if ever, been given an opportunity to use English to express their own thoughts, opinions, interests, or indeed anything personal about their lives. All their writing experience had focused on precisely replicating the models in the textbook, leading to fear of exploring new ways of using language. The culture of the typical Korean classroom penalized errors and inhibited risk-taking, while frowning on individuals "showing off" superior knowledge or skills in front of the group – even though, paradoxically, the nation-wide testing that determined their future educational opportunities made them fiercely competitive.

In short, I learned what I needed to know for my next challenge: teaching English in Seoul, the capital of Korea, to students at Yonsei University, one of the three top universities in the country (Seoul National University, Korea University, and Yonsei). These so-called SKY universities constitute the Ivy League of Korea, and attract the "brightest and best" students.

My Communicative, Second-Language-Acquisition Approach to Teaching English

I was hired as one of several instructors in Yonsei's newly constituted Communicative English Program; its mandate was to prepare students to read and write in English, both formally and informally. When I first began, students had to take two one-term courses. Each course was divided in two parts, "speaking'" and "writing". All of us were required to follow a detailed syllabus using the same two textbooks. They were among the better ones available at that time, presenting a complete process rather than unlinked exercises. For example, the steps of the writing process followed a Prewriting/Drafting/Revising/Proofreading sequence very similar to the one shown in Figure 8.3, but without Weaver's additions on when in the writing process grammar might be taught. I continued to use this sequence and the original schematic (Weaver 1996, p. 83) in all the writing courses I taught during my ten years at Yonsei University.

Although Yonsei students were among the top high school students in the nation, it became clear that their English levels varied drastically, depending on the faculties and departments in which they were enrolled. For example, music students were chosen principally on the basis of their auditions; their English ability was not a consideration. As a result, their English levels ranged from above-average to nonexistent, with the majority at the lower levels. Students in the humanities were much more likely to have superior English ability. Shortly after I began teaching there, the CE Program decided to organize students into groups based on their faculty, and also revised the syllabus so that one course would focus on writing (to include composing essays), and a second on speaking (to include making presentations). These courses would be taken in consecutive terms. Furthermore, the decision was made to allow each teacher to develop his or her own course syllabi, specific to each class they were assigned to teach.

What I implemented was a holistic, communicative, second language acquisition approach. James Gee (1992) has described an SLA approach thus:

> Acquisition is a process of acquiring something subconsciously by exposure to models, a process of trial and error, and practice within social groups, without formal teaching. It happens in natural settings that are meaningful and functional in the sense that the acquirers know that they need to acquire the thing they are exposed to in order to function and that they in fact want to so function. (Gee, 1992, p. 113)

As I began the challenge of designing writing and speaking courses from scratch, my goal was to create a structure and atmosphere to foster this process.

Although each class now consisted of students with similar interests, there was still a wide variation in ability. It was important to me that every student, from the most elementary to the most advanced, be able to learn and progress. I decided to develop a unique curriculum for each group with the following characteristics:

- Students should be encouraged to read, watch, or listen to a massive amount of authentic, natural-language English materials; they chose what to explore themselves, based on their own interests and abilities, with guidance from me, and to reflect on their reading (Krashen's "comprehensible input");

- Students should be provided with tools and techniques enabling them to break down the input into manageable chunks, to help make it comprehensible; these tools should include those used by native speakers of comparable ability, such as dictionaries and grammar reference books (NOT textbooks *per se*); instruction should be provided in their use, as part of preparation for assignments;
- There should be ample opportunities for students to interact with each other, whether discussing issues, giving feedback, or creating something together;
- Both the structure of projects and the way they were graded should reward cooperation, rather than competition, while still recognizing individual excellence;
- The steps and tools for attacking major assignments such as essays, stories, speeches and presentations should be based on how these are approached in the real world by writers, researchers, and working people everywhere, giving them skills they could apply in other aspects of their lives;
- Every major assignment should be sufficiently open-ended that no student should ever have to waste his or her precious energy and time (or mine) working on something artificial, boring, or irrelevant to their personal goals, interests, and concerns;
- Specific teaching of grammar and error correction should be drawn from the specific needs that the students were discovering as they carried out their chosen assignments;
- Every student should be able to experience success as he or she progressed. In fact, I made a promise that no student who attended class regularly, participated actively, and completed all assignments with both diligence and passion would ever fail my course (a promise I was able to keep);
- Students should come away with an arsenal of tools that would enable them to become life-long learners of English, independently.

Teaching Grammar within the Writing Process

Here I focus on how I approached teaching grammar as part of learning to write in English.

First, to encourage students to increase dramatically their exposure to authentic English, they were asked to write a weekly report on a natural text they had personally chosen because of its intrinsic interest. This could be a series of articles, a book, or internet research sources. The students had to describe what it was they had read, comment on what they found easy or difficult about it, and reflect on what they learned. Most important, they needed to express their thoughts and opinions: What did you think or feel about it? How does it relate to your own life and concerns? Is it an issue of importance to Korea, or to the world in general? They discussed these in pairs weekly.

As the term progressed, the students' choices became more demanding and their reports more personal, as well as markedly more fluent. These reports were checked by me (but not corrected) weekly, and shared with a partner. They were submitted at the end of term in a portfolio, along with the final copies of other, more formal, student assignments.

At the same time, students were eased into writing, step by step.

Virtually all students needed to learn what a formal English paragraph was and how it was structured, from topic sentence to conclusion. (The typical literary process in Korean is quite different, with no foreshadowing of the main idea.)

I supplied a general handout and/or web page link explaining how to prepare their assignments for submission, as well as specific handouts for each task.

Next, I introduced the step-by-step *writing process* I outlined earlier. Students were encouraged to think first about expressing themselves clearly and effectively in a way that would communicate with their readers: in order to do this, they had to unlearn the habit of stringing together a sequence of short, perfect and perfectly boring sentences to avoid making any errors.

To encourage fluency of thought and language, I spent a lot of time introducing various techniques of *prewriting* to help the students get past their fear of committing anything to paper that was not perfect. I explained how turning on the editor/critic at the very beginning of the creative process can lead to stilted and unimaginative writing. I taught the students the basics of brainstorming (and later, freewriting), drawing on the instructions outlined by famed writing guru Natalie Goldberg.

At first, the students found the process of writing without worrying about format, grammar or spelling quite terrifying. In the long run, though, they found it liberating, as their previous attempts at writing in English typically came to a halt the first time they encountered a word they couldn't spell.

My track record as a published writer and poet in Korean literary magazines helped to give me credibility with the students, making them more open to trying these new ideas.

Individual writing assignments followed; the topics varied somewhat with the class. Typical assignments included:

- Interview a partner, then choose *one or two* interesting characteristics that you think would describe them well, and expand with details and examples from their appearance, history, hobbies, dreams, and so forth: for example, are they adventurous or cautious? Responsible or carefree? Practical or dreamy? Initially, most students wanted to put everything they had learned in one long, boring list. (Focus on basic paragraph structure; topic sentence and conclusion; backing up your statements with details and examples; subject-verb agreement; sequence of tenses; review of sentence structure)
- Think of a place that has special meaning to you. Describe it as if you were moving through it; let your reader experience it with you. (Focus on descriptive or color writing; show, don't tell; prepositional phrases; adjectives, adverbs, clauses; connotation and denotation; how to choose the appropriate tense and point of view: present tense or past? first or third person singular?)

- Explain how to make or do something, ranging from a craft to a simple meal that could be prepared in your bed-sit or dormitory, for a class cookbook. (Focus on process writing)
- Oral history project. (Focus on narrative voice and style; transitions; sequence of tenses; expressing feelings)
- Opinion essay. (Focus on research, including critical thinking and evaluating source material; essay structure)

Each project was preceded by relevant class, group, or pair exercises to prepare them for the type of writing to follow. At the completion of each project, I created a unique grammar review sheet for each class, choosing one sentence from each student's paper to illustrate a range of typical miscues. Students worked on the sheets individually or in groups to correct them. The students then shared their suggestions of ways to correct the sentences. This was not a test, though some sentences might find their way into later class quizzes.

At the beginning of the term, students were divided into groups of four or five that would become their permanent peer groups. In these groups, they would 'workshop' their various projects.

At the outset of each project, an appropriate prewriting activity was recommended. Students then chose their specific topics and went home to brainstorm and/or research, then brought an outline to the next class to work on with their peer group.

After approval of the prewriting and outline, students began their first drafts. These were started in class and completed at home. In the next class they shared them in their peer groups: each student would read his or her paragraph aloud, while other students offered feedback: Was it easy to understand? Did you feel that you had learned something genuine and unique about the topic? What was the most interesting part? What would you like to know more about? What needs clarification? What, if anything, seemed to be missing? What could have been left out?

The focus at this stage was on content and organization, not on correct grammar. Although I moved from group to group making the occasional suggestion, I did *not* at this stage collect (or correct) the paragraphs.

Students took their work and group comments home to elaborate and improve; first, however, I briefly reviewed grammar points relevant to the type of assignment. At this stage, their assignments were to be word-processed and printed out.

Students then shared their revised texts in their peer groups. The groups worked hard to make sure every student's work was as close to perfect as possible. The overriding rule was that any suggested change needed to be accepted by the author. If there was any disagreement, or if something 'seemed wrong' but no one was sure what to do about it, they could ask me for help, which I would give freely. These 'edited' drafts were handed in to me.

When reviewing the assignment, I would fix non-standard expressions that I considered to be more advanced than the student could reasonably be expected to know. This varied not only with the class, but with the individual student. Other errors I would highlight, indicating particular types of errors, such as wrong word, missing punctuation, capitalization, verb tense, and verb agreement, to mention just a few. Either in the classroom or on the students' papers, I would refer them to the sections of the assigned reference book, so they could review the topic and make their own corrections.

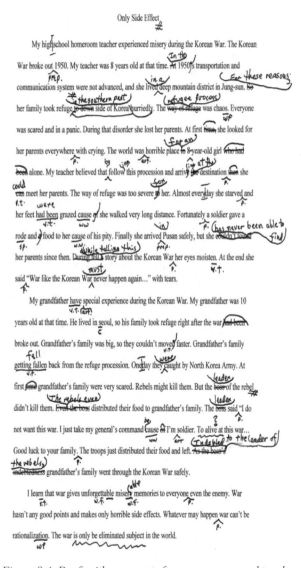

Figure 8.4. Draft with comments from peer group and teacher

The student revised the story based on the comments. This revised version was then printed out and brought to class, ready for the final step: Proofreading. Students exchanged assignments to be reviewed for simple typographical or grammatical errors that they could neatly correct on the paper.

Figure 8.4 shows an example of a draft at the commented stage, with notes from peer reviewers as well as myself. This sample comes from the Oral History Project, described in some detail later; the project description includes the final version of this story.

The final submission to me comprised the marked-up copy as well as the final version with the student's attempt to correct the indicated problems. The student's basic grade was either increased or decreased depending on how well they had managed to correct the errors that I considered to be within their capacity. By this time, their writing had gone through several versions, each one more closely approximating their goal.

I returned the graded assignments to the students, to be placed in their portfolios.

Grammar as Only One Factor in a Broader Context for Promoting Second Language Acquisition

One of the most successful and popular assignments was the Oral History Project. The guidelines were quite simple. Each student chose a topic on which to focus: pretty much anything that they were curious about, from war experiences, to early childhood life, to education, to love and marriage. Then they chose two people *from another generation* to interview at length about the chosen topic. (They did not have to conduct these interviews in English; the interviews were used as source material only.) Having completed the interviews and thought about them, the student needed to select one especially interesting, funny, or poignant event or episode from each person, to write as third-person narratives. The final step was for the student to compose a personal paragraph (or in some cases, a short essay) commenting on the experience, learning, surprises, and personal life lessons they took away from this. Thus, the challenge of communicating in English became very personal for them.

The modern history of Korea has been eventful, to say the least. From the Japanese occupation through the Korean War to the advent of democracy; from a primarily rural populace, to a highly technologically advanced civilization with giant urban areas; from the multi-generational family living together, to the single-family residence; from a society with no divorce to one with one of the highest divorce rates in the world: the lives of the oldest living generation in Korea bear little resemblance to those of modern young adults. Many students had no concept of the lives their parents had led, and the trials they had endured, let alone their grandparents and great-grandparents. One after another, they told me how grateful they were for the opportunity to become closer to the older members of their family, and the awe and respect in which they now held people whom they had previously

Miserable Memories
My high school homeroom teacher experienced misery during the Korean War. The Korean War broke out in 1950. My teacher was 8 years old at that time. In the 1950s transportation and communication system were not advanced, and she lived in a deep mountain district in Jung-sun. For these reasons, her family took refuge hurriedly the southern part of Korea. The refugee process was chaotic. Everyone was scared and in a panic. During that disorder she lost her parents. At first she looked for her parents everywhere, with crying. The world was a horrible place for an 8-year-old girl alone. My teacher believed that by following this procession and arriving at the destination, she would meet her parents. The way of refuge was too severe for her. Almost every day she starved, and her feet were grazed because she walked very long distance. Fortunately, a soldier gave a ride and food to her cause of his pity. Finally she arrived in Pusan safely, but she has never been able to find her parents since then. While telling this story about the Korean War her eyes moistened. At the end she said, "war like the Korean War must never happen again …" with tears.   My grandfather had special experience during the Korean War. My grandfather was 10 years old at that time. He lived in Seoul, so his family took refuge right after the war broke out. Grandfather's family was big, so they couldn't move faster. Grandfather's family fell back from the refuge procession. One day they were caught by North Korea Army. At first, grandfather's family were very scared. Rebels might kill them. But the leader of the rebel didn't kill them. The rebels even distributed their food to grandfather's family. The leader said, "I do not want this war. I just take my general's command because I'm a soldier. Surviving during the war … Good luck to your family". The troops just distributed their food and left. Indebted to the leader of the rebels, grandfather's family went through the Korean War safely.   I learned that war gives unforgettably miserable memories to everyone, even the enemy. War hasn't any good points and makes only horrible side effects. Whatever may happen, war can't be rationalized and war is just madness. War is only the object which has to be removed all over the world.

Figure 8.5. Oral history report, final version

written off as boring. One after another, they told me how ashamed they were of the opportunities and advantages they had taken for granted as their right, and sometimes came close to squandering.

By this point, trained by the weekly reports, students had become fluent at expressing their deeper feelings. Many times, I was moved to tears. William Kern, an American teacher of English at Yonsei's Language Institute, who was a playwright as well as a teacher, heard about my project and became very excited by it. He chose several stories, and after receiving permission from the respective authors, put them together as part of a play called *Mother and Tigers* that was presented at the prestigious Seoul Arts Center in December 1998.

The narrative in Figure 8.5, one of my personal favorites, is the final version of the draft shown above. It is certainly not grammatically perfect, but it is effective in communicating the vivid story that the writer wants to tell.

Through many changes of leadership, syllabi, and recommended or required textbooks at Yonsei University, I remained as close as I could to my initial goals. I was pleased to see significant changes in my students' comfort and skill in English, in both reading and writing. Though students were not able to attain perfect fluency in a single term, much less grammatical accuracy, their enthusiasm and willingness to make an effort speaks well for their future efforts in becoming effective communicators in English. Furthermore, the approaches and tools they acquired will help them become life-long language learners. This, rather than immediate grammatical perfection, is the most realistic goal.

CONCLUSION: LEARNING AND TEACHING GRAMMAR THROUGH READING AND WRITING – REFLECTION UPON PRACTICE AND THEORY

With regard to comprehensible input and the learning of grammar, Stephen Krashen (2013) summarizes:

> Comprehensible, input-based methods have done very well in the published professional research literature. When tests are communicative, students in these classes typically acquire more than those in traditional, grammar-based classes. When grammar tests are used, there is either no difference, or comprehensible input students are slightly better. (2013, p. 6)

We have found from our own experiences and that of other professionals – including Krashen – that explicit attention to some grammatical features in the context of their use can be helpful to intermediate and more advanced English language learners, especially when grammar is addressed in constructivist classrooms and embedded in a rich variety of language and literacy activities, especially writing.

Reflecting upon our teaching practices and how they align with the constructivist principles and theory articulated at the outset, we believe our practices are congruent with theory. Weaver in Michigan, Roche and Gonzales in California, and Gillmeister in Korea addressed "errors" in a way that honored the students' approximations toward the target language and gave them comprehensible grammatical input in stages.

Certain factors in Cambourne's conditions for learning were particularly emphasized in our teaching. Engagement is at the heart of these conditions, several of which are particularly important for the learning and teaching of grammar to those learning English as an additional language:

- Immersion: Learners need to be "saturated" in what is to be learned. This calls for large amounts of comprehensible input, through reading – as much as possible self-chosen – and also through listening. Immersion in a rich language and literacy environment is key. Learners need multiple opportunities to witness actions/artifacts/models of the knowledge and skills to be learned. With respect to grammatical features, addressing them during the writing process is ideal, as we can work with multiple drafts. Furthermore – and very important – grammar can be addressed in a way that does not increase anxiety and thus raise the affective filter.

- Response: Learners need feedback from knowledgeable others. Note that this is feedback. Mere correction seldom works, because it does not provide enough information for a learner to understand what was "wrong" with what he or she wrote (or uttered); we need to provide a fuller explanation and examples (and non-examples) for learners to construct the concepts we want them to grasp. We also need to teach, teach, and reteach each concept multiple times in context, for such extensive reteaching is usually necessary if learners are to master the concepts to the point of being able to use them independently, or at least to edit for them in their writing. One-shot teaching rarely accomplishes this goal.

- Approximation: Learners need the freedom to take risks and to "make mistakes"; this is essential if effective learning is to occur. We do not encourage learners to take risks by correcting them. Rather, we need to scaffold learners in grasping new concepts, grammatical or otherwise. Highly effective scaffolding involves working with the learner to accomplish something the learner could not do him/her self, as demonstrated here by Roche and Gonzales, and by Gillmeister. In addition to guiding writers through multiple phases of editing their own grammar, Gillmeister occasionally substituted an advanced standard construction for what the learner had written. In doing so, she simply acted as an editor. Even while using the term "error" that the student was accustomed to, she recognized that increasingly sophisticated approximations rather than total perfection was the only realistic goal.

There are more factors in Cambourne's model, but we want again to emphasize his observation that engagement is key, and occurs when the learner is convinced that:

- I am a potential doer/owner of this skill or knowledge.
- Engaging with these demonstrations will further the purposes of my life.
- I can try to emulate the skill/knowledge being demonstrated without fear of physical and/or psychological harm if my attempt is not "correct".
- I respect and trust my teacher(s).

The teacher's role in guiding English language acquisition is, we believe, to provide comprehensible input and to make input comprehensible, as well as to adhere to the conditions of learning articulated by Cambourne and advocates of a communicative approach to second/additional language learning. Constructivist theory, based on observations of what best promotes learning, is sound. We encourage its implementation in ESL and EFL classes.

NOTES

[1]   This section is from Weaver (2007, pp. 279–280).
[2]   This first part of this section is from Roche and Gonzales' chapter in Weaver (2008, pp. 278–279).

REFERENCES

Bloomfield, L. (1942). Linguistics and reading. *The Elementary English Review, 19*, 125–130, 183–186.
Cambourne, B. (1988). *The whole story: Natural learning and the acquisition of literacy in the classroom.* Auckland: Scholastic.
Cambourne, B. (1995). Toward an educationally relevant theory of literacy learning: Twenty years of inquiry. *The Reading Teacher, 49*(3), 182–190.
Cambourne, B. (2009). Revisiting the concept of "natural learning". In J. V. Hoffman & Y. M. Goodman (Eds.), *Changing literacies for changing times* (pp. 125–145). New York, NY: Routledge.
Elley, W. B. (1991). Acquiring literacy in a second language: The effect of book-based programs. *Language Learning, 41*, 375–411.
Elley, W. B., & Mangubhai, F. (1983). The impact of reading on second language learning. *Reading Research Quarterly, 19*, 53–67.
Freeman, Y., Freeman, D. E., & Ebe, A. (1998). *ESL/EFL teaching: Principles for success*. Portsmouth, NH: Heinemann.
Freeman, D. E., & Freeman, Y. (2014). *Essential linguistics: What teachers need to know to teach ESL, reading, spelling, and grammar*. Portsmouth, NH: Heinemann.
Gass, S. M., & Selinker, L. (2001). *Second language acquisition: An introductory course* (2nd ed.). Mahwah, NJ: Erlbaum.
Gee, J. P. (1992). *The social mind: Language, ideology, and social practice*. New York, NY: Oxford University Press.
Goldberg, N. (1986/2010). *Writing down the bones: Freeing the writer within*. Boston, MA: Shambhala.
Holdaway, D. (1979). *The foundations of literacy*. Sydney: Ashton Scholastic. (Distributed in the United States by Heinemann)
Krashen, S. D. (1982). *Principles and practice in second language acquisition*. New York, NY: Pergamon Press.
Krashen, S. D. (1998). *Foreign language education: The easy way*. Culver City, CA: Language Education Associates.
Krashen, S. D. (2003). *Explorations in language acquisition and use*. Portsmouth, NH: Heinemann.
Krashen, S. D. (2004). *The power of reading: Insights from the research* (2nd ed.). Westport, CT: Libraries Unlimited.
Krashen, S. D. (2011). *Free voluntary reading*. Westport, CT: Libraries Unlimited.
Krashen, S. D. (2013). *Second language acquisition: Theory, applications, and some conjectures* (Originally prepared by Cambridge University Press). Retrieved from http://www.sdkrashen.com
Krashen, S. D. *Second language acquisition: Theory, applications, and some conjectures* (Originally prepared by Cambridge University Press but not commercially available). Retrieved from http://www.sdkrashen.com
Kroll, B., & Schafer, J. (1978). Error analysis and the teaching of composition. *College Composition and Communication, 29*, 242–248.
MacGowan-Gilhooly, A. (1991a). Fluency before correctness: A whole language experiment in college ESL. *College ESL, 1*(1), 37–47.
MacGowan-Gilhooly, A. (1991b). Fluency first: Reversing the traditional ESL sequence. *Journal of Basic Writing, 10*(1), 73–87.
Richards, J. C. (1971). A non-contrastive approach to error analysis. *English Language Teaching, 25*, 204–219.
Richards, J. C., & Rodgers, T. S. (2001). *Approaches and methods in language teaching* (2nd ed.). Cambridge: Cambridge University Press.
Roche, J., & Gonzales, Y. (2008). The transformative classroom: Rethinking grammar instruction for English language learners. In C. Weaver with J. Bush (Ed.), *Grammar to enrich and enhance writing* (pp. 259–282). Portsmouth, NH: Heinemann.
Rodgers, T. S. (2001, September). *Language teaching methodology*. Retrieved September 12, 2014, from http://www.cal.org/resource-center/briefs-digests/digests/(offset)/60
Rosen, L. M. (1987). Developing correctness in student writing: Alternatives to the error-hunt. *English Journal, 76*, 62–69.

Terrell, T. D. (1991). The role of grammar instruction in a communicative approach. *Modern Language Journal, 75*, 52–63.
Weaver, C. (1990). *Understanding whole language*. Portsmouth, NH: Heinemann.
Weaver, C. (1994). *Reading process and practice: From socio-psycholinguistics to whole language* (2nd ed.). Portsmouth, NH: Heinemann.
Weaver, C. (1996). *Teaching grammar in context*. Portsmouth, NH: Heinemann.
Weaver, C. (2007). *The grammar plan book*. Portsmouth, NH: Heinemann.
Weaver, C. with Bush, J. (2008). *Grammar to enrich and enhance writing*. Portsmouth, NH: Heinemann.

Constance Weaver
Miami University (Retired)
Western Michigan University (Professor Emerita of English)
Kalamazoo, Michigan
USA

Dorothy Gillmeister
Yonsei University (Retired)
Seoul, South Korea

9. REFLECTIVE AND EFFECTIVE TEACHING OF VOCABULARY

There is no "right" or "wrong" way to teach vocabulary.
(Schmitt, 2008)

VOCABULARY SIZE

Learners need to have enough vocabulary size to use a language effectively. To carry out certain tasks in foreign language (FL) such as reading a book, watching a movie, listening to a radio show, communicating with a speaker face-to-face or via an online chat, or engaging in a discussion, learners need to have enough vocabulary. Empirical studies on vocabulary load (also referred to as vocabulary coverage) over the last two decades have clearly showed that the more vocabulary, the greater the learner's comprehension. So, how much vocabulary is necessary? This really depends on what a learner wants to do with the language. Table 9.1 presents vocabulary size (i.e., breadth) necessary to carry out various tasks in English.

Table 9.1. Vocabulary sizes needed for different activities

Activity	Vocabulary Size	
	95% coverage	*98% coverage*
Reading newspapers and novels	4,000–5,000	8,000
Engaging in a conversation	3,000	6,000
Watching movies	3,000	6,000
Watching television programs	3,000	7,000
Academic spoken english	3,000	8,000

All the vocabulary sizes in Table 9.1 include *word families* not individual *words*. One word (*study*) can contain a number of word families that may span different word classes (e.g., *study, studied, studies, studying, studious, studiously*). In addition to word families, proper nouns (e.g., *Iran, Arizona, Behrouz, John*), company names (e.g., *YouTube, Google*), or cartoon characters (e.g., *Shrek, Princess Fiona*) are included into the vocabulary coverage because proper nouns are generally essential to follow a story or understand necessary information in a video or a text

© KONINKLIJKE BRILL NV, LEIDEN, 2018 | DOI:10.1163/9789004380882_009

(Erten & Razi, 2009). Based on the information in Table 9.1, different vocabulary sizes are needed to perform certain tasks. It should be pointed out that 95% and 98% coverage "provide a useful indication of whether or not a text may be understood" (Webb & Nation, 2013, p. 1). In 95% coverage, 1 word out of 20 words will be unknown, while in 98% coverage, 1 word out of 50 words will be unknown. Laufer and Ranvehorst-Kalovski (2010) reported that in reading, 95% coverage provides *adequate* comprehension while 98% coverage provides *good* comprehension. Although teachers want their students to know 98% of the words in a text, a movie or a conversation, it is a challenging task but "probably manageable" (Nation, 2013). Last but not least, vocabulary size as a predictor of comprehension is task- and text-specific. In other words, reading novels or newspapers require relatively more vocabulary than watching movies or engaging in conversations (Nation, 2006).

Food for Thought: Frequency Lists

Achieving a large vocabulary size might be a goal of most learners. In order to achieve this goal, teachers can help their students in the following two ways. First of all, teachers should know their students' initial vocabulary size (Nation & Webb, 2011). To do so, teachers can administer a *Vocabulary Size Test* (Nation & Beglar, 2007). The test has different versions, ranging from 14,000 to 20,000, in both monolingual and bilingual forms. Teachers can download the tests from Paul Nation's website at http://www.victoria.ac.nz/lals/about/staff/paul-nation. Finding out the learners' current vocabulary size provides a useful starting point for determining both the breadth of their knowledge and the lists that will prove most fruitful for expanding their vocabulary. Second, once learners' vocabulary knowledge has been diagnosed, teachers can introduce several frequency lists (Table 9.2). These frequency lists vary in terms of their purposes and the number of words they contain. One option is the updated version of the General Service List (GSL), designed for beginner learners of English (Brezina & Gablasova, 2013). The purpose of this list, comprised of 2,494 *lemmas* (i.e., word forms that belong to the same word class – *develop, develops, developed, developing*), is to familiarize English language learners with the most frequent words in English. Words from the GSL are essential because of their utility, that is, GSL covers around 81% of any English text. Most GSL words can mean different things in different contexts. If you search *go* and *take* in learner dictionaries (see Table 9.4), each verb has from 20 to 25 different meanings, on top of their idiomatic usage. For example, 12 verbs from the GSL (e.g., say, get, go, know, think, see, make, come, take, want, give, mean) are important for conversations because they "account for almost 45% of the occurrences of all lexical verbs" (Biber & Reppen, 2002, p. 205).

Another word list, the *Academic Vocabulary List* (AVL), was put together by Gardner and Davies (2013) with the intention to help learners of English improve their academic vocabulary. Even though another popular list for the same purpose had already been developed, known as an Academic Word List (Coxhead, 2000), the

AVL is perhaps preferable because it is both newer and based on larger corpus and up-to-date methodology. The AVL list comprises around 2,000 word families and covers about 14% of academic texts (compared to AWL's coverage of 10%). This means that in any academic text, ranging from education, history, social sciences to business and finance, 14 words out of 100 can be academic words. Words such as *system, factor, environmental, standard,* and *measure* belong to the AVL list. This interactive website http://www.wordandphrase.info/academic/ allows teachers to input a text and see words that belong to the AVL list, including their parts of speech, definitions, synonyms, collocates, example sentences, and discipline specific technical words (e.g., law, education, business).

Table 9.2. The number of words and text coverage of three lists

List	Number of words	Text Coverage
GSL: Brezina & Gablasova, (2013)	2,494 lemmas	~81% coverage of the general texts in the source corpora (over 12 billion words)
AWL: Coxhead (2000)	570 word families	~10% coverage of the academic materials in the source corpora (351,333 words)
AVL: Gardner & Davies (2013)	2,000 word families (or 3,000 lemmas)	~14% coverage of academic materials in both Corpus of Contemporary American English (120 million + words) and British National Corpus (33 million + words)

WORD KNOWLEDGE

As discussed in the previous section, learners need to recognize and be able to use large numbers of words (i.e., breadth). Learners also need depth of vocabulary knowledge; this means that learners should know about these words if they want to use them well. A mastery of the pronunciation of the word or its spelling does not guarantee that the word has been "learned". It appears that vocabulary size and depth are highly correlated, meaning that the more learners "develop their size of vocabulary knowledge, the more their depth of vocabulary knowledge will increase" (Akbarian, 2010, p. 399). However, developing depth is not a trivial task in part because it involves at least nine different types of knowledge about a given word. Table 9.3 below describes each type.

The components of word knowledge such as *form, meaning,* and *use* are essential aspects. For example, when a learner sees a word *interested,* the learner should recognize its *form,* in other words, its *spelling* (i - n - t - e - r - e - s - t - e - d) and the way the word is pronounced (i.e., /'ɪn·tə‚res·tɪd/). In addition, the learner should

Table 9.3. Aspects of word knowledge (Nation, 2001, p. 27)

Form	Spoken	R	What does the word sound like?
		P	How is the word pronounced?
	Written	R	What does the word look like?
		P	How is the word written or spelled?
	Word parts	R	What parts are recognizable in this word?
		P	What word parts are needed to express the meaning?
Meaning	Form and meaning	R	What meaning does this word form signal?
		P	What word form can be used to express this meaning?
	Concept and referents	R	What is included in the concept?
		P	What items can the concept refer to?
	Associations	R	What other words does this make us think of?
		P	What other words could we use instead of this one?
Use	Grammatical functions	R	In what patterns does the word occur?
		P	In what patterns must we use this word?
	Collocations	R	What words or types of words occur with this one?
		P	What words or types of words must we use with this one?
	Constraints on use	R	Where, when, and how often would we expect to meet this word?
		P	Where, when, and how often can we use this word?

R = receptive knowledge; P = productive knowledge

be able to attach a *meaning* to the form either in English (e.g., a feeling of wanting to know about or take part in something) or in his/her first language. Moreover, the learner should know how to *use* the word in a meaningful way (e.g., *I became interested halfway through the book*). Understanding the *use* of a word also entails grammatical and collocational knowledge, which refer to the syntactic structures we might expect to find the word (e.g., before a noun; as a subject predicative) and words likely to be used in conjunction (e.g., interested *in*; *to be/become* + interested; *very* + interested).

These three major components of vocabulary knowledge, *form*, *meaning*, and *use* can also be divided according to learners' receptive (R) vs. productive abilities (P). It has been shown that FL learners' receptive vocabulary is greater than their productive vocabulary (Laufer, 2005). As a FL learner, you might be familiar with many English words but you might not be sure of how to use them when you write a paper or talk to a speaker. Thus, different aspects of productive and receptive vocabulary knowledge are also important to master words (Nation & Webb, 2011).

Because of the many types of word knowledge that a learner can possess, it is useful to view vocabulary development as an incremental process, rather than simple as present or absent. For example, the parts of the word (e.g., _**uninterested**_), its collocations (e.g., _very; in_), and its syntactic functions (e.g., subject predicative) are learned through multiple encounters with the word, each of which will build on previous encounters. Schmitt (2008) strongly believes that FL learners can improve their word knowledge not only through repeated exposure (i.e., frequency) but also through meaningful _engagement_ (see Plonsky & Loewen, 2013). In other words, learners should encounter the new word many times in many different contexts, each of which will help learners develop their knowledge of the word's collocations, grammatical functions, associations, and word parts. Preferably, the learners have to encounter the different aspects of the word at different times in many different contexts such as while reading a book, watching a movie, listening to a song, talking to a friend, and so forth. The rich information available in learner dictionaries can also promote learner engagement with regards to improving the depth of word knowledge.

Food for Thought: Learner Engagement

The foundation of any word knowledge is establishing an initial form-meaning link (Nation & Webb, 2011; Schmitt, 2010). When a learner sees a word or hears it, the learner should be able to know its meaning either in English or the learner's mother tongue. To help learners improve their independent word knowledge skills, teachers can introduce learner dictionaries to their students (see Table 9.4).

Table 9.4. Online English-English learner dictionaries

1.	Longman Dictionary of Contemporary English (LDOCE) http://www.ldoceonline.com/
2.	Macmillan Dictionary (MD) http://www.macmillandictionary.com/
3.	Merriam-Webster Learner's Dictionary (MWLD) http://www.learnersdictionary.com/

These dictionaries provide necessary information, such as easy-to-understand definitions, audio-friendly pronunciations (both British and North America), example sentences, collocations, and important grammar tips, to improve a learner's word knowledge (Nurmukhamedov, 2012). For effective use, teachers should train their students how to use these dictionaries through guided activities (see Appendix). This activity adapted from Guiterrez Arvizu (2012) engages a learner because a learner can receive comprehensive information about new words by going through the steps in the activity. The learner writes word information one by one and fills out the blanks, the activity that directly contributes to the development of receptive and productive vocabulary (Folse, 2006).

FORMULAIC LANGUAGE

Teachers should not just teach individual words; they also have to focus on teaching *formulaic language*, which is an umbrella term to refer to *collocations, multiword units, lexical bundles*, and *idioms*. Knowing formulaic language for learners is important for at least four reasons. First, formulaic language is everywhere. More specifically, it comprises around 21% to 58% of analysed language in English (e.g., Biber, Johansson, Leech, Conrad, & Finegan, 1999; Erman & Warren, 2000). Second, it is used for a number of purposes, including "expressing a message or idea (*The early bird gets the warm* = do not procrastinate), realizing functions ([*I'm*] *just looking* [*thanks*] = declining an offer of assistance from a shopkeeper), establishing social solidarity (*I know what you mean* = agreeing with an interlocutor)" (Schmitt, 2008, p. 340). Third, it promotes more fluency in production such as in writing (*due to the fact that; on the other hand*), and speaking (*you know what I mean; I'll talk about*). Last but not least, it allows more accuracy and native-like lexical selection in writing and speaking. Some learners write *in one hand ... in other hand*, or say *on other words*, which sound awkward in English. It would be more accurate if learners say or write *on the one hand ... on the other hand* or *in other words*.

Although formulaic language (also known as *phrasal vocabulary*) is important for language learners, vocabulary researchers have not come to agreement on how formulaic language can be most effectively taught to learners (Wray, 2013). However, language teachers have proposed several techniques to develop learners' phrasal vocabulary. First, highlighting, bolding, or italicizing the elements of phrasal vocabulary can raise learners' awareness of formulaic language (Lewis, 2000). Making learners aware of the formulaic language when they listen to a passage or read a text is also beneficial, because this practice will help learners' fluency and accuracy in terms of production (Boers, Eyckmans, Kappel, Stengers, & Demecheleer, 2006). Second, dictionary look-up strategies are particularly useful to promote an accurate production of grammatical collocations (e.g., relevant *to*; warn somebody *against/about* something). Ranalli (2013) introduced strategy instruction that involved the use of a LDOCE dictionary (see Table 9.4) to revise incorrect grammatical collocations in an academic passage. The L2 writers who were trained to use dictionary looking-up strategies performed significantly better than those who did not receive any training. Third, teaching two-word formulaic language such as collocations (e.g., make + effort, appointment, noise) can expose learners' to other types of formulaic language (Nation & Webb, 2011). Thus, we encourage teachers to start with smaller elements (*splendid view; view on*) and to move toward larger ones (*from the point of view of*) to maximize the saliency of phrasal vocabulary in FL language instruction.

Food for Thought: Learning Phrasal Vocabulary

Using corpus-based materials can be particularly useful to teach formulaic language. Teachers can have students learn phrasal vocabulary from the collocation (see

Ackerman & Chen, 2013; Shin & Nation, 2008) or from lists of formulaic language (see Martinez & Schmitt, 2012; Simpson-Vlach & Ellis, 2010). Such lists are specifically designed to improve English language learners' spoken, written, and academic collocations. Teachers can put some collocations or phrases from the abovementioned lists into http://quizlet.com/ and have their students use the website to practice using formulaic language. If learning formulaic language is part of the curriculum, it is even better so that students receive points upon learning the phrasal vocabulary. Using a quizlet website is useful for a number of reasons. First of all, students can access the website in mobile (e.g., cell phone, iPad) as well as any computer devices. Second, this website promotes *spaced learning*, that is, learners can practice the words at different times and at different locations. Instead of learning all the assigned formulaic language in an hour, they can learn them in a piecemeal fashion.

The above-mentioned lists are indeed useful but, in line with the three types of vocabulary knowledge described above (*form, meaning, use*), FL learners should understand the meaning of the phrasal vocabulary as well. FL learners might know both words in the phrase, but the overall meaning of the words might alter when the words co-occur as with much idiomatic language (Cheng, Greaves, Sinclair, & Warren, 2008). For example, learners might recognize the meaning of *role, disappointed*, and *create*, but when these words occur with other words (or collocates), their meanings also change. Because distinguishing collocation meanings is a challenging task for FL learners, teachers should not only discuss the types of collocations (e.g., verb + noun; adjective + noun; noun + noun), but also discuss the overall meanings of collocations. Teachers can use the information in Table 9.5 and talk about the meanings of the collocations with their students.

Table 9.5. Words and their collocates (adapted from McCarthy, O'Keefe, & Walsh, 2010, p. 29)

Adjectives used with ROLE	Adverbs used with DISAPPOINTED	Nouns used as the object of CREATE
Important	Bitterly	jobs
Major	Deeply	atmosphere
Active	obviously	effect
Crucial	extremely	image
Central	Terribly	problems

FOUR STRANDS OF VOCABULARY LEARNING

Goals for vocabulary instruction, such as expanding learners' vocabulary size, raising their awareness about formulaic language, and developing their word knowledge, should be carefully planned. In order to accomplish all these goals, we recommend that teachers follow "the four strands", an approach introduced by Nation (2001):

meaning-focused input; *meaning-focused output*; *language-focused learning*; *fluency development*. Each strand is explained below.

Meaning-focused input involves reading and listening, thus teachers should encourage learners to read and listen to easy-to-understand passages because the purpose is comprehension and enjoyment. The occurrence of new words in a passage should be minimal; preferably, learners should know 98% of the words in the passage. This means that 1 out of 50 words is unknown to a learner. *Meaning-focused output* involves vocabulary use in speech and writing, with the purpose to consolidate vocabulary knowledge of the previously encountered words. In this strand, teachers should organize tasks that encourage students to use those words in meaningful and authentic ways. Activities in this strand should help learners strengthen and deepen all the productive aspects of word knowledge (see "P" items in Table 9.3).

Language-focused learning involves explicit vocabulary teaching. In this strand, the meanings (translation) of low-frequency words are taught explicitly to learners. Because of their low frequency, these words are not likely to be encountered through other sources of input and, for the sake of efficiency, must be taught explicitly. In this strand, teachers can train learners several strategies: word cards, vocabulary notebooks, and dictionaries. A meta-analytic study by Plonsky (2011) on the effectiveness of second language strategy instruction has revealed that vocabulary strategies can be effective if the learners are explicitly taught some strategies and are given enough opportunity to practice them. *Fluency development*: is all about whether words are used or understood in a native-like manner. As a FL learner, you have probably been in a situation (perhaps, more than one time) when you recognize a word in a text but you cannot immediately recall its meaning. This can obviously slow down the word recognition, which makes it almost impossible to understand the flow of the text (Grabe & Stoller, 2013). In speech or writing, likewise, sometimes you cannot produce a word you have recently learned in a timely or native-like manner. In this sense, fluency is one way to distinguish between partial and full mastery of a word. Put another way, "it is one thing to know the meaning of a word and another to be able to use it fluently" (Webb & Nation, 2013, p. 5).

Food for Thought: Four Strands

The application of the four strands in a FL course will help learners explore new words, and then give them opportunities to enhance their vocabulary development through use (Schmitt, 2008; Webb & Schmitt, 2013). A variety of activities belonging to one of these strands are listed below.

• teaching learners how to use bilingual or monolingual learner dictionaries (using tasks that involve receptive and productive skills) facilitate vocabulary learning (Laufer, 2011; Ranalli, 2013)
• deliberate teaching of the highest frequency words (the first and second 1,000) are effective because of their utility across four skills - reading, listening, writing, and speaking (Webb & Nation, 2013)

- having learners explore the meaning(s) of a target word in context helps them notice how English vocabulary works; for example, *break* can mean different things in different contexts: "*he broke his leg* [cracks/separates into pieces]; *Who broke the news* [announce]? *He broke his promise* [failed to keep]; *He broke yet another record* [improved]" (Rott, 2013)
- learning new words using computer programs, mobile phones, electronic pocket dictionaries, and vocabulary notebooks are effective because they encourage spaced learning, and consolidate vocabulary knowledge (see Hayati, Jalilifar, & Mashhadi, 2011; Nakata, 2008)
- assigning learners to produce meaningful sentences by using the target words from a unit in a reading or listening class will "push" learners to orally demonstrate their knowledge of the words (McFeely & Nurmukhamedov, forthcoming)
- giving fill-in-the-blank vocabulary exercises encourage learners to produce the previously encountered words by taking into account the meaning, use, and context which will eventually lead to a improved lexical retention (Folse, 2006)
- encouraging cooperative group learning is beneficial because learners discuss the meaning and usage of previously encountered words from a unit in order to benefit from each other's' input (Mercer, 2005)
- watching movies, specialized TV programs (e.g., http://learningenglish. voanews. com/), and online presentations (e.g., www.ted.com) with captions can help learners improve their vocabulary (Sydorenko, 2010; Webb & Rodgers, 2009)

SUMMARY OF THE VOCABULARY PRINCIPLES

Based on the information in the chapter, it can be inferred that FL learners need to have a large vocabulary size to read, listen, speak and write in English. In addition to learning single words, FL learners should also know word families and their various meanings. Moreover, it is suggested that they be aware of phrasal vocabulary because of the widespread role of formulaic language in both speech and writing and their pragmatic and linguistic functions. With regards to vocabulary instruction, words that have been previously learned should be consolidated using the four strands described above so that learners not only recognize the new words and their meaning, but are also able to produce them in speech and writing in a native-like manner (*fluency*). FL teachers can follow the above-mentioned principles and "food-for-thought" suggestions to help their learners improve their vocabulary knowledge so that FL learners successfully use vocabulary for their future academic and personal endeavours.

REFERENCES

Ackerman, K., & Chen, Y. (2013). Developing the Academic Collocation List (ACL) – A corpus-driven and expert-judged approach. *Journal of English for Academic Purposes, 12*, 235–247.
Akbarian, I. (2010). The relationship between vocabulary size and depth for ESP/EAP learners. *System, 38*, 391–401.

Biber, D., Johansson, S., Leech, G., Conrad, S., & Finegan, E. (1999). *Longman grammar of spoken and written English*. Harlow: Longman.

Biber, D., & Reppen, R. (2002). What does frequency have to do with grammar teaching? *Studies in Second Language Acquisition, 24*, 199–208.

Boers, F., Eyckmans, J., Kappel, J., Stengers, H., & Demecheleer, M. (2006). Formulaic sequences and perceived oral proficiency: Putting a lexical approach to the test. *Language Teaching Research, 10*, 245–261.

Brezina, V., & Gablasova, D. (2013). Is there a core general vocabulary? Introducing the new general service list. *Applied Linguistics* (Online). doi:10.1093/applin/amt018

Cheng, W., Greaves, C., Sinclar, J., & Warren, M. (2008). Uncovering the extent of the phraseological tendency: Towards a systematic analysis of concgrams. *Applied Linguistics, 30*, 236–252.

Coxhead, A. (2000). A new academic word list. *TESOL Quarterly, 34*, 213–238.

Erman, B., & Warren, B. (2000). The idiom principle and the open choice principle. *Text, 20*, 29–62.

Erten, I., & Razi, S. (2009). The effects of cultural familiarity on reading comprehension. *Reading in a Foreign Language, 21*, 60–77.

Folse, K. (2006). The effect of type of written exercise on L2 vocabulary retention. *TESOL Quarterly, 40*, 273–293.

Gardner, D., & Davies, M. (2013). A new academic vocabulary list. *Applied Linguistics* (Online). doi:10.1093/applin/amt015

Grabe, W., & Stoller, F. L. (2014). Teaching reading for academic purposes. In M. Celce-Murcia, D. M. Brinton, & M. A. Snow (Eds.), *Teaching English as a second or foreign language* (4th ed., pp. 189–205). Boston, MA: Heinle Cengage.

Guiterrez Arvizu, M. N. (2012). Online dictionaries rally. In R. R. Day (Ed.), *New ways in teaching reading, revised* (pp. 234–235). Alexandria, VA: TESOL International Association.

Hayati, A., Jalilifar, A., & Mashhadi, A. (2013). Using Short Message Service (SMS) to teach English idioms to EFL students. *British Journal of Educational Technology, 44*, 66–81.

Laufer, B. (2005). Focus on form in second language vocabulary learning. *EUROSLA Yearbook, 5*, 223–250.

Laufer, B. (2011). The contribution of dictionary use to the productive and retention of collocations in a second language. *International Journal of Lexicography, 24*, 29–49.

Lewis, M. (2000). *Teaching collocation: Further developments in the lexical approach*. Hove: Language Teaching Publication.

Martinez, R., & Schmitt, N. (2012). Phrasal expressions list. *Applied Linguistics* (Online). doi:10.1093/applin/ams010

McCarthy, M., O'Keeffe, A., & Walsh, S. (2010). *Vocabulary matrix: Understanding, learning, teaching*. Andover, MN: Heinle CENGAGE Learning.

McFeely, W., & Nurmukhamedov, U. (forthcoming). Developing fluency of target vocabulary through meaningful sentence production. In A. Coxhead (Ed.), *New ways in teaching vocabulary, revised*. Alexandria, VA: TESOL International Association.

Mercer, S. (2005). Vocabulary strategy work for advanced learners of English. *English Teaching Forum, 43*, 24–45.

Nakata, T. (2008). English vocabulary learning with word lists, word cards and computers: Implications from cognitive psychology research for optimal spaced learning. *ReCALL, 20*, 3–20.

Nation, P. (2001). *Learning vocabulary in another language*. New York, NY: Cambridge University Press.

Nation, P. (2006). How large a vocabulary is needed to reading and listening? *The Canadian Modern Language Review, 63*, 59–82.

Nation, P. (2013). Vocabulary size in a second language. In C. Chapelle (Ed.), *The encyclopedia of applied linguistics* (pp. 1–4). Malden, MA: Wiley-Blackwell.

Nation, P., & Beglar, D. (2007). A vocabulary size test. *The Language Teacher, 31*, 9–13.

Nation, P., & Webb, S. (2011). *Researching and analyzing vocabulary*. Boston, MA: Heinle.

Nurmukhamedov, U. (2012). Online English-English learner dictionaries boost word learning. *English Teaching Forum, 50*, 10–15.

Plonsky, L. (2011). The effectiveness of second language strategy instruction: A meta-analysis. *Language Learning, 61*, 993–1038.

Plonsky, L., & Loewen, S. (2013). Focus on form and vocabulary acquisition in the Spanish L2 classroom. *Language, Interaction, and Acquisition, 4*, 1–24.

Ranalli, J. (2013). Online strategy instruction for integrating dictionary skills and language awareness. *Language Learning & Technology, 17*, 74–99.

Rott, S. (2013). Incidental vocabulary acquisition. In C. Chapelle (Ed.), *The encyclopedia of applied linguistics* (pp. 1–5). London: Wiley-Blackwell.

Schmitt, N. (2008). Review article: Instructed second language vocabulary learning. *Language Teaching Research, 12*, 329–363.

Schmitt, N. (2010). *Researching vocabulary: A vocabulary research manual.* New York, NY: Palgrave Macmillan.

Shin, D., & Nation, P. (2008). Beyond single words: The most frequent collocations in spoken English. *ELT Journal, 62*, 339–348.

Simpson-Vlach, R., & Ellis, N. (2010). An academic formulas list: New methods in phraseology research. *Applied Linguistics, 31*, 487–512.

Sydorenko, T. (2010). Modality of input and vocabulary acquisition. *Language Learning & Technology, 14*, 50–73.

Webb, N., & Nation, P. (2013). Teaching vocabulary. In C. Chapelle (Ed.), *The encyclopedia of applied linguistics* (pp. 1–7). Malden, MA: Wiley-Blackwell.

Webb, S., & Rodgers, M. (2009). The vocabulary demands of television programs. *Language Learning, 59*, 335–366.

Wray, A. (2013). Research timeline: Formulaic language. *Language Teaching, 46*, 316–334.

Ulugbek Nurmukhamedov
Northern Illinois University
DeKalb, Illinois
USA

Luke Plonsky
Georgetown University
Washington, DC
USA

APPENDIX

ONLINE DICTIONARIES RALLY HANDOUT
(adapted from Gutierrez Arvizu, 2012, p. 235)

1. Go to this website: _____

2. Find this **word**. _____

3. What is the word's **part of speech**?

   _____

4. How many **definitions** did you find?

   _____

5. Write down the **definition** you need to learn (*in English*).

_____

6. How do you say that word in your language? (*write the meaning in your language*)

_____

7. How is the word **pronounced**? (*Br/Am*)

_____

8. How can you **use** this word? (*grammar*)

_____

9. Provide an example sentence (*from the dictionary*).

_____

10. Find two or three **collocations** for the word from the example sentences.

_____

11. Compare your sheet with your friend and talk about the differences.

JOHN I. LIONTAS

10. REFLECTIVE AND EFFECTIVE TEACHING OF IDIOMS THROUGH A PRAGMATIC PERSPECTIVE

INTRODUCTION

To bridge the gap between pragmatic theory and idiom pedagogy, this chapter begins with three general tenets regarding the content, construction, and dependence of idioms on the contexts in which they are uttered during conversations. First, all idioms contain ever-evolving social, cultural, and historical material through which a language's sociocultural pulse through the passage of time may be taken. Second, all idioms are constructed and co-constructed in an extralinguistic context; that is, against the background of shared beliefs and assumptions that are intuitively exploited by both speaker and audience, signifying a particular communicative purpose in a particular situation. Third, the selection and use of all idioms depends on the immediate context, linguistic or otherwise, of a given dialog or text, and on the communicative functions idioms fulfill during a conversational exchange.

To scaffold reflective and effective teaching of idioms, this chapter delineates specific pragmatic concepts for incorporating these three idiom tenets within conversational contexts.

More specifically, it is argued that using a pragmatic theory of idiomaticity can help SLA researchers and language teachers alike to circumvent the predominant view that language pedagogy can be firmly constructed only upon a base of either a semantic or a syntactic theory.

While one could easily postulate a semantic theory that leads from syntactic surface structure to meaning, one could also postulate a pragmatic theory that leads from what is conveyed literally by the idiom in context to what is implied idiomatically by the dictionary definitions of the individual words comprising the idiom, a meaning that cannot be deduced from the ordinary meanings of the words in it. It is such a pragmatic theory that is presented here.

This theory proposes classroom conditions that are most likely to facilitate the development of native-like *idiomatic competence* – the ability to understand and use idioms appropriately and accurately in a variety of sociocultural contexts, in a manner similar to that of native speakers, and with the least amount of mental effort – so defined by Liontas (1999, 2015a), in second and foreign languages. Its aim, however, is not to suggest specific techniques or activities that language teachers can employ. Rather, its aim is to consider pedagogy in terms of what

© KONINKLIJKE BRILL NV, LEIDEN, 2018 | DOI:10.1163/9789004380882_010

kinds of classroom behaviors language teachers need to adopt in order to promote idiomatic competence in their students, albeit in different learning environments and with different levels of success, not to suggest that such a pragmatic theory of idiom pedagogy is the only viable one.

This chapter therefore focuses attention on H. P. Grice's (1968, 1975) pragmatic concept of the *Cooperative Principle* (CP). Using Grice's CP (especially the Maxim of Manner), it is shown how idioms can be 'worked out' successfully on the basis of the principles of conversation. In the process, some claims are made about how idioms act in communicative contexts, and about the ways contexts constrain the interpretation of idioms. The ensuing discussion seeks to reveal how Grice's CP may be used effectively in the second and foreign language (henceforth SL) classroom. In particular, authentic text examples are used to examine.

Grice's CP and to show how the conversational maxims underlying the CP can enhance the teaching and learning of idiomatic knowledge. Throughout this chapter, it is argued that idioms should be analyzed pragmatically not only in terms of the semantic content expressed, but, perhaps even more importantly, in terms of the extralinguistic contexts and shared background knowledge of conventionalized norms, practices, and cultural beliefs in which idioms are used by interlocutors to express meaning at particular points in a conversational transaction.

PRAGMATICS: A LOOK BEHIND A SPEAKER'S COMMUNICATIVE INTENTIONS

Pragmatics has long been haunted by definitions too broad to be of any specific use to researchers who work in applied linguistics. In fact, the term pragmatics may be in danger of becoming a useless catch-all term. Consider, for example, the definition of pragmatics offered by Charles W. Morris (1971) in *Foundations of the Theory of Signs*: [T]he biotic aspects of semiosis, that is, ... [the study of] all the psychological, biological, and sociological phenomena which occur in the functioning of signs (p. 43). Two decades later, Davis (1991) correctly points out that the problem with such a broad view of pragmatics is that it covers almost "any human activity involving language" (p. 3). He thus suggests that if 'pragmatics' is to be a useful term, "its domain must be restricted" (p. 4).

Accordingly, Davis's (1991) definition of pragmatic theory is adopted for the purposes of this discussion here. As he states,

[A] pragmatic theory is part of a theory of a speaker's linguistic competence. As such, it is part of a psychological theory that plays a role in accounting for what speakers tacitly know which enables them to understand and to use sentences of their language. (p. 4)

To this definition of pragmatic theory this researcher adds additional facets of pragmatics such as the cognitive, social, and cultural study of language and communication.

According to the definition above, we understand a given human language because we have knowledge of the syntactic rules of that language that allows us to understand one another.

Based on the syntactic rules we can say with a degree of confidence whether or not a string of words constitutes a well-formed sentence in that language. This tacit knowledge is referred to as linguistic *competence* (Chomsky, 1965). But, while the syntactic rules of a language allow one to construct a sentence using, for instance, well-accepted tree-diagrams, such knowledge does not necessarily *require* the ability to understand language per se. To understand language, one must understand the very sentences one is producing (encoding) or hearing (decoding). This, by definition, is the domain of semantics, which allows us to understand the meaning of the individual words of our language, as well as the rules that allow us to combine these meanings into larger units such as phrases and sentences.

If, however, all that is needed for successful communication is knowledge of syntax (i.e., rules of grammar and the resulting relations of linguistic units, structures of phrases, and sentences to one another) and semantics (i.e., knowledge of the meanings of words), why do we more often than not fail to grasp each other's meaning during conversations? Expressed more precisely, if *conversational meaning* is found in the lexical units informed by the syntactic/ semantic 'definitions' we offer for each of the words which, in combination, form the meanings of larger units, why do we time and again still fail to understand what is being expressed by individual words or by word combinations? Is it because knowledge of semantics alone is not sufficient to determine what each word or sentence means in a particular situation? If not, what determines how we communicate with and understand one another?

It is proposed that a major role in successful interaction is played by *communicative context* and *pragmatic knowledge*. The communicative context in which a conversation takes place shapes the particular meaning of a word or a cluster of words; therefore, implied meaning will vary considerably from context to context and from occasion to occasion. Coupled with one's pragmatic knowledge, which includes knowing the rules that govern conversational exchanges, as well as the multiple nuances of meaning that communicative intentions can have on a particular occasion, human communication generally succeeds, although not without some room for ambiguity.

Successful communication thus includes more than simple "context-independent linguistic knowledge" (Davis, 1991, p. 6). It also involves conversational knowledge, or knowledge of pragmatic aspects, including, but not limited to, such aspects as "deixis (i.e., the ways in which language encodes features of the context of utterance), conversational implicature and presupposition (i.e., the way language is used to convey meanings that are not actually encoded linguistically), illocutionary acts (i.e., the use of language to perform speech acts such as stating, questioning, and directing), conversational structure (i.e., the way in which conversations are organized across turns), and repairs (i.e., the conversational work undertaken to deal with miscommunication of various kinds)" (Ellis, 1994, p. 23). The end result is that we can carry on a conversation and progress from *linguistic competence* to *socio-pragmatic performance*. In short, *performance* is the result of linguistic competence at work. Consider, for example, the following conversational exchange between a husband and a wife:

A Newlywed Couple Returns Home after a Night on the Town

Husband: How come the front door is open? Didn't you close it before we went out?
Wife: I'm sure I did. I can't understand it.
Husband: Frankly, *I smell a rat.*
Wife: Me, too. We'd better call the police.
Husband: Yeah! I think you are right. Give me your cell phone!

Anyone familiar with the American idiom *to smell a rat* (i.e., to feel that something is wrong) immediately recognizes that the newlywed couple here is not talking about an actual rat or about the fact that now the house has the 'smell of a rat' because Speaker B (Wife) forgot to close the exterior door. Nor is the couple seriously considering the option of calling the police because of the smell left behind by a 'rat'. Instead, Speaker B is very much aware of the fact that

Speaker A (Husband) is not talking about his superb sensory ability to 'smell a rat'. This is clearly evident by the follow-up remark of Speaker B to call the police immediately, but not before she too concedes 'smelling a rat'. Her very acknowledgment of the same 'smell' indicates her shared knowledge of the conversation, that is, the interplay between referential and communicative intentions that allows her to initiate her own conversational move. This conversational move is dependent upon the context of the conversation. Speaker A is by no means trying to mislead his conversational partner when he suggests that he 'smells a rat'. The fact that their conversation continues without any communicative ambiguity – although the potential for it is clearly there – shows that both of them share the background and cultural knowledge that allows them to see that 'I smell a rat' in fact means 'there is something wrong here'. The first two sentences of the conversation clearly make possible only one kind of possible meaning for 'I smell a rat', that is, the idiom is used in such a way as to be the only logical summation of the preceding lines. In short, what is being said and ultimately communicated relies on the immediate extralinguistic context of the conversation in question, as well as on the shared background knowledge the two interlocutors take for granted.

Successful human communication, then, occurs when both speaker and hearer share linguistic (i.e., phonology, morphology, syntax, grammar), semantic (i.e., lexicon and etymology), and pragmatic knowledge (i.e., cultural beliefs of norms and practices about how language is used in communication). In addition, both speaker and hearer observe the rules that govern conversation (implying a knowledge of pragmatics) and the truth conditions (implying a knowledge of semantics) that semantic referents have in a particular context.

Moreover, while the non-deictic referents of an expression are fixed within the conventions of a language, the speaker's intentions are only fixed by what the speaker intends to refer to on a particular occasion and in a particular context. If the rules that govern conversation are not observed, the interplay between referential and communicative intentions (the speaker's intentions) becomes the source of communicative ambiguity. Not only do speakers have to make sure that their audiences recognize what they are trying to communicate, more importantly, audiences have to recognize speakers' communicative intentions (Grice, 1975, p. 45). Again, *context* plays a crucial role. As Davis (1991) correctly asserts:

> Pragmatics will have as its domain speakers' communicative intentions, the uses of language that require such intentions, and the strategies that hearers employ to determine what these intentions and acts are, so that they can understand what the speaker intends to communicate. (p. 11)

The discussion now turns to these communicative intentions, and to what an utterance can both explicitly (*what is said* in a particular context) and implicitly (*what is implicated* by how the utterance is said) convey.

Grice's Cooperative Principle (CP)

Paul Grice's (1968, 1975) theory of conversational implicatures was a major development in the field of pragmatics. Grice's primary aim was to show that the meaning of an utterance often results from an unconscious constructive inferential process whose input is the linguistic meaning of the sentence uttered. Seeking to draw attention to the nature and importance of the conditions governing conversation, Grice introduced the notion of 'implicature' (cf. *implicate*).

Implicatures, according to Grice, can be conventional and conversational. *Conventional* implicatures include all non-truth-conditional aspects of what is conveyed by the words or forms a sentence contains (i.e., the presuppositions of a sentence in the strict sense). In other words, what is conveyed is determined by the particular lexical items or linguistic constructions in an utterance. In contrast, *conversational* implicatures are only indirectly associated with the linguistic content of utterances. They are derived from the content of sentences and owe their existence to the fact that participants in a conversation are constrained by their common goal of communication as a cooperative venture.

Since conversational implicatures are closely connected with features of human discourse, Grice posits that discourse is not simply a succession of disconnected remarks, for if it were, it would not make sense. To some degree, then, verbal exchanges are cooperative efforts guided by a set of purposes. These purposes may be fixed from the start or may evolve during the exchange; they may also be fairly definite, or indefinite as in casual conversation. Yet, any deviation from generally accepted moves during the various stages of the exchange between

Speaker A and Speaker B would be considered conversationally unsuitable. In the 'I smell a rat' example given earlier, it was shown how the exchange between Speaker A and Speaker B is guided by the same purpose: to call the police. This purpose was not predetermined at the outset but evolved during the conversational exchange. Had Speaker A said 'No, let's open the windows to air out the house!', it would have been extremely difficult for Speaker B to 'work out' the intended meaning of her husband's utterance.

In effect, this means that both speakers observe a general principle of conversation, which Grice terms the *Cooperative Principle* (CP). This principle counsels both interlocutors to make their conversational contribution "such as it is required, at the stage at which it occurs, by the accepted purpose or direction of the talk exchange in which you are engaged" (Grice, 1975, p. 45). The important difference between *conventional* and *conversational* implicatures is that the conventional implicatures are arbitrarily stipulated, whereas conversational implicatures are recoverable through reasoning. As Grice (1975) further states:

> The presence of a conversational implicature must be capable of being worked out; for even if it can in fact be intuitively grasped, unless the intuition is replaceable by an argument, the implicature (if present at all) will not count as a conversational implicature: it will be a conventional implicature. (p. 50)

Accordingly, conversational implicatures follow from the general maxims of informativeness (Quantity), truthfulness (Quality), relevance (Relation), and clarity (Manner) that speakers are assumed to heed during conversations. These categories and their more specific maxims are briefly summarized below.

The Cooperative Principle and Its Maxims

Quantity: This category relates to the quantity of information provided. The following two maxims fall under this category:

1. Make your contributions as informative as is required (for the purposes of the current exchange).
2. Do not make your contribution more informative than is required.

Grice points out that the validity of the second maxim may be questionable due to its over informativeness effect; that is, the hearer might be lead to thinking that there is some particular point at which information provided becomes excessive. However, the effects of this maxim may be minimized by the Maxim of Relation (discussed below). In the 'I smell a rat' example, the use of the idiomatic utterance by Speaker A (Husband) is only as informative as is required for that particular situation. Neither Speaker A nor Speaker B (Wife) engage in lengthy unwarranted explanations of the expression uttered, given the content and context of their conversation and their shared knowledge that the idiom means 'there is something wrong here'.

Quality: Under this category, Grice offers a 'supermaxim' – "Try to make your contribution one that is true" (Grice, 1975, p. 46) – and two submaxims:

1. Do not say what you believe to be false.
2. Do not say that for which you lack adequate evidence.

In the 'I smell a rat' example, Speaker A does not really smell a rat. If this was indeed the case, that is, if Speaker A wanted Speaker B to recognize only his referential intention, Speaker B's next conversational move would have been more productive had she uttered 'Me, too. We'd better call the exterminator first thing tomorrow morning!' Clearly, if Speaker A had categorically detected the odor of a large rodent in the house, such a response by Speaker B would have been most appropriate here. However, the front door of their house is open and Speaker B suggests calling the police rather than the exterminator. Clearly, Speaker B is capable of successfully 'working out' her husband's communicative intentions in this particular context.

Furthermore, the conversation between Speaker A and B is guided by a mutual purpose: to call the police, given the eerie feeling they have upon realizing that someone may have broken into their house. Through this example, it can be seen that the processing of an idiom depends critically on the larger context of which it is part. As a result, it is easier to perceive idioms in context than it is to perceive idioms that stand alone. This line of argument is well supported by the maxim below.

Relation: Under this category, Grice places a single maxim: "Be relevant" (Grice, 1975, p. 46).

This maxim he calls 'terse', since its formulation may conceal a number of questions such as: (1) what different kinds and focuses of relevance are in a talk exchange; (2) how these shift in the course of a talk exchange; and (3) how to allow for the fact that subjects of conversation are legitimately changed. Again, in the 'I smell a rat' example, it is the relevance of the situation and the communicative context in which the expression is uttered that allows Speaker B to ignore the literal referential meaning of the expression 'I smell a rat' and thus recover her husband's idiomatic communicative intention. The meaning of an idiom is always cross-referenced with other semantic and pragmatic indicators in a conversation or text that prompt a hearer (reader) who is constructing meaning, to take apart the sentence meaning and the speaker's (writer's) utterance meaning. It would be a grave mistake to assume that the figurative meaning of an idiom is supplied solely by the words surrounding it. Semantic and syntactic constraints facilitate idiom identification because idioms are embedded in the broader context of human experience.

In short, idiom interpretation demands recognition of contextual and pragmatic inferences that are greater than a given conversation or text. Paradoxically, this is also why the particular figurative meaning of an idiom is specific to a given text.

Manner: Grice posits that this category, unlike the previous three categories, relates not to what is said, but rather, to *how* what is said is to be said. He once again postulates a supermaxim – "Be perspicuous" – and some submaxims such as:

- Avoid obscurity of expression.
- Avoid ambiguity.
- Be brief (avoid unnecessary prolixity).
- Be orderly.

To anyone unfamiliar with American culture, expressions such as 'I smell a rat' may appear obscure when interpreted literally only at the sentence level (i.e., the level of simple semantic knowledge of the meanings of the words). Idioms are used both consciously and unconsciously by speakers of a language because they (1) avoid unnecessary prolixity and can be executed with reasonable dispatch; (2) are only as informative as is required; (3) are genuine since they are culturally and socially conventionalized, and thus easily recognized; and lastly, (4) are relevant to the immediate needs of a conversational transaction and to any shifts in its course due to changes in conversational and situational contexts.

Given these reasons, in addition to the rules that govern conversation and the truth conditions that speakers many a time share in a particular communicative context, it is logical to postulate that both speakers in the 'I smell a rat' example are constrained by a common goal: to be cooperative. In turn, this also explains why their discourse is not a succession of disconnected remarks. Not only is their talk exchange a cooperative effort, but it is also guided by a mutual purpose (to call the police) that evolved during their conversation. This clearly suggests that both speakers observe Grice's pragmatic concept of conversation – the *Cooperative Principle* (CP).

Grice's CP can be summarized by the conversational maxims in Table 10.1.

Table 10.1. Grice's cooperative principle (CP)

Maxim of Quantity	Make your contribution neither more nor less than is required.
Maxim of Quality	Make your contribution to be genuine and not spurious.
Maxim of Relation	Make your contribution to be appropriate to the immediate needs at each stage of the transaction.
Maxim of Manner	Make your contribution clear and execute it with reasonable dispatch.

Conversational Maxims at Work

Grice believes that speakers, in the absence of indications to the contrary, advance their conversational transactions by adhering to the principles discussed above. Such conversational behavior is not reconstructed each time speakers converse; rather, this behavior is learned early in childhood. Conversation, proceeding appropriately by observing the CP and its maxims, relies on speakers' often tacit knowledge that underlies the transitory conversational interests of the talk exchange. Conversation continues until both parties decide that they have arrived at a point at which the conversation should be terminated or until they decide that a mutually acceptable new topic is needed.

While Grice's assumption that talk exchanges are generally conducted in accordance with the CP and its maxims can be largely substantiated by analyzing large excerpts of natural conversational data, one should bear in mind that the very maxims which offer support to the CP may at times be (and often are) violated. In other words, a participant in a talk exchange may fail to heed a maxim in various ways. As Grice cautiously points out, s/he may violate a maxim and in doing so may mislead his or her conversational partner. S/he may also *opt out* of the operation both of the maxim and of the CP or may be faced with a *clash* of maxims in conflict with one another. Consider, for example, the first Maxim of Quantity with regard to the second Maxim of Quality. What is the point of being as informative as required if one does not have adequate evidence for what s/he is saying?

In the 'I smell a rat' example, the expression *I smell a rat* is both a sentence (S) and an utterance (U). As a sentence, it is an abstraction made up of grammar and semantics (context independent linguistic knowledge), but as an utterance, it includes a contextual reality (context dependent extralinguistic knowledge) and has more than one meaning – a literal, referential semantic meaning (SM) and a non-literal, figurative utterance meaning (UM). That is, the speaker says an S (sentence) by expressing the SM, all the while implicating the UM, the supposition of which, based on the other conversationalist's linguistic and socio-pragmatic competence, may be 'worked out' or grasped intuitively.

It can therefore be argued, as Grice does, that conversational implicatures must be capable of being worked out and that the *implicatum* (cf. *what is implied*) must be derived without lapsing into ambiguity that could further hinder how a particular implicature is ultimately interpreted and understood. Such an argument raises several questions:

- How is the overall Cooperative Principle (CP) observed at the level of what is implicated? Said differently, how does the hearer who hears an S, and should understand the conventional literal meaning (SM), arrive at the 'post-conventional' figurative meaning (UM)?
- How does s/he work out the supposition implied in the SM?
- What is the unstated connection between an S and a UM?

To answer the above questions, let us take a close look at an example from real-life communication.

This example violates the 'Maxim of Manner' because of what is said at the end. The text, therefore, imposes on the hearer two stages of interpretation: a literal one and a figurative one. Speaker A says 'She has put his two feet into one shoe', intending the hearer to interpret this phrase figuratively – as 'She has wrapped him around her little finger' – rather than literally.

Speaker A, therefore, expects the ambiguity of the literal meaning to be recognized by his hearer.

The hearer, on the other hand, assumes that the Maxim of Manner is still in force. As a result, upon hearing S 'She has put his two feet into one shoe', he believes that

Table 10.2. Excerpt from an authentic text

Modern Greek text	English text (translation)
A: Ο Μίλτος παντρεύτηκε.	**A:** Meltos got married.
B: Αλήθεια; Βρέθηκε γυναίκα να τον παντρευτεί;	**B:** Really? A woman was finally found that wanted to marry him?
A: Βέβαια.	**A:** Sure.
B: Την καημένη! Πολύ τη λυπάμαι!	**B:** Poor soul! I feel sorry for her!
A: Τον καημένο να λες, γιατί τον κάνει ότι θέλει.	**A:** You should feel sorry for him, because she does with him whatever she wants.
B: Σοβαρά; Το Μίλτο, το σκληρό άντρα;	**B:** Are you serious? Melto, the tough guy?
A: Μάλιστα. Το Μίλτο, το σκληρό άντρα του **έχει βάλει τα δυο πόδια σ∏ ένα παπούτσι.**	**A:** Yeah. Melto, the tough guy. She has **put his two feet into one shoe.**

the conversational game is still being played and that therefore the ambiguity of SM cannot be entertained seriously. The fact that Speaker A is deliberately flouting the Supermaxim of Manner – 'Be perspicuous' – and its submaxims is a good indication to Speaker B that these maxims are being purposefully violated by Speaker A. In other words, the supermaxim is, as Grice (1975) asserts, "flouted for the purpose of getting in a conversational implicature by means of something of the nature of a figure of speech" (p. 52).

In essence, for the CP to operate, the hearer has to be able to understand what is being said despite the obvious obscurity imported into the SM. It can therefore be argued that although the Supermaxim of Manner is violated at the level of what is said literally in a particular context, the hearer, given the conversational data available to him or her, can easily assume that the Supermaxim of Manner is observed at the level of what is implicated, which is UM and *not* SM. Expressed differently, the hearer assumes that the talk exchange continues to be conducted in accordance with the overall conversational principles of the CP, leading him or her to a search for an interpretation away from the literal SM to the implicated UM. Consequently, the implicated UM 'She has wrapped him around her little finger' presupposes a prior knowledge of the conventional meaning for that expression and, even more importantly, an appropriate extralinguistic context which cogently disambiguates the SM.

It can be safely argued that the hearer, concerned with appropriateness of what is said (and how what is said is to be said) in a particular context, goes beyond the strict semantic content of the sentence SM and, on the basis of contextual assumptions and pragmatic principles, recovers the intended UM. In other words, the hearer will select an interpretation consistent with the presumption that the speaker is trying to say something true and relevant to the conversation.

With idioms in general, one arrives at the idiomatic meaning directly, without any inferential processing. This is due to the fact that the meaning of an idiom, which through the passage of time has become socially and culturally conventionalized, is already entrenched in the mental lexicon and, thereby, part of the knowledge one has as a speaker of a language. A key point worth mentioning here is that virtually all native speakers have easy access to such figures of speech and need not process all data sequentially to arrive at the desired figurative interpretation. Having access to and utilizing various figures of speech appropriately and within the proper sociocultural contexts is what underlies native speakers' linguistic and cultural proficiency.

In contrast, as shown in the Liontas (1999, 2001, 2002a, 2002b, 2002c, 2002d, 2002e, 2003, 2007, 2008, 2013, 2015b) studies, SL learners will make use of their translation skills first. When they fail to understand the conventional meaning of the words used, they will then – with various degrees of success – rely on the context, linguistic or otherwise, of the utterance to determine an idiom's meaning. In fact, they use context as the organizing framework for comprehending and interpreting Vivid Phrasal (VP) idioms (i.e., imageable-rich multiword lexemic units) in context. This, combined with their background experience and world knowledge, may then allow them to correctly detect and interpret the idiom in question.

Furthermore, both the experimental data and the variety of introspective/ retrospective reports analyzed in these studies strongly suggest that SL learners use (either consciously or unconsciously) pragmatic strategies such as their own experiences in a similar situation, cultural and world knowledge, text organization, and patterns of naturally-occurring discourse features to decipher contextually based VP idioms. On this basis, it was deduced that since participants made continuous use of such knowledge, SL students would profit greatly from instruction in metacognitive awareness and retention strategies for idioms in general and pragmatics in particular. Within the specific domain of the CP, Grice (1975) similarly states that to "work out that a particular conversational implicature is present, the hearer will rely on the following data" (p. 50):

- The conventional meaning of the words used, together with the identity of any
- references that may be involved;
- The CP and its maxims;
- The context, linguistic or otherwise, of the utterance;
- Other items of background knowledge; and
- The fact (or supposed fact) that all relevant items falling under the previous headings are available to both participants and both participants know or assume this to be the case.

These types of data were clearly employed by the adult second- and third-year participants of the Liontas studies cited above. Participants were repeatedly found to employ the underlying maxims of conversation and the pragmatic strategies of Grice's CP successfully throughout the three experimental tasks.[1] The maxims of Relation and Manner amassed the most attention in the metalinguistic citations received. For example, one participant commented during the Idiom Detection Task with respect to the German idiom *wie die Katze um den heißen Brei herumreden* (lit. to walk like a cat round hot porridge; fig. to beat around the bush), "I choose this one because it again has a reference to an animal. I also believe from the context of the paragraph, that it may mean 'to beat around the bush'". With respect to the German idiom *ein Haar in der Suppe finden* (lit. to find a hair in one's soup; fig. to split hairs), another participant observed, "This expression is easy to spot because the clerk is all of the sudden talking about a hair in the soup, and this does not go along with the rest of the context". Similarly, another German SL participant wrote, "Hair and soup are out of strict context. 'B' is making an evaluative statement about 'A' that is not relevant to cars". With respect to the Modern Greek idiom χτύπα ξύλο (lit. to knock/throw wood, to beat someone; fig. to knock on wood) a participant noted, "Because it directly translates to the English expression 'knock on wood'. Also, the only phrase which is not a matter of fact in the passage. The other sentences are straightforward and cannot be interpreted differently". (For additional Modern Greek metalinguistic citations, see Liontas, 2001, in particular appendix A, p. 31.)

Many more such supporting comments can be presented here, but the point is clear.

Language teachers interested in using such metalinguistic data in their own teaching are counseled to spend more class time on metacognition, discussing the pros and cons of different idiom-detection strategies. What should be emphasized, however, is not so much the relative accuracy of the participants' detections as the different ways in which these detections were made. In other words, SL learners need to become aware of how to isolate an idiom in a text and to analyze its contribution to the context. It is precisely this gap that astute language teachers can begin to fill with more focused, meaning-based language-use activities and strategies training that, it is predicted, will lead to more effective inferencing. Repeated exposure to idioms and the contexts in which they are used positively influences idiom learning. Indeed, teachers need to be concerned equally with the conventions of a language (i.e., the linguistic matters of literal meaning) and the conventions of usage (i.e., the cultural matters of idiomaticity such as occasion, purpose, and means) if reflective and effective teaching of idioms is to be achieved across the curriculum (see also Alexander, 1987; Bortfeld, 2003; Cacciari, Padovani, & Corradini, 2007; Caillies & Butcher, 2007; Palmer, Shackelford, Miller, & Leclere, 2007).

As SL learners move through higher levels of education and proficiency, language teachers should consider the need for learners to infer the purpose-meaning connections made between occasions of usage and expressions used. In the process of learning, certain appropriate figurative expressions can become part of one's background knowledge, with no other plausible paraphrases any longer serving the same purpose. Over time, such expressions become 'common knowledge' and need not be inferred from supporting contextual cues: There is more to knowing 'how to do things with words' than just knowledge of literal meaning. Besides knowledge of the conventions of word meanings and the semantic rules of combination, language users also have knowledge about the use of particular expressions or classes of expressions. This second kind of knowledge sometimes involves convention, but conventions of usage, conventions governing the use of meaning-bearing expressions on certain occasions, for certain purposes. These two kinds of knowledge are not mutually exclusive. They are involved simultaneously in the full understanding of many utterances (Morgan, 1978, p. 279).

Nearly four decades later, as first asserted by Morgan, developing these two kinds of knowledge in SL learners may at first appear to be a lofty goal. It may be useful to note that while conventional idiomatic expressions normally take a native speaker only milliseconds to grasp (see, for example, Bobrow & Bell, 1973; Colombo, 1993; Cronk & Schweigert, 1992; Gibbs & Raymond, 1980, 1984; McGlone, Glucksberg, & Cacciari, 1994; Petersen & Burgess, 1993; Swinney & Cutler, 1979; Titone & Connine, 1999), non-native speakers unfamiliar with these meaning-bearing expressions have to labor intensely to grasp the meaning of different classes of idiomatic expressions (Irujo, 1986; Cieślicka, 2006a, 2006b, 2015; Kecskes, 2006; Laufer, 2000; Liontas, 1997, 1999, 2001, 2002a, 2002b, 2002c, 2002d, 2002e, 2003, 2007, 2008, 2013, 2015b; Malt & Eiter, 2004; Vespignani, Canal, Molinaro, Fonda, & Cacciari, 2010).

While this was evident in all three experimental tasks involved in the Liontas studies, it was especially clear in the Zero Context Task (ZCT) data. In the ZCT, participants quite frequently reported having a hard time interpreting VP idioms based solely on their imperfect knowledge of the conventions of word meanings and the semantic rules of combination.

Regarding the Spanish idiom *costar un ojo de la cara* (lit. to cost an eye of the face; fig. to cost an arm and a leg), one participant said, "I can't think of an English idiom that has something to do with an eye of the face". Another participant reported with respect to the Spanish idiom *la última gota que hace rebosar la copa* (lit. the last drop that makes the glass overflow; fig. the straw that broke the camel's back), "I have tried to find cognates. I have tried to remember expressions I may know that may relate to this one, but I am having no luck". Others expressed frustration and annoyance with interpreting certain idioms. With regard to the Spanish idiom above, one of them wrote: "I find myself very confused/annoyed!" Trying to interpret the Spanish idiom *subirse a la parra* (lit. to climb up the grapevine; fig. to blow one's top, to hit the ceiling), another participant said, "This is so frustrating to me. I have no idea what most of these idioms are". Similar comments were also made by the Modern Greek participants. With respect to the Modern Greek idiom *του ψήνω το ψάρι στα χείλη* (lit. I fry the fish on his lips; fig. to torment someone) one participant commented, "I have no idea what's going on here … something about frying a fish on someone's lips".

Collectively, these comments and others like them have profound implications for language pedagogy. They suggest that SL learners have distinct difficulties in interpreting certain types of idioms, especially if such idioms are presented to them without any contextual support.

Appertaining to this, two questions deserve serious consideration here:

- How can language teachers help SL learners reach the formidable goal of understanding idioms as well as the occasions and purposes for which such idioms are used in natural discourse?

- What can language teachers do specifically to facilitate SL learners' comprehension of the process of human communication?

These concerns and the pedagogical implications resulting from their consideration are discussed next.

BECOMING AWARE OF IMPLICATED MEANING:
PEDAGOGICAL IMPLICATIONS

Incontestably, encouraging SL learners to become aware of implicated meaning during conversational exchanges is challenging. Nevertheless, there are at least three distinct ways in which this formidable goal can be attained. They are presented here in the form of three 'broad" lessons which language teachers can adopt when teaching idioms to students. It is highly recommended that before discussing the specific lessons with students, language teachers first review with them, what is generally meant by having a conversation. Such a discussion provides a point of departure for the systematic clarification of the consequences of the pragmatic lessons examined below. It also provides a firm foundation upon which a pragmatic framework of theory and pedagogy may be pursued to advance the reflective and effective teaching of idioms.

According to Stalnaker (1978), a conversation is "a process taking place in an everchanging Context" (p. 322). Given a conversation's context dependence, people converse with one another in various expressive ways in order to communicate something. Teachers should point out to students that at any stage in a well-run conversation, a certain amount of information is always presupposed. In turn, these presuppositions can be upheld or destroyed in the course of that conversation. As Stalnacker (1974, as cited in Davis, 1991) reminds us, communication, whether linguistic or not, normally takes place against a background of beliefs or assumptions which are shared by the speaker and his audience, and which are recognized by them to be so shared (p. 472).

Then, during the evolving communicative process, certain things are taken for granted, making communication more efficient. The more common ground that is taken for granted, the more efficient communication will be. The presumed background information (the set of presuppositions which help define a linguistic context) naturally imposes constraints on what can reasonably or appropriately be said in the way it is said in that context. Keeping the above in mind, instructors can now proceed with presenting to students the three key lessons this researcher deems indispensable to idiom teaching and learning. Combined, these idiom lessons, while assuredly not exhaustive in nature, help language teachers reexamine their contexts of teaching and pedagogical practices while also expanding the pragmatic propositions advanced herein and, in particular, the pedagogical constructs upon which successful teaching of idiomatic knowledge may be attained in the SL classroom and beyond.

Idiom Lesson 1: *'What is said' is context dependent. Therefore, try to figure out as best as you can the context, linguistic or otherwise, of what you hear or read.*

In discussing speech acts, Searle (1965, as cited in Davis, 1991) astutely asserts that in "speaking a language I attempt to communicate things to my hearer by means of getting him to recognize my intention to communicate just those things" (p. 258). He further posits that meaning "is more than a matter of intention, it is also a matter of convention" (p. 259), a view echoed in the work of Morgan (1978). The goal for SL learners is therefore to perceive both the intentional and conventional aspects of what is meant in a particular context, and to understand the relationship between them. According to Searle (1975), [the] simplest cases of meaning are those in which the speaker utters a sentence and means exactly and literally what he says .... But notoriously, not all cases of meaning are this simple: In hints, insinuations, irony, and metaphor – to mention a few examples – the speaker's utterance meaning and the sentence meaning come apart in various ways (p. 59).

In the Gricean framework, conversational implicatures are contextual implications of the utterance act: they are the assumptions that follow from the speaker's saying what s/he says, together with the presumption that s/he is heeding the maxims of conversation. The fact that a given expression receives different interpretations in different contexts does not necessarily imply that it is semantically ambiguous. These differences in meaning can be accounted for at the semantic level, by positing the expression's literal meaning against a figurative meaning, but they can also be explained at the pragmatic level, by positing a conversational implicature that in some cases, combines with what is literally said. Therefore, what is said depends not only on the conventional meaning of the words contained in the expression, but also on the immediate context of the utterance expressed. Said another way, once the context is known, what is said can in most cases be automatically decoded. In short, 'what is said' is context dependent. This is why there is no ambiguity present in the conversational exchange between husband and wife in the 'I smell a rat' example, despite the potential for such ambiguity. This is the *first* idiom lesson SL learners need to learn (and subsequently observe) in their reading of and/or listening to authentic target-language texts.

Idiom Lesson 2: *Locate and work out the identity of reference cues that are available in a text and that a speaker is intuitively exploiting.*

If 'what is said' within the lexical items comprising the idiom is indeed context dependent, then that which is said must attempt to communicate something more than the literal, referential semantic meaning (SM). Affirming earlier discussion, there is a need for a pragmatic process to be involved not only to get from what is said to what is communicated, but also to get from the SM to non-literal, figurative utterance meaning (UM). Using only a semantic approach, one could locate ambiguity at the level of the SM, but such an approach is inadequate to explain what is said (i.e., the SM) against what is communicated (i.e., the UM): the latter is the domain of a pragmatic approach. Here, a pragmatic approach is preferred to a semantic approach because idioms always mean more than the sum of the lexical items comprising them. The question to answer is: How does one bridge the gap between literal meaning stated and figurative meaning attempted?

According to Récanati (1989), there are three levels of meaning: "sentence meaning, what is said, and what is communicated. What is communicated includes not only what is said but also the conversational implicatures of the utterance" (p. 298). What is said is identified intuitively; we have 'intuitions' concerning what is said that serve as a starting point for determining the linguistic meaning of a sentence (Récanati, 1989, p. 311). This process is enhanced by the cues that a competent and attentive addressee will reasonably assume the speaker is exploiting. In other words, what the speaker says, and thus his reference, is determined by the cues available to the addressee. In the 'I smell a rat' example, the door being 'open' serves both as a starting point and as the identity of a reference cue for what is being communicated by Speaker A on that particular occasion. Therefore, the bridging of the gap between Speaker's A literal and intended meanings comes from how his hearer (Speaker B) treats the available context. This is the *second* idiom lesson SL learners need to understand when faced with texts containing 'hard-to-crack' idioms.

Idiom Lesson 3: *Go beyond the literal meaning of an idiom and try to infer the speaker's communicative intentions behind an utterance through the immediate context and pragmatic knowledge available to you.*

If a speaker were to fail to make clear what was communicated to the hearer through the immediate context, this would indicate that his intended meaning was defective. Thus, even the best intentions of the hearer would not be able to remedy this situation. This does not mean, however, that taking care of linguistic contexts alone solves potential meaning defects. Indeed, it is often social and cultural contexts, in combination with other features of communication, such as a speaker's tone of voice, posture, facial expressions, and other subtle nonverbal cues, that provide added information for correctly interpreting an utterance and the text that surrounds it.

This is especially important for deciphering sentences containing hints, insinuations, irony, sarcasm, and stylistic effects. In accord with this view, Morgan (1978) observes that a good part of comprehension must be ascribed not to the rules of language that assign meanings to sentences as a function of the meanings of the parts, but to our ability to somehow infer what the speaker's intentions were in saying what he said, with the literal meaning it has (p. 264).

For Morgan, comprehension is demonstrably a mixture of pragmatic and semantic matters, a view deserving serious consideration in idiom study. Since meaning may take many forms, training in pragmatics should be added to the study of second and foreign languages.

Learners' knowledge of pragmatics can help with the accurate deciphering of potentially ambiguous communication. For example, students could learn that in the "I smell a rat" exchange, ambiguity is not a problem by and of itself precisely because the wife is capable of inferring her husband's utterance meaning (UM) based on her set of presuppositions which help define a linguistic context (i.e., conventions governing the use of particular meaning-bearing figurative expressions or classes of expressions). This is the *third* idiom lesson SL learners need to follow in pursuit of meaning creation.

The section that follows next demonstrates how Morgan's view of comprehension, combined with Grice's (1968, 1975) conversational maxims, affirm Grice's claim that background knowledge plays a key role in the way conversational implicatures are "worked out".

It will also be shown how the conventional meaning of words determines what is being implicated, thus helping a hearer to distinguish between what is said and what is ultimately communicated.

APPLYING THE CONVERSATIONAL MAXIMS TO IDIOMS IN SECOND AND FOREIGN LANGUAGES: A PRAGMATIC ACCOUNT OF IDIOMATICITY

To understand the significance of the three idiom lessons discussed above, consider the following text. The text is first provided in its original published language (Table 10.3).

Table 10.3 contains a side bar with corresponding text annotations (Numbers 1–8) which are discussed in Table 10.6. The original German dialogue is followed by its

Table 10.3. German text (Burke, 1996, p. 88)

1	*Im Supermarkt*
2	*Matthias:* Guck mal! Ist das nicht Klaus an der Kasse? Er war doch mal Direktor der größten Sparkasse in der Stadt. **Da bleibt mir ja die Spucke weg!**
3	*Michel:* Ich weiß. Er hat all sein Geld an der Börse verloren. Den einen Tag hat er **Geld wie Heu**, den anderen Tag ist er **arm wie eine Kirchenmaus**. Warum mußte er auch **alles auf eine Karte setzen**? Ich **gehe immer auf Nummer sicher**, wenn ich Geld in irgend etwas investiere.
4	*Matthias:* Das ist ja wirklich **in die Hose gegangen**. Na, nach sowas kann man nur **die Ohren steif halten** und **darf die Flinte nicht ins Korn werfen**.
5	*Michel:* Er sieht auch ganz zufrieden aus. Ich schätze, er **schiebt hier eine etwas ruhigere Kugel** als bei einer großen Bank.
6	*Matthias:* Kassierer zu sein ist nicht so einfach wie es aussieht. Dafür muß man ganz schön **auf Draht sein**.
7	*Michel:* (Witzelnd) Deshalb warst du nie Kassierer!

Table 10.4. Literal translation of dialogue (Burke, 1996, p. 89)

At the Market

Matthias: Look! Isn't that Klaus working at the cash register? He used to be the president of the biggest bank in the city. That **leaves me without spit!**

Michel: I know. He lost all of his money in the stock market. One day he's got **money like hay** and the next day he's **poor as a churchmouse**. Why would he **bet all on one card**? I always go **on number safe** when I invest my money in anything.

Matthias: That really **went into the pants**. Well, after something like that, all you can do is to **keep the ears stiff** and **not to throw the rifle in the corn**.

Michel: He sure does look happy. I guess, he's **pushing a calmer sphere** here, compared to a big bank.

Matthias: Being a cashier isn't as easy as it looks. You really have to be **on wire**.

Michel: (Jokingly) So that's why you've never been a cashier!

Table 10.5. Idiomatic translation of dialogue (Burke, 1996, p. 90)

At the Market

Matthias: Look! Isn't that Klaus working at the cash register? He used to be the president of the biggest bank in the city. I'm **flabbergasted!**

Michel: I know. He lost all of his money in the stock market. One day he was **rich** and the next day he was **broke**. Why would he **put all his eggs in one basket** like that? I always **play it safe** when I invest my money in anything.

Matthias: His whole life **went up in smoke**. Well, after something like that, all you can do is to keep a **stiff upper lip** and not **throw in the towel**.

Michel: He sure does look happy. I guess, he has **it easy** working here compared to a big bank.

Matthias: Being a cashier isn't as easy as it looks. You really have to **be on the ball**.

Michel: (Jokingly) So that's why you've never been a cashier!

literal English translation (Table 10.4). To fill the gap between 'what is said literally' and 'what is being communicated figuratively', an idiomatic translation of the dialog (Table 10.5) is offered, replacing where necessary the target German idioms (given in bold typeface) with their appropriate idiomatic counterparts (also given in bold typeface) in the English language.

At first glance, it is clear that the text follows the rhetorical conventions of casual communication. It has a clearly defined situation (At the Market), topic (the mutual acquaintance Klaus), and theme (Klaus's new workplace). Both speakers take turns speaking and there is a clear progression of thought.

A hearer generally builds on what has already been said: this is clearly the case here. For the purposes of this illustration let us assume that the following two conditions were equally true with regard to this dialog: (1) a third person shopping at the market where the conversation takes place listens in; and (2) this listener, whom we shall name Lexis, is highly proficient in German.

He is in fact an advanced-mid speaker of German as determined by an ACTFL Oral-Proficiency Interview test. (For a more complete account, see Buck, Byrnes, & Thompson, 1989.) Given these conditions, it can be reasonably assumed that Lexis would immediately access the appropriate background knowledge necessary to follow the conversation. He would also become familiar with some of the predispositions of the two participants. Yet it is still highly questionable whether or not Lexis would be able to make sense of some of the statements highlighted in bold typeface in Table 10.3. Most likely, Lexis would declare many of the statements plain *nonsense*.

Lexis would of course only reach this conclusion if he took these statements literally, that is, solely within their semantic domain. Therefore, some of the immediate questions that he would have to answer in this case would be: Is Matthias lying when he says that he is "without spit"? Can money be like "hay"? Is being a 'churchmouse' a precondition for being 'poor'? *What* 'went into the pants'? Do people in Germany actually 'throw their rifles in the corn'? *What* 'sphere' is Klaus 'pushing'? Is Matthias not working as a cashier because he is afraid of 'wires'? Is that even a logical explanation?

However, instead of answering these 'off the wall' questions, it would be more productive for Lexis to attempt to recognize, or assume, something about the *intentions* behind Matthias's and Michel's utterances. Based on the contextual support offered throughout the development of the text, he could try to identify the utterances as idioms and classify them (according to the Maxim of Manner) as literal, metaphoric, ironic, hyperbolic, and so on. When the understanding of idioms is at issue, 'context' induces not only the communicative exchanges in which the idioms occur, but also the actual propositions asserted and the hearer's (in this case, Lexis's) background knowledge. Most importantly, however, Lexis must recognize that the expressions uttered may be either semantically or contextually anomalous if taken literally.

Following Grice, Lexis may say that, in this talk exchange, it is especially the conversational Maxim of Manner – 'Make your contribution clear and execute it with reasonable dispatch' – that has been flouted. If this were the case indeed, Lexis would deem the literal content of the idiomatic sentences conversationally inappropriate. *Being perspicuous* certainly does not mean to fill one's conversation with obscure expressions and lexical ambiguities.

Hence, *understanding idioms* requires more than *understanding word meaning;* it clearly relies on context rather than simply on semantic knowledge alone. Emphatically, correct idiom interpretation depends on shared knowledge – namely cultural, social, and historical beliefs of conventionalized norms and practices – that are so shared among speakers from the same linguistic and cultural community.

By extension, Lexis must distinguish between the literal, referential semantic meaning (SM) of the words spoken and the speakers' non-literal, figurative utterance meaning (UM) expressly implied. He therefore needs to discover the relation between the idiomatic utterances used and the propositions asserted. In fact, what he must do to avoid 'getting stuck' in a merely literal translation of the dialogue (Table 10.4) is to 'work out' the UM from the SM. What Lexis must ultimately accomplish is as follows: using his linguistic and socio-pragmatic competence and his cultural knowledge, coupled with the CP and its maxims, and given the context in which these utterances occur, Lexis must summarily realize that the maxims of conversation are being *exploited* by both speakers. Veritably, both speakers very skillfully observe the overall CP by engaging in conversational implicatures, using idiomatic as opposed to literal statements.

Relying on the pragmatic strategies just discussed *may* lead Lexis to the intended meaning of the idiomatic utterances given in Table 10.5. The main verb 'may' is used resolutely here because arrival at the UM in second languages is *not* always guaranteed.[2] What is guaranteed, however, is that anyone following the conscious inferential process given above will not end up only with the literal translation of the dialogue given in Table 10.4.

Table 10.6. Reading tips

---

1   Skim the dialog and try to get a general feel for the text. Who is talking to whom? Are they talking about something personal or about someone else? What is the relationship of the two speakers? What is their topic of conversation? What general information does the text provide?

2   Scan the text carefully now! What specific information is Matthias offering Michel? Whom is he talking about? What do we know about this person?

3   How does Michel respond to Matthias' remarks? What new information is he offering? What comparison is he making?

4   How does Matthias respond? What concrete suggestions is he making? Do you (dis)agree?

5   How does Michel describe the psychological state of the person in their conversation? What assumptions is he making? Do you share his opinion?

6   Does Matthias agree with Michel? What are his views on the subject? What is your opinion on that?

7   How does the dialog come to a logical end? What new insight does Michel now have that he did not have before?

8   ***Beyond Reading:*** Can you think of a personal situation in which you could have used any or all of the idioms presented in this dialog? Have you ever been *flabbergasted*? Do you *put all your eggs in one basket*, or do you *play it safe*? When was the last time that *something went up in smoke*, or that you had to *keep a stiff upper lip*? Have you ever *thrown in the towel*, or do you always try to *be on the ball*? Please think about these questions, and try to create your own personal dialog or narrative by using some (or all) of the idioms given above.

Regardless of one's deductive reasoning skills or how closely a given L2 idiom matches a native L1 idiom, the likelihood of arriving at the correct interpretation of the L2 idioms presented in Table 10.5, or at least at an interpretation near the figurative domain of the L2 idioms, depends on how closely one follows the three idiom lessons discussed above. This is because the processes of pragmatic hypothesis formation and confirmation are clearly context dependent. Second language learners may also be greatly helped by text-tailored guiding questions (interspersed throughout the text), which aid in making the text connections from one conversational turn to the next more pronounced. The sample reading tips given below in Table 10.6 correspond to the side bar numbers 1 through 8 in the original German text presented in Table 10.3.[3]

Just as a metaphor may be "used for aesthetic reasons (it conjures up a pleasing or disturbing image), or rhetorical ones (an expression in the metaphor has strong emotive connotations) ... because it is believed to be rich, to be fecund, or to have considerable organizing power", as Bergmann (1982, p. 243) contends, idioms may be similarly used for their built-in explanatory power which makes them literally unique among other tropes of figurative language. Liontas (2015a) asserts that idioms have their origins in the fabric of human communication. Peculiar to a language, these forms of expression – from the ancient to the most recent – owe their creation to the inventive workings of human thought and language evolution. They possess extraordinary communicative effectiveness and rhetorical power yet convey complex realities and human behavior with the help of simple but colorful, and very powerful, figures of speech that are to a large extent frozen in time (pp. 621–622). Because idioms do not mean what they literally state, it is easier and more economical (linguistically speaking) to *take the bull by the horns* (fig. to confront a difficult problem or situation head on in a brave and determined way) than to flounder in literal meanings. With imageable-rich idioms, just as with metaphors (e.g., Blasko, 1999; Cacciari, 1993; Chen & Lai, 2014; Dong, 2004; Glucksberg & McGlone, 1999; Hussey & Katz, 2009; Shen, 1999), certain words take on new and extended meanings: the individual lexemes that constitute idioms are with a hidden second, or figurative, coded meaning in addition to their literal meaning.

Our purported inconspicuous listener, Lexis, as we have seen heretofore, will have to go beyond the literal meanings of the words if he is to capture the intended meaning(s) of what is really being communicated. What distinguishes idioms from other facets of figurative speech (e.g., metaphors, proverbs, indirect speech acts, sarcasm, irony, insinuations, and metonymy), however, is that their semantic meaning is not fixed by context, but instead by actual pragmatic *use*, a point echoed since the late 1970s in such works as Davidson (1978), Lakoff and Johnson (1980), Searle (1982), Martinich (1984), Colston and O'Brien (2000), Gibbs (2002), Schauer (2006), and Kecskes (2013). Unlike metaphoric meaning, which is not exclusively singular, idiomatic meaning is to a large extent *frozen,* or so Cutler (1982) would have us believe, by historical, social, and cultural conventionalized practices in a way that makes more than one figurative meaning impossible.

CONCLUSION

Using a pragmatic rather than a strictly semantic approach, this chapter on *Grice, Idioms,* and *Conversational Implicatures* featured a pragmatic account of idiomaticity to advance reflective and effective teaching of idioms. Toward this end, the chapter has shown that the concept of 'conversational implicatures' and its underlying principles, as developed by H. P. Grice, can be effectively applied in the second and foreign language classroom. It has been argued throughout that the conversational maxims offered by Grice provide researchers and language teachers alike with a pragmatic lens through which the process of in-context idiomatic interpretation can be viewed more systematically. By extending Grice's theory of conversation to account for idioms, this chapter has demonstrated that idiomatic meaning, in addition to the semantic and linguistic components, is recoverable only when the pragmatic component of idioms is accessed. It follows logically that the pressing issue here is not one of semantics versus pragmatics, linguistics versus pragmatics, or even linguistics versus semantics, but of the necessity that all three concepts work in concert with one another to allow SL learners to grasp idiomatic meaning in the best possible way, with a minimum of effort, and as the need arises. (For a detailed methodological framework for developing idiomatic competence, see Liontas, 2008, 2015a. For a discussion concerning the anatomy of knowledge systems for idiom learning, see Liontas, 2006.)

What a speaker says (or makes as if to say) and what s/he implies, both directly and indirectly, are the two crucial elements that must be considered here when a SL teacher explains the literal-figurative meaning and intent of an idiom, its use or function in communicative context nothwithstanding. The important point to underscore here is that if SL learners are to *understand and use idioms appropriately and accurately in a variety of sociocultural contexts, in a manner similar to that of native speakers, and with the least amount of mental effort* (Liontas, 2015a, p. 623), they may first have to 'work out' the communicational intents of given conversations before idiomatic interpretations can be successfully rendered. They may do so with the assistance of the rules of conversation and the maxims offered by Grice more than four decades ago. How they may do this most effectively and, more broadly, how the conditions that are most likely to facilitate the development of native-like idiomatic competence can be promoted in the second and foreign language curriculum remains the subject of future empirical investigations and pedagogical discussions. And yes, the jury is still out on whether *taking the bull by the horns* was a stroke of genius worth writing home about. Only time will tell for time only knows.

Food for Thought

As the heading suggests, this section aims to provide mental stimulus for thinking of what has been perceived, discovered, or learned in this chapter. To this end, it offers emphatic intellectual nourishment in the form of specific questions that will help you to reflect and analyze your own thought processes and understandings pertaining to *Reflective and Effective Teaching of Idioms.*

Pragmatic in nature, the content of the questions posed below deals with theoretical and pedagogical constructs sensibly and realistically in accordance with proven instructional pragmatism and reflective reason. Collectively, these ten questions epitomize to the old adage, *in for a penny, in for a pound.* Even so, they only ask *a penny for your thoughts.*

As we have seen in this chapter, the concept of pragmatics includes multiple phenomena and components warranting serious consideration. To this day, the concepts and theories of pragmatics remain prevalent in the research literature. Over the past 40 years, a great many pragmatics frameworks, models, theories, and phenomena have been proposed and researched within applied linguistics. Yet the concept of pragmatics has proved particularly difficult to define coherently despite wide acknowledgement and general agreement that pragmatic and idiomatic competence are both crucial aspects of communicative language ability. On the basis of the discussion presented in this chapter then, peruse the ETS Research Report No. RR-15-06 (Timpe Laughlin et al., 2015) and propose your very own construct definition of pragmatic competence for the development of idiomaticity for second and foreign language learners, who many a times are either ill-prepared for or uninformed of pragmatic/idiomatic challenges.

- How do the domains discussed in the ETS Research Report No. RR-15-06 (e.g., L2 pragmatics instruction, development of L2 learners' pragmatic competence in different languages, cross-cultural pragmatic differences, and L2 pragmatic assessment) now influence your thinking concerning pragmatic phenomena in general?
- In what ways do speech acts and functions over *implicatures, routine formulae, register, politeness, lexis, deixis,* and *genre,* for example, influence matters of idiomaticity in general and the reflective and effective teaching of idioms in particular?
- What constitutes a pragmatically competent L2 learner? How are language teachers supposed to know what knowledge of idiomaticity to foster in their second/foreign language learners?
- How would you situate pragmatic principles and pragmatic-functional knowledge within the larger context of general language ability and idiomaticity?
- What do second and foreign language learners need to know in pragmalinguistics and sociopragmatics in order to be pragmatically competent and to communicate appropriately and effectively in a given language use situation?
- Following Grice, Liontas, and other pragmatists, which principles of pragmatic learning would you acclaim as quintessential conditions for felicitous idiomatic behavior?
- To attain communicative reality and social relevance in everyday discourse, which conditions for optimal idiom learning would you pursue in language

instruction and how would you implement these pedagogical constructs in your own classroom to make them compatible with and supportive of the way language learners learn best?

- What type(s) of idiom learning materials and resources underlying essential knowledge of idiomaticity both in comprehension and production would you employ in your language or academic curriculum to develop in your students the ability to communicate both effectively and appropriately in context-sensitive language use situations without violating the conventions of social appropriacy?

- If *idiomatic competence* is indeed a "dynamic, complex, and multifaceted phenomenon of language acquisition" and its development an "arduous and cumbersome process that extends over many years", as Liontas (2015a, p. 627) affirms, what types of interactions and idiom learning tasks would you expect your language learners to be able to perform in what settings in order to promote the development of idiomatic competence across the curriculum while effusively observing and supporting the individual learner and psychological factors believed to contribute to differing degrees in different learners?

- One last penny for your thoughts please! What three big ideas were you able to perceive, discover, or learn from reading the chapter, *Reflective and Effective Teaching of Idioms?*

- What would you want the author to know about the content and ideas presented in this chapter?

NOTES

[1] The aim of the Idiom Detection Task (IDT) was to determine how well SL learners strategize when confronted with reading texts (made up of either a short narrative six to ten sentences long or of a short dialog with three to seven interactional exchanges) containing a range of VP idioms, and what context cues and principles of communication they employ in identifying these idioms. Every narrative and dialog contained only one idiomatic expression. The aim of the Zero Context Task (ZCT) was to provide evidence for the importance of context in determining the meaning(s) of VP idioms. Furthermore, it was to ascertain which subtypes of VP idioms – Lexical Level (LL), Semi-Lexical Level (SLL), or Post-Lexical Level (PLL) – are the fastest and easiest to understand, and why this is the case even in the absence of contextual support. Finally, the aim of the Full Context Task (FCT) was to evaluate the effect of context on the comprehension and interpretation of VP idioms. Participants were presented with the same idioms from the previous ZCT along with the texts (narratives or short dialogs) from which they had been previously extracted.

[2] In the Liontas (1997, 1999, 2001, 2002a, 2002b, 2002c, 2002d, 2002e, 2003, 2007, 2008, 2013, 2015b) studies, adult second- and third-year learners of second languages appear to have certain difficulties interpreting VP idioms correctly, even if these idioms are presented in context. This was clearly evident from the analysis of data from the Idiom Detection Task and the Full Context Task.

[3] Reading Tip Number 8 asks students to go beyond the text and build on their own emerging understanding by relating the text and the idioms therein to their personal 'real-life' experiences. As noted in the introduction, more often than not, participants in the Liontas studies made use of such a metacognitive pragmatic strategy to enhance their idiom understanding prior to rendering an idiomatic interpretation. Post-reading tasks and expansion activities should build on such understanding if acquiring idiomatic language is to be a viable goal of SL learning.

REFERENCES

Alexander, R. J. (1987). Problems in understanding and teaching idiomaticity in English. *Anglistik und Englischunterricht, 32*, 105–122.

Bergmann, M. (1982). Metaphorical assertions. *Philosophical Review, 91*, 229–245.

Blasko, D. G. (1999). Only the tip of the iceberg: Who understands what about metaphor? *Journal of Pragmatics, 31*, 1675–1683.

Bobrow, S. A., & Bell, S. M. (1973). On catching on to idiomatic expressions. *Memory and Cognition, 1*, 343–346.

Bortfeld, H. (2003). Comprehending idioms cross-linguistically. *Experimental Psychology, 50*(3), 217–230.

Buck, K., Byrnes, H., & Thompson, I. (Eds.). (1989). *The ACTFL oral proficiency interview tester training manual.* Yonkers, NY: ACTFL.

Burke, D. (1996). *Street German-1: The best of German idioms.* Berkeley, CA: Optima Books.

Cacciari, C. (1993). The place of idioms in a literal and metaphorical world. In C. Cacciari & P. Tabossi (Eds.), *Idioms: Processing, structure, and interpretation* (pp. 27–55). Hillsdale, NJ: Lawrence Erlbaum.

Cacciari, C., Padovani, R., & Corradini, P. (2007). Exploring the relationship between individuals' speed of processing and their comprehension of spoken idioms. *European Journal of Cognitive Psychology, 19*, 417–445.

Caillies, S., & Butcher, K. (2007). Processing of idiomatic expressions: Evidence for a new hybrid view. *Metaphor and Symbol, 22*, 79–108.

Chen, Y.-c., & Lai, H.-l. (2014). The influence of cultural universality and specificity on EFL learners' comprehension of metaphor and metonymy. *International Journal of Applied Linguistics, 24*, 312–336. doi:10.1111/ijal.12021

Chomsky, N. (1965). *Aspects of the theory of syntax.* Cambridge, MA: MIT Press.

Cieślicka, A. B. (2006a). Literal salience in on-line processing of idiomatic expressions by second language learners. *Second Language Research, 22*(2), 115–144.

Cieślicka, A. B. (2006b). On building castles on the sand, or exploring the issue of transfer in interpretation and production of L2 fixed expressions. In J. Arabski (Ed.), *Cross-linguistic influences in the second language lexicon* (pp. 226–245). Clevedon: Multilingual Matters Ltd.

Cieślicka, A. B. (2015). Idiom acquisition and processing by second/foreign language learners. In R. R. Heredia & A. B. Cieślicka (Eds.), *Bilingual figurative language processing* (pp. 208–244). New York, NY: Cambridge University Press.

Colombo, L. (1993). The comprehension of ambiguous idioms in context. In C. Cacciari & P. Tabossi (Eds.), *Idioms: Processing, structure, and interpretation* (pp. 163–200). Hillsdale, NJ: Lawrence Erlbaum Associates.

Colston, H. L., & O'Brien, J. (2000). Contrast and pragmatics in figurative language: Anything understatement can do, irony can do better. *Journal of Pragmatics, 32*, 1557–1583.

Cronk, B. C., & Schweigert, W. A. (1992). The comprehension of idioms: The effects of familiarity, literalness, and usage. *Applied Linguistics, 13*, 131–146.

Cutler, A. (1982). Idioms: The older the colder. *Linguistics Inquiry, 13*, 317–320.

Davidson, D. (1978). What metaphors mean. In S. Sacks (Ed.), *On metaphor* (pp. 29–46). Chicago, IL: University of Chicago Press.

Davis, S. (Ed.). (1991). *Pragmatics: A reader.* Oxford: Oxford University Press.

Dong, Y. R. (2004). Don't keep them in the dark! Teaching metaphors to English language learners. *English Journal, 93*(4), 29–35.

Ellis, R. (1994). *The study of second language acquisition.* Oxford: Oxford University Press.

Gibbs, R. W. (2002). A new look at the literal meaning in understanding what is said and implicated. *Journal of Pragmatics, 34*, 457–486.

Gibbs, R. W., & Raymond, W. (1980). Spilling the beans on understanding and memory for idioms in conversation. *Memory and Cognition, 8*, 149–156.

Gibbs, R. W., & Raymond, W. (1984). Literal meaning and psychological theory. *Cognitive Science, 8*, 275–304.

Glucksberg, S., & McGlone, M. S. (1999). When love is not a journey: What metaphors mean. *Journal of Pragmatics, 31*, 1541–1558.

Grice, H. P. (1968). Utterer's meaning, sentence-meaning, and word-meaning. In J. Searle (Ed.), *The philosophy of language* (pp. 54–70). Oxford: Oxford University Press.

Grice, H. P. (1975). Logic and conversation. In P. Cole & J. L. Morgan (Eds.), *Syntax and semantics 3* (pp. 41–58). New York, NY: Academic Press.

Hussey, K., & Katz, A. (2009). Perception of the use of metaphor by an interlocutor in discourse. *Metaphor and Symbol, 24*, 203–236.

Irujo, S. (1986). Don't put your leg in your mouth: Transfer in the acquisition of idioms in a second language. *TESOL Quarterly, 20*, 287–304. doi:10.2307/3586545

Kecskes, I. (2006). On my mind: Thoughts about salience, context and figurative language from a second language perspective. *Second Language Research, 22*(2), 219–237.

Kecskes, I. (2013). *Intercultural pragmatics.* Oxford: Oxford University Press.

Lakoff, G., & Johnson, M. (1980). *Metaphors we live by.* Chicago, IL: University of Chicago Press.

Laufer, B. (2000). Avoidance of idioms in a second language: The effect of L1-L2 degree of similarity. *Studia Linguistica, 54*(2), 186–196.

Liontas, J. I. (1997, November). *"Building castles in the air": The comprehension processes of modern Greek idioms.* Paper presented at the 15th International Symposium on Modern Greece, Kent State University, Kent, OH.

Liontas, J. I. (1999). *Developing a pragmatic methodology of idiomaticity: The comprehension and interpretation of SL vivid phrasal idioms during reading* (Unpublished doctoral dissertation). The University of Arizona, Tucson, AZ.

Liontas, J. I. (2001). That's all Greek to me! The comprehension and interpretation of modern Greek phrasal idioms. *The Reading Matrix: An International Online Journal, 1*(1), 1–32.

Liontas, J. I. (2002a). Vivid phrasal idioms and the lexical-image continuum. *Issues in Applied Linguistics, 13*(1), 71–109.

Liontas, J. I. (2002b). Context and idiom understanding in second languages. In S. H. Foster-Cohen, T. Ruthenberg, & M.-L. Poschen (Eds.), *EUROSLA yearbook: Annual conference of the European second language association* (Vol. 2, pp. 155–185). Amsterdam: John Benjamins.

Liontas, J. I. (2002c). Reading between the lines: Detecting, decoding, and understanding idioms in second languages. In J. H. Sullivan (Ed.), *Literacy and the second language learner: Research in second language learning* (Vol. 1, pp. 177–216). Greenwich, CT: Information Age Publishing.

Liontas, J. I. (2002d). Transactional idiom analysis: Theory and practice. *Journal of Language and Linguistics, 1*(1), 17–53.

Liontas, J. I. (2002e). Exploring second language learners' notions of idiomaticity. *System, 30*, 289–313.

Liontas, J. I. (2003). Killing two birds with one stone: Understanding Spanish VP idioms in and out of context. *Hispania, 86*, 289–301.

Liontas, J. I. (2006). Artificial intelligence and idiomaticity. *The APAMALL Higher Education Journal, Language Learning Technologies, 1*(1), 1–33.

Liontas, J. I. (2007). The eye never sees what the brain understands: Making sense of idioms in second languages. *Lingua et Linguistica, 1*(2), 25–44.

Liontas, J. I. (2008). Toward a critical pedagogy of idiomaticity. *Indian Journal of Applied Linguistics, Special Issue on Strategies in Learning and using English as a Foreign/Second Language, 34*(1–2), 11–30.

Liontas, J. I. (2013). Educating educators about SL idiomaticity through action research. *Iranian Journal of Language Teaching Research, 1*(2), 1–35.

Liontas, J. I. (2015a). Developing idiomatic competence in the ESOL classroom: A pragmatic account. *TESOL Journal, 6*(4), 621–658.

Liontas, J. I. (2015b). Straight from the horse's mouth: Idiomaticity revisited. In R. R. Heredia & A. B. Cieślicka (Eds.), *Bilingual figurative language processing* (pp. 301–340). New York, NY: Cambridge University Press.

Malt, B. C., & Eiter, B. (2004). Even with a green card, you can be put out to pasture and still have to work: Non-native intuitions of the transparency of common English idioms. *Journal of Memory and Cognition, 32*(6), 896–904.

Martinich, A. P. (1984). A theory of metaphor. *Journal of Literacy Semantics, 13*, 35–56.

McGlone, M. S., Glucksberg, S., & Cacciari, C. (1994). Semantic productivity and idiom comprehension. *Discourse Processes, 17*, 167–90.

Morgan, J. L. (1978). Two types of convention in indirect speech acts. In P. Cole (Ed.), *Syntax and semantics 9* (pp. 261–280). New York, NY: Academic Press.

Morris, C. W. (1971). Foundations of the theory of signs. In C. W. Morris (Ed.), *Writings of the general theory of signs* (pp. 17–74). The Hague: Mouton.

Palmer, B. C., Shackelford, V. S., Miller, S. C., & Leclere, J. T. (2007). Bridging two worlds: Reading comprehension, figurative language instruction, and the English-language learner. *Journal of Adolescent & Adult Literacy, 50*(4), 258–267.

Peterson, R. R., & Burgess, C. (1993). Syntactic and semantic processing during idiom comprehension: Neurolinguistic and psycholinguistic dissociations. In C. Cacciari & P. Tabossi (Eds.), *Idioms: Processing, structure, and interpretation* (pp. 201–225). Hillsdale, NJ: Lawrence Erlbaum Associates.

Récanati, F. (1989). The pragmatics of what is said. *Mind and Language, 4*, 295–329.

Schauer, G. A. (2006). Pragmatic awareness in ESL and EFL contexts: Contrast and development. *Language Learning, 56*, 269–318. doi:10.1111/j.0023-8333.2006.00348.x

Searle, J. R. (1975). Indirect speech acts. In P. Cole & J. L. Morgan (Eds.), *Syntax and semantics: Speech acts* (pp. 59–82). New York, NY: Academic Press.

Searle, J. R. (1982). Metaphor. In A. Ortony (Ed.), *Metaphor and thought* (pp. 92–123). Cambridge: Cambridge University Press.

Shen, Y. (1999). Principles of metaphor interpretation and the notion of 'domain': A proposal for a hybrid model. *Journal of Pragmatics, 31*, 1631–1653.

Stalnacker, R. C. (1978). Assertion. In P. Cole (Ed.), *Syntax and semantics 9* (pp. 315–332). New York, NY: Academic Press.

Swinney, D. A., & Cutler, A. (1979). The access and processing of idiomatic expressions. *Journal of Verbal Learning and Verbal Behavior, 18*, 523–534.

Timpe Laughlin, V., Wain, J., & Schmidgall, J. (2015). *Defining and operationalizing the construct of pragmatic competence: Review and recommendations* (ETS Research Report No. RR-15-06). Princeton, NJ: Educational Testing Service. Retrieved from http://dx.doi.org/10.1002/ets2.12053

Titone, D. A., & Connine, C. M. (1999). On the compositional and noncompositional nature of idiomatic expressions. *Journal of Pragmatics, 31*, 1655–1674.

Vespignani, F., Canal, P., Molinaro, N., Fonda, S., & Cacciari, C. (2010). Predictive mechanisms in idiom comprehension. *Journal of Cognitive Neuroscience, 22*, 1682–1700.

John I. Liontas
University of South Florida
Tampa, Florida
USA

ANNE BURNS

11. REFLECTIVE TEACHING OF SPEAKING

INTRODUCTION

Speaking is a complex and multidimensional skill that needs to be taught and practised explicitly. Goh and Burns (2012) argue, however, that in many second language classrooms around the world, teachers may be "doing speaking" rather than "teaching speaking". Doing speaking involves introducing speaking tasks that simply get learners to speak, while teaching speaking means systematically focusing on the skills and strategies of speaking that students lack and assisting students to understand and practise them.

"Doing speaking" could be considered to be an unreflective approach to teaching speaking, as it does not consider in sufficient depth the various dimensions of speaking that need to be highlighted if learners are to improve their speaking repertoires. "Teaching speaking", on the other hand, means that teachers are reflecting deliberately and constructively on the current speaking needs of their students, and addressing these needs explicitly through interesting, creative and sequenced activities. In this chapter, I outline some of the key dimensions of the skills of speaking and suggest ways for teachers to assist their learners.

SPEAKING: A "COMBINATORIAL" SKILL

Speaking is complex because it requires the simultaneous use of several discourse skills and strategies, all of which must be produced in "real time": in other words, it is combinatorial. Unlike writers, speakers do not get the leisure to redraft and restructure what they produce, but must express meaning spontaneously and rapidly. Speakers must also take into account how their oral output is understood and evaluated by others, which constrains the process of producing speech accurately and fluently. Johnson and Morrow (1981, p. 11), writing at the beginning of the communicative language teaching movement, summed up succinctly what a competent second language speaker needs to be able to do:

Apart from being grammatical, the utterance must also be appropriate on very many levels at the same time; it must conform to the speaker's aim; the role relationships between the interactants; to the setting, topic, linguistic context, etc. The speaker must also produce his (sic) utterance within severe constraints; he does not know in advance what will be said to him (and hence what his utterance will be a response to); yet, if the conversation is not to flag, he must respond quickly. The

© KONINKLIJKE BRILL NV, LEIDEN, 2018 | DOI:10.1163/9789004380882_011

rapid formulation of utterances which are simultaneously "right" on several levels is central to the communicative skill.

From a pedagogical point of view, there are three key areas of speaking competence that teachers need to consider when planning a speaking program for their students.

KNOWLEDGE OF LANGUAGE AND DISCOURSE

Learners need sufficient knowledge of the structure, meaning and use of the language they are learning. This means having: grammatical knowledge; phonological knowledge; lexical knowledge and discourse knowledge.

Grammatical knowledge means knowing about how words are strung together, and how different structures are used to express different meanings (e.g. making a request, asking a question). Grammatical knowledge also helps listeners to deconstruct and understand the messages they are hearing.

Another important kind of knowledge is phonological, knowing how the sounds of the language are formed and the stress, and intonation patterns at word (micro) and utterance (macro) levels, and what communicative functions are served by chunking sounds (tone) and placing emphasis on certain sounds and words (prominence).

Lexical knowledge is to do with the number of words and their meanings at the speaker's disposal (vocabulary size) and whether a learner knows these words as part of their productive vocabulary (produced when speaking/writing) or receptive vocabulary (recognised during listening/speaking). Vocabulary development is helped by knowing the meaning relationships between words (e.g., word families, opposites) and fixed, formulaic or idiomatic expressions that speed up the speech process (e.g., *nice to meet you, you're in the know*).

Finally, discourse knowledge requires knowing about the genre structures common in extended speech (e.g., telling stories, jokes or anecdotes, or recounting an interesting event) and how conversational exchanges follow typical patterns of interaction (e.g., three part exchanges: *How are you? Fine, that's good*). In a world where English is now a globalised language, having an appreciation of intercultural and cross-cultural variations in speech use (e.g. typical features of how greetings are exchanged in different languages) is now a valuable addition in discourse knowledge if cross-cultural interactions are to operate effectively.

CORE SKILLS

These skills involve more than just knowing about language and discourse. They are to do with using this knowledge, or "putting it into action", in different communicative contexts. There are four broad areas that learners need to develop: pronunciation (producing the sounds of the language); speech functions (performing different kinds of speech acts); interaction management (managing the flow of speech; and discourse organisation (creating socioculturally appropriate stretches of speech).

Pronunciation skills are important enabling skills in speech production. They involve articulating the sounds of the language, as well as adopting appropriate stress patterns at the word level (segmental), and intonation patterns at the utterance level (suprasegmental). Research has shown that in general suprasegmental skills have a greater impact on a speaker's intelligibility than segmental skills (Hahn, 2004). Even though the concept of the native speaker is alive and well in many English language classrooms, so-called native speaker pronunciation may not be a realistic goal for learners. Teachers can raise learners' awareness that, in a situation where English is now used as a global language, different accents and varieties of the language are common. It is more realistic to aim for intelligibility so that meaning can be effectively communicated.

Another important skill for speakers is to manage speech functions, such as disagreeing, thanking, explaining, complimenting, greeting, declining, complaining and so on. Many of these functions, which are frequently found in English textbooks, involve the use of formulaic or fixed expressions (e.g. *Thanks for that*, *Sorry, I can't make it*), which teachers can usefully introduce to their learners. Speech functions may differ from culture to culture in the way they are expressed, so it is valuable to raise learners' awareness of how speech functions used in native speaker examples might be used differently with speakers from their own culture. These uses might depend on issues such as seniority, age, closeness of relationships, gender, life experience and so on.

Interaction management is to do with negotiating the flow of speech among the different speakers involved. Speakers influence the direction the interaction takes by initiating turns, giving their turns to someone else, changing the topic, or closing down the conversation. Some of these interactions involve reading verbal and non-verbal clues, such as changes in posture, eye-gaze and other body language. Speakers also need to know how to avoid break-down in communication by asking for clarification, reinterpreting what they think a speaker has said, summarising a point or giving positive or negative feedback.

Lastly in the area of core skills, discourse organisation involves structuring the flow of talk in relation to widely recognised social and linguistic conventions. This involves producing speech genres in ways that other speakers and listeners anticipate (e.g. retelling past events in a time sequence) and using relevant vocabulary and grammar that relates to the genre. Speakers and their listeners expect a spoken text to have coherence (showing the thread of meaning through the use of related vocabulary items or pronoun substitutions) and also cohesion (e.g. providing expressions such as time, place or linking markers, so that so that the text hangs together).

COMMUNICATION STRATEGIES

Speaking is a very demanding cognitive process. Communication strategies are used to prevent speakers becoming overloaded through having to produce too much speech (reduction strategies) or to give them access to whatever means they have to communicate (achievement strategies). Three types of communication strategies in speech are cognitive strategies, metacognitive strategies and interaction strategies.

Cognitive strategies are used to compensate for the processing problems involved in being able to say something. Speakers may use similar words to the one they are trying to remember (substitution), use descriptions of a thing or person (circumlocution), coin new words to express an idea (coinages), restate something using other words (paraphrase), or even use the same expression in another language (code-switching or translanguaging). All these strategies are to do with mentally manipulating the meanings the speaker wishes to convey and are valuable for learners to be aware of.

Metacognitive strategies refer to thinking about cognition. These are strategies used to manage and evaluate the thinking involved in speech production. For example, speakers may plan what to say in advance (planning) so that they are more prepared, or note how well their words are being understood during a conversation (self-monitoring), and reflect on how they could express their meanings more effectively in a similar situation (self-evaluating). These are all strategies that can be usefully employed to develop learner autonomy for speaking development.

Whereas cognitive and metacognitive strategies are to do with psycholinguistic aspects of speaking, interaction strategies relate to social behaviours and the pragmatic (contextualised) meanings created between speakers. Effective speaking is highly dependent on the way speakers negotiate meanings with each other as they interact during the flow of speech, using strategies such as repeating each other's utterances, checking comprehension, providing examples, asking for clarification, and using gesture and facial expressions.

We can see that speaking requires a speaker to manage many dimensions of communication at the same time. It requires knowing the language as a system at different levels, being aware of the contextual demands, employing various skills to produce fluent and appropriate utterances, and using strategies to compensate for speaking problems.

A major implication for reflective teachers of speaking is that they need to be knowledgeable about these various dimensions, to analyse their learners' speaking needs carefully, and identify where to focus attention on gaps in knowledge or skill. It is very important not to overload learners or to make unrealistic demands when they do not have the required abilities. It is also not sufficient to get learners simply to 'practise' speaking, the 'doing speaking' I referred to earlier. In reflective speaking lessons, teachers will include a structured and explicit focus on assisting learners to develop the knowledge, skills, or strategies they need.

Reflective teachers of speaking will also be aware of the affective factors involved. Speaking in class often causes learners great anxiety, which teachers may see as a reluctance, unwillingness or lack of motivation to speak. It is very important to reassure learners that it is normal to feel nervous and to make sure that they are carefully supported. Therefore, before they undertake particular tasks in the classroom, the teacher needs to 'scaffold' or 'apprentice' them into the knowledge, skills and strategies they need for success. In the next section of this chapter, I present a teaching-speaking cycle outlined by Goh and Burns (2012) that assists teachers to plan and develop a sequence of activities that take into account holistically the ideas I have discussed so far.

THE TEACHING-LEARNING CYCLE

Teachers can use the cycle described below to guide their students to:

- Use a wide range of core skills
- Develop fluency in expressing meaning
- Use grammar flexibly to produce a wide range of utterances that can express meaning precisely
- Use appropriate vocabulary and accurate language forms relevant to their speaking needs
- Understand and use social and linguistic conventions of speech for various contexts
- Employ appropriate oral communication and discourse strategies
- Increase awareness of genre and genre structures
- Increase metacognitive awareness about L2 speaking
- Manage and self-regulate their own speaking development
  (Based on Goh & Burns, 2012, pp. 151–152)

The cycle is organised into a sequence of seven stages which are not intended to be covered in a single lesson. Instead, the cycle can be used over a series of lessons or a unit of work.

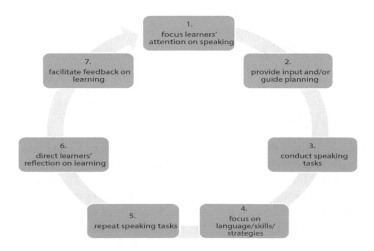

Figure 11.1. The teaching-speaking cycle

Stage 1: Focus Learners Attention on Speaking

This stage focuses on two areas of metalinguistic strategies: encouraging learners to plan for overall developments in speaking (Task 1); preparing them for a specific speaking task (Task 2). In the first task, the teacher gets learners to think about their experiences of speaking, using questions such as the ones below; they can write notes, or their ideas can be discussed in groups or with the whole class.

Example Task 1: Reflecting on speaking experiences

Think about your own learning processes for speaking

1. Do you feel nervous when you speak?
2. What helps you to feel less nervous?
3. What kinds of activities do you like in speaking lesson?
4. What would you like your teacher to do to help you speak more in class?

Etc.

The second area focuses attention on a task they are about to do and activates learners' prior knowledge. The length of time for this task will depend on whether learners prepare individually or discuss their ideas in groups.

Example Task 2: Activating knowledge about a spoken genre

You will need to speak for one minute on one of these topics. Think about the way you would organise the information and what you could say about the topic.

1. Describe the street where you live.
2. Explain how you get to school
3. Talk about an unusual event that happened to you

Etc.

Stage 2: Provide Input and/or Guide Planning

This is a pre-task stage that scaffolds learners' preparation for the task they will perform. Teachers can provide them with the vocabulary they will need, or give them time to research information required to complete the task. The teacher can also talk about how they would go about preparing for the task, or model the task for the learners. For example, if the task is about describing the city they live in, the teacher can discuss where to find information, through library resources or the Internet, and then give their own short description. Teachers can also break down parts of the task and learners can then prepare their plans by deciding what they would say at each stage. Depending on whether the task is a dialogue or monologue, they could also, for example, think about how they would handle breakdowns in communication or identify the content for a particular genre. Task 3 illustrates a task for preparing and rehearsing a procedure genre (how to do or make something).

Example Task 3: Pre-task plan for giving a talk

In this task you will need to talk about how to do something (e.g. making your favourite recipe; using a mobile phone).

Part 1

1. Identify a topic you know a lot about.
2. Write down the main points you want to cover.
3. Write down expressions to say you are moving from one stage of the process to the next.
4. Write down key words you will need to use.
5. Note any other words or expressions that you need for your talk.

Part 2 (optional)

Practise your talk, using the points you have written down and any other expressions you want to bring in.

Stage 3: Conduct Speaking Task

This stage encourages fluency and provides a context to practise spoken communication skills. The preparation in Stage 2 should make this stage easier. Learners need a reason to speak, so this task is best performed in groups or pairs where they can talk about things that are not already known to their listeners. Teachers should stress that at this stage learners also do not need to worry about accuracy, but rely on whatever linguistic knowledge, skills or strategies they already possess to express meaning.

Stage 4: Focus on Language/Skills/Strategies

In many speaking classes it is typical for teachers to provide some input (Stage 2) and then get students to practise speaking (Stage 3) – and that is where speaking activities stop. Alternatively, in some classes, learners are only involved in Stage 3. They simply practise speaking as it arises in their text book, sometimes on topics that are unrelated to other parts of the unit. This means that learners receive no preparation for tasks or feedback on their performance and their further development is limited. In a reflective speaking class, the teacher follows up the fluency practise in Stage 3 by focusing on improving accuracy. This not only provides feedback but helps learners to identify where they can improve. For example, performance in Stage 3 can be recorded by teachers or learners, who can then self-assess their accuracy for various parts of the task (e.g. how they introduced the text, how well they used the vocabulary they had prepared). Alternatively, the teacher may want to select different aspects of the performance where he or she noticed students were having trouble (e.g. use of a particular grammar structure, pronunciation, or question forms) and provide some remedial practice. Another option would be to play a recording or read a transcript of a competent speaker performing the same task (e.g. the teacher, or a colleague) and ask learners to notice features they can develop for themselves.

Stage 5: Repeat Speaking Task

Too often in speaking classes, learners are only given one opportunity to perform a task. Stage 5 is the point when learners do the task again, this time having practised both accuracy and fluency, to improve their performance. The teacher can use different forms of repetition: repeating parts of the original task; repeating the entire task; performing a different task focusing on the same genre or grammatical feature. To keep things fresh, learners can change groups or partners. This kind of practise can help learners to develop atomicity in handling spoken tasks, complete the task again more effectively, and build their confidence and motivation.

Stage 6: Direct Learners' Reflection on Learning

This stage encourages learners, either individually, in pairs or groups, to self-regulate their own learning by monitoring and evaluating their performance and consolidating their new knowledge of language, skills and strategies. Reflection can focus on aspects such as areas of speaking that have improved demands of the task they have become aware of, or what they need to focus on next. Teachers can provide prompts such as the following to guide learners' reflections:

Example Task 4: Learner reflections on speaking development

Reflections on my learning in this lesson:

1. I learned to do the following in speaking:
2. I learned the following useful expressions:
3. I used the following strategies to prepare for speaking:
4. This is how I feel about my learning:
   a. I am confident I can do this task again
   b. I am not very confident I can do this task again
   c. I am still unsure what to say
5. This is how I feel about speaking
   a. I still feel nervous about speaking
   b. I feel less nervous about speaking

Stage 7: Facilitate Feedback on Learning

The final stage is where feedback is provided to learners on how well they have performed. Formative feedback should create a process of assessment-for-learning (Black & William, 1998), the type of input from teachers which enables learners to 'feed-forward' into future development of their skills. Summative feedback is the kind that encapsulates how a learner has performed over a period of time; it sums up where learners have arrived in their learning in relation to various criteria. Often summative feedback is in the form of test or examination results.

In this cycle, formative assessment is an important component as it provides information on what learners can focus on further in their learning and can increase motivation. In large classes it may be difficult for teachers to offer immediate feedback to all learners, but teachers do not have to be the only ones supplying feedback. Learners can be involved in peer feedback where they are asked to focus on specific aspects of each other's performance, or the teacher can respond over time to the kind of written prompts used in Stage 6. Other types of feedback include comments or grades on particular skills or language features, teacher's consolidated feedback to the whole class on their performance and areas for further development, or feedback on observation sheets such as the one below, which can provide learners with different ratings for different aspects of their performance and provide a picture of strengths and weaknesses.

Example Task 5: Feedback performance sheet

	1	*2*	*3*	*4*	*5*
Language Structure and organisation Grammar and vocabulary Accuracy					
Production Fluency Syllable/word pronunciation Intonation, stress and rhythm					
Participation Turn-taking Maintenance of interaction Feedback					
Expression Clarity of ideas Quality of ideas					
Coherence Linking of ideas Justification of point of view					

CONCLUSION

As I have argued in this chapter, a reflective teacher of speaking is one who teaches speaking, rather than merely does speaking. Speaking in a second language takes time to develop tasks it is a highly complex skill with multiple dimensions. Effective speaking skills will not be developed in the classroom without the teacher's constructive intervention. Therefore, it is vitally important for teachers, especially those who specialise in teaching speaking, to expand their knowledge of the discourse features, genres, grammar patterns, skills and strategies that are used in speaking and to share this knowledge with their learners. In the holistic approach to teaching speaking advocated in this chapter (see Goh & Burns, 2012), teachers, materials and learners all play a part in reflective practice. Teachers must be aware of learners' speaking needs, social, cognitive and linguistic, and provide motivating activities that structure and support learning experiences and provide effective feedback. Materials need to provide extensive speaking practice, promote language and skills learning, and facilitate metacognitive development. Reflective teachers of speaking scrutinise the materials in textbooks carefully to ensure they provide opportunities for all three kinds of learning, and where necessary supplement these material with others that build on learners' cultural and social experiences, and provide topics of interest and relevance to them. Finally, learners need to be encouraged to overcome their anxiety or nervousness about speaking, to develop responsibility for their own speaking development by becoming familiar with the demands of speaking, and be aware of strategies they can use to assist themselves. As the number of speakers of English grows across the world, it is vital that teachers and learners create optimal classroom conditions that will facilitate and enhance the reflective teaching and learning of speaking.

REFERENCES

Black, P., & Wiliam, D. (1998). Assessment and classroom learning. *Assessment in Education: Principles, Policy and Practice, 5,* 7–74.

Goh, C. C. M., & Burns, A. (2012). *Teaching speaking: A holistic approach.* New York, NY: Cambridge University Press.

Hahn, L. D. (2014). Primary stress and intelligibility: Research to motivate the teaching of suprasegmentals. *TESOL Quarterly, 38*(2), 201–223.

Johnson, K., & Morrow, K. (1981). *Communication in the classroom.* London: Longman.

Klippel, F. (1984). *Keep talking: Communicative fluency activities for language learning.* Cambridge: Cambridge University Press.

Anne Burns
University of New South Wales
Sydney, Australia

MITRA ZERAATPISHE AND MARYAM AZARNOOSH

12. REFLECTIVE AND EFFECTIVE
TEACHING OF WRITING

INTRODUCTION

A developmental view of teaching based on Farrell (2013) identifies teaching as an art along with the craft of teaching. Accordingly, teachers find themselves professionally develop along a continual intellectual, experiential, and attitudinal continuum. This chapter takes a reflective-based approach to teach writing skill to EFL learners. Reflection is regarded as a process through which teachers observe their beliefs and practices, assess, restructure their teaching and learning so that they can better situate themselves as agents of change in the immediate contexts of teaching. After introducing some cognitive and metacognitive strategies of teaching writing, the authors propose a model based on which teachers can practice teaching writing reflectively and hence move toward their own professional development to act more effectively.

TOWARD A POST-PROCESS APPROACH TO TEACH WRITING

A glance back through the history of language pedagogy reveals that common to most dominant teaching methods of the 20th century was a crucial emphasis on writing either as a language learning activity or an evaluative technique. In more traditional methods of the first half of the twentieth century with a major focus on language subskills. But in the last quarter of the century, during the heyday of more communicative teaching methods, a communicative skill of converting ideas to language became dominant. The natural consequence of viewing "writing as a language learning and evaluative technique" became known as product writing approach where writing was merely treated as an invaluable practice activity to help learners develop the habits of producing correct words and sentences in a controlled manner (Li, 1998, p. 33). According to Panofsky, Pacheco, Smith, Santos, Fogelman, Harrington, and Kenney (2005), controlled composition writing is an umbrella term that covers various product-oriented writing approaches which reflect traces of the behavioral, habit-formation theory of learning with a focus on sentence-level structure and the arrangement of sentences into paragraphs based on prescribed templates, giving no freedom for the learners to make mistakes. The focus in the product approach is on grammar and correctness (Panofsky et al., 2005).

With the advent of the Communicative Language Teaching (CLT) and subsequent approaches such as Task-based Instruction (TBI), Strategic-based Instruction (SBI), and Content-based Instruction (CBI), this overemphasis on language sub-skills and components gave way to a due focus on language skills as communication devices that would enable the learners to put their knowledge of language components to everyday use. The gradual tendency toward the process view, witnessed in many fields since the late 1960s (Williams, 2004), initiated an incipient shift of emphasis in the communication era away from accurate written skills to fluent oral skills. Writing, hence, initially faded into the background and lost ground. Yet, further research findings in second language acquisition (SLA) soon underscored the need for a balanced attention to both fluency and accuracy in ESL and EFL contexts, especially in the writing skill (Ashwell, 2000; Ferris, 1999; Piri, Barati, & Ketabi, 2012; Robb, Ross, & Shortreed, 1986; Truscott, 2007). Moreover, researchers came to acknowledge language learning as an active process highly influenced by various cognitive and affective learner characteristics, and hence, learner engagement was proposed as a prerequisite for the efficiency of the process (Crooks & Gass, 1993; Richards & Rodgers, 2001; Zhu, 2011).

Process writing is characterized by pre-writing, multi-drafts, peer collaboration, feedback, and revisions (Li, 1998). Ziahosseiny and Salehi (2008) have stated that writing is an exceedingly complex cognitive activity in which the writer is required to attend to and demonstrate the control of a number of features simultaneously while converting his/her thoughts to language.

Despite the valuable merits, process-writing approach has not been devoid of its critics. Cahyono (2004) has proposed that process writing can become cumbersome and over-lengthy in class, since too much prominence is given to the process. Besides, the emphasis on multiple drafts can make the work on a particular text tedious to students, especially when they know that the audience is still the teacher (Li, 1998). Not only the students but also teachers find it lengthy and difficult to apply process writing approach in the classroom because they have to provide constructive individual feedback during the writing process. Furthermore, the process approach is not suitable for writing examination essays and is not applicable to all types of writers and tasks.

Attempts to address weaknesses of the process-writing approach on the one hand and the empirical investigation of the writing process in many areas of research including applied linguistics, cognitive psychology, sociolinguistics, rhetoric, text linguistics, and educational ethnography on the other led the researchers and experts to think deeply about the discrepancy between process and product. In addition integrating the theory of metacognition into writing instruction could best reconcile the manipulation of product versus process-oriented approaches, which Devine (1993) believes to complement each other.

166

Metacognition refers to the knowledge, awareness and control of one's own learning (Brown, 1987). Metacognitive strategies help learners develop their metacognition by planning, monitoring, and evaluating their learning process (Hamzah & Abdullah, 2009). They are considered as the most essential strategies in developing learners' skills and establishing meaningful learning since learners are actively involved in the learning process (Negretti & Kuteeva, 2011). Students who can identify appropriate learning strategies in the proper situation are using metacognition. For instance, a student may confront difficulties in linking between key concepts within a story. If graphic organizer like a concept map is taught to him/her, then he/she can categorize the main ideas and can link them through some lines. In this way, the learner has used metacognition to complete the task. Metacognitive strategies are mental operations or procedures that learners apply to regulate their learning (Wenden, 1991) and through which they think about their learning process. In general, metacognition is the engine that drives self-directed learning.

These strategies account for the execution of a writing task which include three main stages of planning, monitoring, and evaluating as defined below:

• Planning: It refers to strategies by which the writer plans and talks outwhat ideas will come next, and explicitly states his or her objectives for organization and procedures (Victoria, 1995).
• Monitoring: They are "strategies the writers use when checking and verifying their process in the composing process and when identifying oncoming problems" (Mu, 2005, p. 4).
• Evaluating strategies: They refer to "strategies undertaken when reconsidering the written text, previous goals, planned thoughts, as well as changes undertaken to the text" (Maftoon & Seyyedrezaei, 2012, p. 1599).

These three metacognitive strategies can be well manipulated to ensure one about his or her success in utilizing cognitive strategies. Metacognition is referred to as "thinking about thinking" and involves overseeing whether a cognitive goal has been met. While metacognitive strategies are used to ensure that the goal has been reached (e.g., quizzing oneself to evaluate one's understanding of that text), cognitive strategies are used to help an individual achieve a particular goal (e.g., understanding a text). Cognitive strategies are mental operations or steps learners take to learn new information and apply to accomplish a writing tasks. They are as auxiliary tools to contend with the obstacles in their way.

Metacognitive experiences usually precede or follow a cognitive activity. They often occur when cognitions fail, such as the recognition that one did not understand what one just read. Metacognitive and cognitive strategies may intersect with each other in a way that one gets confused whether he utilizes cognitive or metacognitive strategy (Livingston, 2003). He exemplifies questioning which could be regarded as either a cognitive or a metacognitive strategy depending on what the purpose for using that strategy may be. While reading, the learner's aim is to obtaining knowledge (cognitive), or to monitor what he has read (metacognitive).

Now after introducing the three metacognitive strategies of planning, monitoring, and evaluating, we find it appropriate to bring together a list of cognitive strategies that an EFL teacher can utilize in a writing class. Mingling these cognitive strategies with metacognitive ones could equip the teacher to attain effectiveness in their teaching experiences.

CORE SKILLS OF WRITING (COGNITIVE STRATEGIES)

Besides metacognition as an engine that drives self-directed learning, EFL teachers should take some other skills into account to ensure an effective teaching of writing. These include cognitive, communicative, and social/affective strategies.

Cognitive strategies are used to cope with the hindrances and difficulties learners encounter along the way. They are auxiliary strategies that aid in the implementation of the metacognitive strategies. Cognitive strategies that can be implemented in the writing process are as follows:

• Concept Mapping:

Using concept mapping, students construct a model for organizing and integrating the information that they are learning. Concept mapping can be used prior to an assignment as a brainstorming activity or during an assignment as an organizing strategy.

How to create a concept map? Choose a topic and write it on the board. Ask learners to think of as many words and ideas as they can relate to the focal word. Write the words on a map in clusters or categories through labeling the categories. Then scaffold the learners with organizing their paragraphs through shaping their first draft from the final map. In this way, at least learners can easily write their topic sentences for each paragraph and can go further into details for developing their supporting sentences.

• Organizing strategies

They include the organization of the whole essay, introduction, body and conclusion. Some formulaic speech can be taught on how to start an introduction, or conclusion. Here teaching the transitional markers and cohesive ties are suggested to language teachers such as use of conjunctions (therefore, furthermore, …).

• Resourcing strategies

Resourcing strategies are those using reference materials such as dictionary to look up or confirm doubts (lexicon, grammatical, semantic or spelling doubts), or to look for alternatives (synonyms). They can refer to an encyclopedia to search the definitions or a specific classification. Available textbooks can also be utilized. The teacher can ask the learners to have a dictionary while they prepare their drafts.

- Repeating strategies

"Repeating strategies are strategies repeating chunks of language in the course of composing, either when reviewing the text or when transcribing new ideas" (Maftoon & Seyyedrezaei, 2012, p. 1599). Teachers can help students organize a coherent composition by teaching them how to repeat the main idea and key concepts while they are writing their drafts. This can be a good strategy for learners to make a strong link between the paragraphs and also to have clear smooth flow of ideas in their minds.

- Reduction strategies

Reduction strategies are strategies used to discard or remove a problematic structure or word. Reduction can be done through substituting a phrase or a word or avoiding that structure totally.

- Deferral strategies

According to Wenden (1991), they refer to learners' thinking in their own native language about the piece of work produced. They reduce writers' stress and give them a second thought of the whole idea in their minds.

- Visualization

A picture in which different processes, parts, categories, etc are displayed in the class to give students a mental image of the whole essay they are going to write. In this way, the teacher can provide a visual map of what the learners aim to write about.

- Self-Questioning

This strategy makes students ask themselves questions that increase the development of metacognitive strategies. Through self-questioning, students can consciously raise awareness of their thinking processes starting from the initial stage of preparing, monitoring, and evaluating.

As facilitators, teachers should lead students to ask reflective questions that trigger their metacognition such as what follows (Hartman, 2001, p. 150):

How much time do I need to complete this task?
What strategies am I using?
Should I use a different way/strategy to complete this task?
When students are evaluating their task, they can ask themselves:
How well did I do?
What did I learn from doing this task?
Was what I learned more or less than I had expected?
Do I need to redo the task?
What could I have done differently?

According to Beckman (2002), when students become strategic, they trust their minds, know there is more than one right way to do things, admit their mistakes, try to correct them, assess their products and behavior, enhance their memories, increase their self-esteem, feel a sense of power, become more responsible, know how to try, and become more engaged.

Based on the discussions raised above on a post-process model of writing which is a blend of process writing approach with cognitive and metacognitive strategies, EFL teachers can follow a completely reflective step by step process to teach writing in a way that at every point of their teaching they could reflect, evaluate, self-regulate themselves and then adjust their techniques accordingly. Such a reflective way of teaching writing not only leads to the training of good writers but also to the training and restructuring of the teachers to be as effective as possible in their jobs. This model could be used by both novice and experienced teachers because through the process of reflection they can gain a lot more experience regardless of the years they work. Also this model is applicable for any context whether EFL or ESL since it generally attempts to focus on the teacher as the agent of immediate change in situation, the one who can be effective through the beneficial stages of reflection, self-regulation and self-criticality. What follows is the proposed model of reflective and effective teaching of writing.

THE PROPOSED MODEL OF REFLECTIVE AND EFFECTIVE TEACHING OF WRITING

Teachers can use the following model described below to guide their students to provide a self- and peer-edited writing while at the same time evaluate and improve their own teaching (see Figure 12.1).

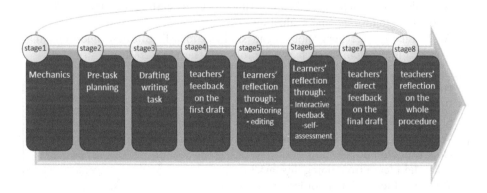

Figure 12.1. Proposed model of reflective and effective teaching of writing

Stage 1: Teaching Mechanics of Writing

At this stage teachers are to focus on presenting mechanics of writing to the learners. These include: accuracy (grammar or word order), fluency (appropriate choice of structures and vocabulary consistently), organization (clear progression of ideas well-linked), mechanics of writing such as punctuation and discourse markers.

At the first stage, from those above mentioned cognitive strategies, the teacher can focus on repeating and organizing strategies. This can help the learners find that how it is important to repeat the key terms of the title all through their essays to make their writing more coherent. And organizing strategies show them that they can have a categorized well-developed plan before they start to write.

Stage 2: Pre-Task Planning

This is the stage at which the teacher should present some cognitive strategies to help learners gain enough information and as a result enough confidence to develop internal procedures that enable him/her to perform the writing task (Rosenshine, 1995). In this stage, cognitive strategic instruction can set in motion learners' remembering and applying information from course content, constructing sentences and paragraphs, editing written work, paraphrasing, and classifying information to be learned. One of the common strategies that can be taught by the teacher is concept mapping which can be really useful for the learners to plan their writing before they start to prepare their first draft. Another cognitive strategy that the teacher can focus on is visualization. In other words, he/she can bring a picture to the class through which they could visualize a draft in their minds.

Stage 3: Drafting/Writing Task

Here, the teacher asks students to start to write their first draft based on the ideas gained in the previous stage. Through writing the first draft, learners are expected to create well-formed sentences and structures that could best include the information they gained from the planning stage. The topic sentences are formed and they have to write appropriate supporting sentences for each topic sentence. Here, they are scaffolded by the teacher again by reminding them of the strategies they got familiar with such as repeating strategy that help them reiterate the key terms to maintain the coherence of their written work.

Stage 4: Teacher's Feedback on the First Draft

At this stage, the teacher provides some coded feedback on the learners' erroneous forms. Coded feedback is suggested because it makes learners reflect on their mistakes and bring challenge to their minds. The point here is that not all mistakes are coded, but only those that harm the content, organization, or serious grammatical mistakes. The teacher could start to keep a record of the students' mistakes and the way they correct them in the form of a journal. This journal can be a good basis for teacher's reflections and self-regulating actions.

These codes should be introduced to the learners at the initial sessions of the writing course so that learners get familiar with them. To give some examples, the teacher can use T for tense, V for wrong vocabulary, Conj for conjunction, Org for organization, etc.

Stage 5: Learners' Reflection through Monitoring and Editing

Now it is the time for the learners to start to reflect on what they prepared for their drafts after the teacher's first revision. They have to focus on the coded parts to correct those erroneous forms. It is recommended to edit their errors on the same paper beside the codes so that whenever they turn back they could remind their problems better. They can submit their edited papers next session.

Stage 6: Learners' Reflection through Interactive Feedback and Self-Assessment

This stage keeps learners concentrated on their drafts through reflecting and discussing the errors of a selected paper chorally in the class. Such a learner-learner and learner-teacher interaction pave the way for a better understanding of the mistakes and broadens learners' minds to pick up and manipulate different ways of correction. Teachers can select one or two papers each session randomly and display them on the projector so that coded parts could be discussed in the class. This phase is crucial in increasing learners' critical thinking abilities and enhancing teachers' evaluative perspectives toward their learners' recognition abilities in editing their drafts. In other words, it is a step towards both teacher's and learners' self-regulating abilities. Both can reflect on the whole process and can modify their current status based on the gained understanding. This reflective approach for sure make them be more effective.

Stage 7: Teacher's Direct Feedback on the Final Draft

The last draft of the learners are suggested to receive the direct correction type. The teacher should focus on the learners' revisions and if they could not still correct their mistakes, the teacher should write the correct form to finalize their revisions. Since learners pass through several revision steps, they become more eager to see whether they are on the right way or not. In this way, not only they find their mistakes preventive and demotivating but also they learn from their own mistakes in a reflective way.

Stage 8: Teachers' Reflection on the Whole Procedure

The whole process of reflective teaching of writing goes on with the teacher's reflection in action and reflection on action. In other words, not only should a teacher plan and make decisions on the techniques before the class but also he he/

she should react to, reflect on, and self-regulate the whole procedure during the process of teaching. This can be done in two ways, individually and collaboratively. According to Nunan (2010), reflection can be enhanced with collaboration. Teachers are encouraged to exercise their professional development through being agents of immediate situation and this phase is where collaboration and collective agency come to help. What follows are those tools teachers can use in the final stage of teaching writing reflectively.

Tools for Individual Reflection

There are some tools that teachers can use to reflect on the whole process of teaching, giving feedback to leaners, and evaluating techniques they utilized. Two tools for individual reflection are suggested as follows.

• Reflective journals

A journal is the impeccable place to jot down and record feelings, reflections and thoughts. In a reflective journal, one can write about the newly learned experience. It is an effective instrument to develop metacognition through a reflective cycle. This journal can be kept by both teachers and learners. Teachers can continuously keep a record of the writing class events and include their own feelings toward each session on-goings. Teachers can also include a self-assessment part to their own acts, feedbacks they gave to the learners, the success of the whole session.

Teachers are then suggested to include their thoughts, feelings, beliefs, attitudes in regards to the lesson and comment on how learners have dealt with the difficulties in their learning processes.

• Video Recording

It is a self-reflection tool that teachers can use in their writing courses to take a more scrutinized approach to evaluate themselves. Video recording enables the teacher to watch the unwatched and unnoticed events and help them find the flaws and weaknesses. Through video recording, teachers can find which students were not focused, how his voice and gestures were, how the interactive feedback on the written works went on, how much time was allocated for each section, etc.

Tools for Collaborative Reflection

Besides individual reflection, teacher can benefit from collaborative reflection which takes place among their colleagues. They can be effective tools for their professional growth. Tools are suggested.

• E-portfolio

It is "one of the web-based technologies that can be used for the documentation of teaching evidence from a diversity of sources" (Amzat & Valdez, 2017, p.

298). E-portfolios are tools that contribute to a teacher to both reflect on and improve on the teaching process. They are constructive tools which enable the whole community of language teachers have access to individual teaching practices and as a result ease collective learning and knowledge sharing of the TEFL teachers. Therefore, it is a technology for enhancing teachers' reflectivity toward professional development and consequently toward their effectiveness. Amzat and Valdez (2017) believe that e-portfolios are multifaceted since they give teachers the power of reflection, assessment, exposure, collective/peer learning.

• Peer coaching

Brown (2015, p. 560) defines peer coaching as "structured by which faculty members voluntarily assist each other in enhancing their teaching within an atmosphere of collegial trust and candor". According to Amzat and Valdez (2017), it is a cycle of professional growth of teachers which starts from assessing the needs of the teachers in a writing classroom, getting prepared for observation, then observing the colleagues, and finally reflecting on the whole procedure.

To complete the proposed model for reflective teaching of writing, there should be a scale based on which teachers should provide feedback on the learners' written works. What follows is an adopted evaluation checklist from Brown (2015) that can be used by the teachers.

TEACHER FEEDBACK SCALE

There have been various checklists to rate students' writing. We suggest the writing evaluation checklist by Brown (2015).

Table 12.1. Categories for evaluating writing (adapted from Brown, 2015, p. 457)

	0	1	2	3	4	5
Content						
Thesis statement						
Related ideas						
Development of ideas						
(personal, experience,						
illustration, facts, opinions)						
Use of description, cause/						
effect, comparison/contrast						
Consistent focus						
Organization						
Effectiveness of introduction						
Logical sequence of ideas						
Conclusion						
Appropriate length						

Table 12.1. (Continued)

	0	1	2	3	4	5
Discourse						
Topic sentences						
Paragraph unity						
Transitions						
Discourse markers						
Cohesion						
Rhetorical conventions						
Reference						
Fluency						
Economy						
Variation						
Syntax						
Vocabulary						
Mechanics						
Spelling						
Punctuation						
Citation of references (if applicable)						
Neatness and appearance						

CONCLUSION

Through a reflective post-process approach to writing, EFL teachers of writing pass eight stages of teaching mechanics of writing, pre-planning, drafting, giving feedback to the drafts, learners' reflecting on the drafts, peer editing, giving feedback to the final drafts, and teacher's reflecting on the whole process. Teaching writing in such a reflective way enhances the quality of teaching and learning of this skill since careful and continuous guided reflection bring about opportunities for EFL teachers to be self-directed and move toward their own professional development. Farrell (2013) believes that teacher reflection is closely linked to self-worth and self-efficacy. Writing teachers find themselves actively involved in the process of shaping and reshaping their ideas and techniques exactly based on the needs of the immediate context. A reflective teacher becomes a learner of his own teaching. As Brown (2015, p. 570) mentions, "all growth and change involve learning and you develop your craft and practice your art, as you raise questions and discover more about language and teaching, and as you benefit from the wisdom of students, you learn". Besides all the merits this reflective approach has for teachers to be effective in their profession, learners can also benefit. They can improve their self-regulating abilities and move toward gaining autonomy. Through a cycle of teacher reflection, students learn how to be reflective themselves and they find themselves all the time scaffolded by the teacher and their peers.

REFERENCES

Amzat, I. H., & Valdez, N. P. (2017). *Teacher empowerment toward professional development and practices: Perspectives across borders.* Singapore: Springer Nature, Singapore Pte Ltd.

Ashwell, T. (2000). Patterns of teacher response to student writing in a multiple-draft composition classroom: Is content feedback followed by form feedback the best method? *Journal of Second Language Writing, 9*(3), 227–257.

Beckman, P. (2002). *Strategy instruction.* Arlington, VA: ERIC Clearinghouse on Disabilities and Gifted Education.

Brown, A. (1987). Metacognition, executive control, self-regulation, and other more mysterious mechanisms. In F. E. Weinert & R. H. Kluwe (Eds.), *Metacognition, motivation, and understanding* (pp. 65–116). Hillsdale, NJ: Lawrence Erlbaum.

Brown, H. D. (2015). *Teaching by principles: An interactive approach to language pedagogy.* White Plains, NY: Pearson Education.

Cahyono, B. Y. (2004). Research studies in second language writing and in contrastive rhetoric. *k@ ta, 3*(1), 39–52.

Crookes, G., & Gass, S. (1993). *Task in a pedagogical context: Integrating theory and practice.* Clevedon: Multilingual Matters.

Devine, J. (1993). The role of metacognition in second language reading and writing. In J. G. Carson & I. Leki (Eds.), *Reading in the composition classroom: Second language perspectives* (pp. 195–127). Boston, MA: Heinle & Heinle.

Farrell, T. S. C. (2013). *Reflective practice in ESL teacher development groups: From practices to principles.* New York, NY: Palgrave Macmillan.

Ferris, D. (1999). The case for grammar correction in L2 writing classes: A response to Truscott (1996). *Journal of Second Language Writing, 8*(1), 1–11.

Hamzah, M. S. G., & Abdullah, S. K. (2009). Analysis on metacognitive strategies in reading and writing among Malaysian ESL learners in four education institutions. *European Journal of Social Sciences, 11*(4), 676–683.

Hartman, H. J. (2001). Teaching metacognitively. In H. J. Hartman (Ed.), *Metacognition in learning and instruction: Theory, research and practice* (pp. 149–172). Boston, MA: Kluwer Academic.

Li, Y. (1998). *Using task-based email activities in developing academic writing skills in English as a second language oral* (Unpublished doctoral dissertation). University of Arizona, Tucson, AZ.

Livingston, J. (2003). *Metacognition: An overview.* Retrieved from https://files.eric.ed.gov/fulltext/ED474273.pdf

Maftoon, P., & Seyyedrezaei, S. H. (2012). Good language learner: A case study of writing strategies. *Theory and Practice in Language Studies, 2*(8), 1597–1602.

Mu, C. (2005, May 30). *A taxonomy of ESL writing strategies.* Proceedings Redesigning Pedagogy: Research, Policy, Practice, Singapore. Retrieved March 2, 2015, from http://eprints.qut.edu.au/view/person/Mu,_Congjun.html

Negretti, R., & Kuteeva, M. (2011). Fostering metacognitive genre awareness in L2 academic reading and writing: A case study of pre-service English teachers. *Journal of Second Language Writing, 20,* 95–110.

Nunan, D. (2010). Thomas Farrell: Reflective language teaching: From research to practice. *Applied Linguistics, 31*(3), 474–475.

Panofsky, C., Pacheco, M., Smith, S., Santos, J., Fogelman, C., Harrington, M., & Kenney, E. (2005). *Approaches to writing instruction for adolescent English language learners: A discussion of recent research and practice literature in relation to nationwide standards on writing* (ERIC Document Reproduction Service No. ED491600). Providence, RI: The Education Alliance at Brown University.

Piri, F., Barati, H., & Ketabi, S. (2012). The effects of pre-task, on-line, and both pre-task and on-line planning on fluency, complexity, and accuracy–the case of Iranian EFL learners' written production. *English Language Teaching, 5*(6), 158–167.

Richards, J. C., & Rodgers, T. S. (2001). *Approaches and methods in language teaching* (2nd ed.). Cambridge: Cambridge University Press.

Robb, T., Ross, S., & Shortreed, I. (1986). Salience of feedback on error and its effect on EFL writing quality. *TESOL Quarterly, 20*(1), 83–95.

Roberts, M. J., & Erdos, G. (1993). Strategy selection and metacognition. *Educational Psychology, 13*, 259–266.

Rosenshine, B. (1995). Advances in research on instruction. *Journal of Educational Research, 88*, 262–268.

Truscott, J. (2007). The effect of error correction on learners' ability to write accurately. *Journal of Second Language Writing, 16*(4), 255–272.

Wenden, A. L. (1991). Metacognitive strategies in L2 writing: A case for task knowledge. In J. E. Alatis (Ed.), *Georgetown University round table on languages and linguistics 1991* (pp. 302–322). Washington, DC: Georgetown University Press.

Williams, J. (2004). Tutoring and revision: Second language writers in the writing center. *Journal of Second Language Writing, 13*(3), 173–201.

Zhu, H. (2011). The application of multiple intelligences theory in task-based language teaching. *Theory and Practice in Language Studies, 1*(4), 408–412.

Ziahosseini, S. M., & Salehi, M. (2008). An investigation of the relationship between motivation and language learning strategies. *Pazhouhesh-e Zabanha-ye Kareji, 41*, 85–107.

Mitra Zeraatpishe
Islamic Azad University
Mashhad Branch
Iran

Maryam Azarnoosh
Islamic Azad University
Semnan Branch
Iran

CHRISTINE C. M. GOH AND LARRY VANDERGRIFT[†]

13. REFLECTIVE AND EFFECTIVE TEACHING OF LISTENING

INTRODUCTION

What is listening and how can it be taught? This article attempts to answer the questions by inviting language teachers to reflect on the characteristics of foreign language (FL)/second language (L2) listening and how listening can be taught and learnt effectively. Part 1 explains what teachers need to know about the listening comprehension process in order to better understand what their students need to learn to comprehend what they hear. Part 2 offers suggestions on how to teach listening in ways that is personally meaningful for learners and helpful for their listening performance.

PART 1
REFLECTING ABOUT LISTENING: HOW DOES FL LISTENING COMPREHENSION WORK?

In this section, we will discuss the cognitive processes that come into play during the process of FL listening comprehension. These processes describe what listeners do during the act of listening, how they can do this efficiently, and how they regulate these processes. Although listening can be one-way (with a speaker or an oral text) or two-way (in interaction with a speaker), our discussion, due to space limitations, will be limited to one-way listening.

TOP-DOWN AND BOTTOM-UP PROCESSING

In order to understand how FL comprehension works, we need to begin by distinguishing between bottom-up and top-down processing. These two cognitive processes apply different types of knowledge to the comprehension process and each one is used by the listener to varying degrees, depending on the purpose for listening.

Bottom-up processing is a decoding process where listeners segment the sound stream into meaningful units in order to comprehend the message. This view of listening assumes that the comprehension process begins with information from the sound stream, with minimal contribution of information from the listener's prior (or world) knowledge. In bottom-up processing, listeners draw primarily on linguistic knowledge which includes phonological knowledge (phonemes, stress, intonation),

© KONINKLIJKE BRILL NV, LEIDEN, 2018 | DOI:10.1163/9789004380882_013

vocabulary knowledge and syntactic knowledge (grammar) of the FL. Used alone, this approach to comprehension is obviously not adequate since listeners cannot keep up with the speed of the sound stream.

Top-down processing, on the other hand, is an interpretation process where listeners apply context and prior knowledge to comprehend the message. This view of listening assumes that the comprehension process begins with listener expectations about information in the text, based on topic, discourse and pragmatic knowledge. Used alone, this approach to comprehension is not adequate either, since listeners may not possess the required knowledge to interpret accurately.

In real-time comprehension, top-down and bottom-up processes rarely operate independently. Linguistic information gathered from the decoding process and prior knowledge applied during the interpretation process are managed in parallel fashion as listeners build a mental representation of what they hear. These processes occur so rapidly that listeners must learn to do this automatically if their proficiency in FL listening is going to grow. Over time, through frequent practice, listeners implicitly learn that certain patterns and categories in the FL are more possible than others (Hulstijn, 2003). This makes processing more fluent: easier, faster, and more accurate.

The degree to which listeners may use one process more than another will depend on their purpose for listening. A listener who is looking for a specific detail, such as a weather forecast, will likely do more bottom-up processing than a listener who is interested in the overall plotline of a movie. FL listeners need to learn how to use both processes to their advantage, depending on the purpose for listening and the context of the listening event. This is why it is important in teaching listening to give students a clear purpose for listening so that they know which process to apply in order to quickly identify the desired information.

CONTROLLED AND AUTOMATIC PROCESSING

When listening is fluent, as in first language (L1) listening, cognitive processing occurs extremely rapidly, moving back and forth between top-down and bottom-up processes as required achieving the desired level of comprehension. Successful FL listening depends, obviously, on the degree to which listeners can efficiently coordinate these processes. L1 listeners do this automatically (particularly bottom-up processing), with little conscious attention to individual words. FL listeners, on the other hand, usually have limited language knowledge; therefore, they are not able to automatically process everything that they hear. Depending on their FL proficiency or their familiarity with the topic of the text, listeners may need to focus consciously on some aspects of the text or learn to direct their attention to basic elements of meaning, such as important content words.

Controlled (as opposed to automatic) processing involves conscious attention to elements in the speech stream. A cognitive skill, such as listening, becomes automatic with practice, like other skilled behaviours (Johnson, 1996). For example, when we first begin driving a car, we need to pay deliberate attention to coordinating the clutch, the gas pedal, the stick shift and the steering wheel as we move the car forward smoothly to regular speed. Eventually this becomes automatic and we no longer need to pay conscious attention to the different elements of the driving skill. Similarly, in listening, processing initially requires conscious attention (controlled processing) to the different elements in the sound stream. However, because controlled processing cannot keep up with the rapid incoming input, comprehension either breaks down or listeners resort to compensatory strategies to guess at what they did not understand. That is why it is important to guide students in discovering the most productive strategies to use when comprehension breaks down.

As suggested so far in our discussion of the listening processes, memory plays a crucial role in comprehension. Traditionally, the concept of memory has been divided into two components: long-term memory (LTM) and working memory (WM, formerly called short-term memory). LTM, as noted in the discussion of top-down processing, is the bank of information (world knowledge) that listeners access to interpret what they are trying to understand. This bank of information is comprised of accumulated prior knowledge and life experiences of the listener, organized as schemata. Appropriate schemata are activated when listeners identify the relevant topic. While knowledge from LTM shapes the interpretation of what listeners hear, WM influences the efficiency of the cognitive processing and allows the listener to process chunks of information (instead of individual words) and, in the case of interactive listening, to think about an appropriate response. This is why it is so important to provide students with the topic of a listening text so that they can activate their prior knowledge and apply it to the comprehension process.

In contrast to LTM, WM has restricted capacity; listeners can only hold a limited number of units of information in memory before they fade and new information has to be processed (Call, 1985). Listeners hold the retained units of information in a phonological loop for a few seconds until the sounds can be segmented into words or larger chunks of meaningful speech through links with LTM. How much information a listener can hold in WM will depend on their level of language proficiency. As their level of language proficiency increases, listeners are able to retain and process increasingly larger chunks of meaningful speech.

Cognitive activity in WM is overseen and regulated by an executive control responsible for high level activities such as planning, coordinating flow of information, and retrieving knowledge from LTM (Baddeley, 2003). The more familiar the units are to listeners, the more quickly LTM can supply previously acquired linguistic and prior knowledge for listeners to process. An example of this phenomenon is the difference we experience in processing a new telephone number, in contrast to processing a sentence with the same number of individual units. We process the sentence more efficiently because the links between the units are meaningful and easier to retain, due to the rapid links with semantic and syntactic components of our linguistic knowledge store in LTM. The digits of the telephone number, on the other hand, need to be processed individually since the digits, although meaningful as individual numerals, are new information to LTM as a combined unit. Once we have more experience with this telephone number, it will be stored in LTM and processed in WM as one meaningful unit; for example, the phone number of a newly-discovered restaurant. Processing the telephone number as a single unit leaves more attentional resources (room in WM) for additional information, thereby it increases the efficiency of cognitive processing.

The link between WM and LTM plays a critical role in successful listening comprehension. The more listeners process information automatically, the more they can allocate the limited attentional resources of their WM to processing new information. Increased WM space also allows listeners to think about the content of what they are hearing, which is essential for critical listening. This is why it is important to offer students many opportunities for listening practice so that, over time, the skill becomes more and more automatic. The relationship between WM and L2 listening comprehension is, however, an area that is still under researched. A better understanding of how WM interacts with other listening comprehension processes will be invaluable to strengthening future pedagogical directions for listening.

PERCEPTION, PARSING AND UTILISATION

Another perspective on cognitive processes that can provide further insight into how listeners construct meaning is Anderson's (2000) differentiation of listening comprehension into three interconnected phases: perceptual processing (perception), parsing and utilization. Although this model may suggest a sequence of phases, the three phases have a two way relationship with one another which, in fact, reflects the integrated nature of bottom-up and top-down occurs (see Figure 13.1).

During the perception phase, listeners use bottom-up processing to recognize sound categories (phonemes) of the language, pauses and acoustic emphases (prosody) and hold these in memory. Listeners decode incoming speech by (1) attending to the text, to the exclusion of other sounds in the environment; (2) noting similarities, pauses and prosody relevant to a particular language; and then (3) grouping these according to the categories of the L2. This is the initial stage in the word segmentation process. A phonetic representation of what is retained is passed on for parsing.

Development of word segmentation skills is a major challenge for L2 listeners. Unlike readers, listeners do not have the luxury of spaces to help them determine word boundaries. Listeners must parse the sound stream into meaningful units when word boundaries are difficult to determine, due to stress patterns, elisions and reduced forms. Even if they can recognize individual words, when spoken in isolation, listeners may not always be able to recognize those same words in connected speech. Furthermore, word segmentation skills are language-specific and acquired early in life. They are so solidly engrained in the listener's processing system that their L1 segmentation strategies are involuntarily applied when listening to a non-native language. Difficulties reported by L2 listeners during the perception phase include: (1) not recognizing words; (2) neglecting parts of speech that follow; (3) not chunking the stream of speech; (4) missing the beginning of a sentence or message; and, (5) concentration problems (Goh, 2000). This is why it may be important to provide listeners with some simple word recognition exercises in the early stages of language learning.

During the parsing phase, listeners parse the phonetic representation of what was retained in memory and begin to activate potential word candidates. Listeners use the parsed speech to retrieve potential word candidates from LTM, based on cues such as word onset; perceptual salience; or, phonotactic conventions (rules that apply to the sequencing of phonemes). Using any one or more of these cues, listeners create propositions (abstract representations of an idea) in order to hold meaning of these words in WM as new input is processed. Meaning is often the principal clue in segmentation. As language proficiency develops, listeners can more quickly activate successful word candidates related to the context or topic, and hold meaning in increasingly larger chunks. With regard to the identification of function and content words, L2 listeners appear to be more successful in identifying content words (Field, 2008). This is not surprising, since content words carry meaning and, because of the limitations of WM, L2 listeners need to be selective. Difficulties reported by listeners during this phase include: (1) quickly forgetting what is heard; (2) being unable to form a mental representation from words heard; and (3) not understanding subsequent parts because of what was missed earlier (Goh, 2000). Improving perception and parsing may require teachers to provide listeners with some simple word recognition exercises in the early stages of language learning.

Finally, in the utilisation phase, listeners relate the resulting meaningful units to information sources in LTM in order to interpret the intended or implied meanings. This phase primarily involves top-down processing of the parsed speech. An important characteristic of this phase is that listeners use information from outside the linguistic input to interpret what they have retained (the parsed speech). Using pragmatic and prior knowledge (stored as schemata in LTM) and any relevant information in the listening context, listeners elaborate on the newly parsed information and monitor this interpretation for congruency with their prior knowledge and the evolving representation of the text in memory, as often as necessary within the time available.

During the utilisation phase, listeners generate a conceptual framework against which to match their emerging interpretation of the text or conversation and to go beyond the literal meaning of the input, when warranted. Fluent listeners then automatically reconcile linguistic input with their accumulated store of prior knowledge, in order to determine meaning. When the automatic processes break down, due to a comprehension problem, listening becomes a problem-solving activity. Listeners, for example, may need to reconsider inferences made. Difficulties reported by listeners during this phase include: (1) understanding the words but not the message, and (2) feeling confused because of seeming in congruencies in the message (Goh, 2000). This is why, as suggested above, it is so important to provide

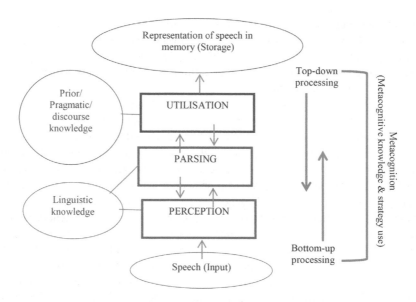

Figure 13.1. Cognitive processes and knowledge sources in listening comprehension (based on Vandergrift & Goh, 2012, p. 27)

students with the topic of a text so that, as they do in real-life listening, they can use knowledge of the context to inference on what they have not understood clearly.

These processes neither work independently nor in a linear fashion. Cognitive processing at each level can influence and be influenced by the results of cognitive processing that precedes or follows (see Figure 13.1).

METACOGNITION

Listeners control or regulate these comprehension processes through their use of metacognitive knowledge. Metacognition refers to listener awareness of the cognitive processes involved in comprehension, and the capacity to oversee, regulate and direct these processes (Goh, 2008). In addition to the ability to reflect on these processes generally, it includes knowledge about the task- , person- and strategy-related factors that come into play during any cognitive activity (Flavell, 1979). Applied to L2/FL listening, person knowledge concerns internal factors that affect learners and their listening comprehension and includes personal beliefs as L2/FL listeners. Task knowledge concerns the nature and purpose of a listening task, the demands that listening makes on learners themselves and the procedure(s) required for accomplishing a listening task. Strategy knowledge is knowledge about strategies that can help learners themselves in achieving listening comprehension and learning goals. The control dimension of metacognition involves use of cognitive processes, initially activated as L2 listening strategies, such as planning, monitoring, problem-solving and evaluating to effectively regulate listening comprehension. The overarching role of metacognition is that of an executive function overseeing the cognitive processes described (see Figure 13.1).

The ability to apply metacognitive knowledge to a learning task is a characteristic shared by successful learners; in fact, Vandergrift, Goh, Mareschal, and Tafaghodtari (2006) found that approximately 13% of variance in listening achievement could be explained by metacognition. A similar level of variance (15%) was also reported by Zeng (2012). Listeners who can apply metacognitive knowledge about listening during the cognitive processes of comprehension described above are better able to regulate these processes and draw on the relevant knowledge sources in an efficient manner to build text comprehension. It is important therefore to teach students *how* to listen because they become acquainted with the processes that characterize successful listening.

KNOWLEDGE SOURCES IN LISTENING

As listeners engage in the cognitive processes described above, they draw on different knowledge sources: linguistic knowledge, pragmatic knowledge, prior knowledge and discourse knowledge (see Figure 13.1). Information retrieved from these 'data banks' will influence the quality and the direction of the cognitive processing and therefore important to guide students in accessing these resources to facilitate their listening efforts.

Linguistic Knowledge

Linguistic knowledge is fundamental to listening comprehension; vocabulary knowledge is a strong predictor of L2 listening success (Staehr, 2009). In addition to vocabulary, linguistic knowledge includes phonological knowledge (phonemes, stress, intonation, and speech modifications such as assimilation and elision) and syntactic knowledge (grammar) of the L2. Phonological and syntactic knowledge help listeners parse the sound stream for meaningful units of language and assign semantic roles to words. Application of all three components of linguistic knowledge helps listeners assign meaning to word-level units and to the relationship between words. However, listeners need to know how to use this knowledge as rapid speech unfolds. Recognizing a word in its written form or hearing it in isolation does not necessarily mean that L2 listeners will recognize that same word in the context of rapid speech. This is the real challenge of listening comprehension: L2 listeners need to be able to rapidly identify words from a stream of sound. Some words are easily parsed and can be quickly mapped onto LTM, such as: cognates for linguistically similar languages; sound effects and paralinguistics that are not culturally bound; and, increasingly, English words related to technology or the media (e.g., i-pod) that are becoming universally understood. Other words will require deeper processing to infer their meaning in the context of the text.

Pragmatic Knowledge

Listening often involves more than just the comprehension of a word. Listeners use pragmatic knowledge when they apply information that goes beyond the literal meaning of a word to interpret the speaker's intended meaning. It is informed, for example, by interpretation of tone (e.g., sarcasm and questions). L2 pragmatic knowledge helps the listener to infer the speaker's intention, particularly if there is any ambiguity in the literal meaning. Pragmatic knowledge is often culturally-bound and, therefore, closely related to sociocultural and sociolinguistic knowledge (e.g., formal or informal registers, idioms and slang) which listeners use to further interpret an utterance (Buck, 2001). Listeners usually apply pragmatic knowledge during the utilisation phase of the comprehension process and if students do not have that knowledge, it is important that they be given this knowledge before a listening activity begins.

Listeners use pragmatic knowledge to enrich the linguistic input. During the utilisation phase, listeners generate familiar 'conceptual events' or scenarios from LTM and match the emerging meaning of the text or utterance against them (Dipper, Black, & Bryan, 2005). In adapting this scenario, listeners go beyond semantic meaning to consider the contextualized meaning intended by the speaker. A statement such as "It's cold in here" as someone enters a room may suggest that the speaker would like someone to close the window.

Prior Knowledge

Prior knowledge plays a powerful role in listening comprehension (e.g., Macaro, Vanderplank, & Graham, 2005). Listeners match what they hear (the linguistic input) with what they know about how things work in the world (their prior knowledge). This knowledge source plays a critical role at the utilisation phase of the listening process. For example, before listening to a phone conversation enquiring about rental space or watching a video about visiting the apartment and talking to the landlord, students can greatly benefit from a discussion about experiences in renting an apartment to activate vocabulary and types of scenarios. For this reason, it is important to provide listeners with the context of a listening text or event, before they begin listening. Contextualized listeners then have the necessary information to activate their prior knowledge on the topic and to develop a conceptual framework in order to identify potential words and content. Contextual information can help listeners process the linguistic input more efficiently, freeing up WM resources to process larger chunks of information.

Although prior knowledge is important for facilitating comprehension, it can also be misleading when used inflexibly. Listener use of prior knowledge can lead to inaccurate comprehension when it is not supported by corroborating evidence that matches the listener's expectations (Macaro et al., 2005). This underscores the importance of flexibility in the comprehension process. Using a combination of questioning and elaboration (activating prior knowledge), listeners must continually consider different possibilities and monitor the emerging interpretation for congruency with their expectations and prior knowledge (Vandergrift, 2003).

Discourse Knowledge

Discourse (textual) knowledge involves comprehension at the level of text organization. Awareness of the kind of information found in certain texts and how that information is organized can facilitate listener ability to process this information. A restaurant advertisement, for example, is likely to include name, address, phone number and the restaurant's specialty or current specials, in addition to other information. Listeners use this kind of knowledge when they consider and apply knowledge of text types to the comprehension process.

Depending on the nature of the text, discourse knowledge can include knowledge of and attention to discourse markers that signal the beginning (e.g., first of all) or conclusion (e.g., in sum) of a set of arguments, an opposing argument (e.g., on the other hand) or a hypothesis (e.g., if). Such signals give listeners some idea of what type of information they can expect to hear. Discourse knowledge can be used proactively by the listener to anticipate the kinds of information that might be found in a text and is often used in combination with prior knowledge. A listener, for example, can use knowledge about how an interview with a soccer player might begin, what questions are asked and how the interview will likely end as a guideline to anticipate what he will hear in an interview with a hockey player.

Discourse knowledge is very important in interactive listening. In these contexts, listeners use discourse knowledge to facilitate the processing of what they might likely hear and how they may be asked to respond. For example, in an information exchange, such as at a fast food restaurant, listeners can use their knowledge of the script that is likely to unfold to anticipate the questions that will be asked and the answers they will need to provide for the exchange to be successful. Furthermore, in these contexts, listeners use discourse knowledge when to take their turn in conversation, and decide when and how to ask clarification questions.

LISTENING SKILLS AND STRATEGIES

Different knowledge sources work together with the cognitive processes to help listeners arrive at a meaningful interpretation of a listening text. Some of these knowledge sources, such as prior knowledge, can be transferred from L1. In other cases, depending on the similarities between the languages (root language, script system and cultural conventions), some elements of pragmatic, discourse and linguistic knowledge may also transfer. As L2/FL listeners gain more language experience and their language proficiency develops, they are able to process information more efficiently and access knowledge sources more rapidly. In doing this, they are also able to engage in specific ways of listening which the literature refers to as listening skills, listening sub-skills or enabling skills. Here we suggest six core skills which are central to listening comprehension and whichlisteners need to use according to their purposes for listening:

- *Listen for details*: Identify specific information
- *Listen for global understanding:* Understand the overall general idea
- *Listen for main ideas:* Understand key points or propositions
- *Listen and infer:* Make up for missing or unclear information with various forms of knowledge
- *Listen and predict:* Anticipate what is going to be said
- *Listen selectively*: Pay attention to particular parts of the listening text

When L2/FL learners anticipate or experience problems with their listening comprehension, they can either give up trying to make sense of what they hear or they can use some strategies to help them compensate for their lack. For example, when they are unable to process sounds in the perception stage as words that they recognise, learners can apply comprehension strategies to fill in the gaps where possible. When they are practising their listening on their own or in class, learners can also make use of learning resources to support their comprehension. Strategies are typically engaged by language learners who lack different kinds of knowledge to achieve adequate comprehension during a specific listening event. Strategies are conscious and goal-directed ways of listening and learning to listen. The following strategies are important to many language learners:

- *Planning:* Think of what needs to be done to overcome anticipated challenges
- *Focussing attention*: Concentrate on the spoken input and avoid distractions
- *Monitoring*: Check, confirm, or correct comprehension , or check the progress of learning
- *Evaluation*: Check the outcomes of listening and study plans for listening
- *Inferencing*: To guess the meaning of unfamiliar words or fill in missing information
- *Elaboration*: Use prior knowledge to extend and embellish an interpretation
- *Prediction:* Anticipate the contents of what one is going to hear
- *Contextualization:* Relate what is heard in a specific context
- *Reorganizing:* Transfer what is understood into other forms to facilitate further understanding, storage, and retrieval
- *Using linguistic and learning resources:* Support listening with knowledge of other languages and learning aids
- *Cooperation*: Get other people's help in comprehension and learning
- *Managing emotions*: Acknowledge negative emotions linked to listening and prevent them from affecting learning

PART 2
TEACHING LISTENING EFFECTIVELY: HOW CAN
STUDENTS LEARN TO LISTEN?

Part 1 of this chapter has described the processes that interact to enable listening comprehension to take place. Teachers can become more effective in teaching listening when they understand these processes and reflect on how they can facilitate their students' listening comprehension and overall development. With this knowledge, they can teach their students how to reflect on and assess their own listening processes, as well as demands and challenges they experience, so the students themselves can play an active role in enhancing their own learning.

A BRIEF OVERVIEW OF LISTENING INSTRUCTION

Over the past six decades the focus of llistening instruction has shifted from a heavily text- and comprehension-based approach to one where listening is practiced as a communication skill. More recently, emphasis is paid to helping language learners develop their listening systematically and holistically by tapping the power of metacognition. These changes demonstrate further understanding of the listening construct, the characteristics of spoken discourse and the science of learning. In the early text comprehension approach, learners first listened to written passages read aloud and then showed their understanding by giving what are hopefully the correct answers, not unlike a reading comprehension test. These texts contained many features of written grammar, for example, long sentences with embedded ideas that made processing difficult in real time listening. While most listening instructional materials have largely shifted away from such text- and comprehension-based techniques, remnants of the approach may still exist in some classrooms today due to the washback effects of high-stakes listening examinations.

Radical changes came in the late 1970's and 80's as a result of the Communicative Language Teaching methodology that gained popularity in many countries in Europe and Asia. Listening texts were chosen because they were authentic or had a high degree of authenticity. Authentic listening texts were chosen from the media and other non-teaching sources and included recordings such as movie or video clips, songs and radio programmes. Scripted texts for listening activities would possess features of spontaneous speech found in real-life interaction, such as repetitions, hesitations and shorter or incomplete utterances. Listening activities became closer to real-world tasks, such as taking notes while listening to a talk or a voice message on the telephone. To facilitate the planning of listening lessons, listening sub-skills were selected from available taxonomies reflecting various communicative language functions.

Following these changes, listening instruction became heavily influenced by a socio-cognitive paradigm of learning that addresses learner needs such as cognitive

189

processing demands, contextual factors and learner anxiety. Within this paradigm, language learners are taught to use listening strategies to handle the cognitive and social-affective demands of listening. They are also shown how to reflect on their own listening processes and challenges, and to consider ways of improving their comprehension and learning processes. More details on this approach, which we refer to as the metacognitive approach, will be discussed in the rest of this article.

PRINCIPLES AND STRATEGIES FOR TEACHING L2/FL LISTENING

The following principles and teaching strategies can be identified based on our current understanding of how listening comprehension takes place:

- *Give students a clear purpose for listening so that they know which process or strategies to apply in order to achieve reasonable comprehension or compensate for linguistic difficulties*

Listening comprehension is achieved through bottom-up and top-down cognitive processes that frequently occur in an interactive manner but also, where necessary, on its own. Students can listening for details by recognising only key words if they know their purpose is just to focus on a small piece of information such as the time or a name. Students who understand their purpose for a specific listening task can also prepare themselves to use strategies that can compensate for or enhance their comprehension. For example, when students know they are required to understand only the gist of a difficult listening text, they may use some of the key words they have through bottom-up word recognition and apply their knowledge of the context or topic to constructing a reasonable broad interpretation of what they hear. Teachers should therefore begin each listening task by helping students identify their purpose for listening.

- *Provide students with the topic of a listening text so that they can activate their prior knowledge and apply it to the comprehension process.*

Although many L2/FL learners are still struggling to master the language, they would all undoubtedly bring with them factual knowledge and relevant experiences. Young language learners whose prior knowledge may not be as extensive would still possess adequate knowledge about things in their world. Teachers can also help them by choosing topics that are relevant to these children. In situations where teachers suspect or know that their L2/EFL learners (adult and children alike) may have little or no knowledge about a certain topic, the teacher should provide activities before the listening task to help learners generate and create the knowledge that they can use to bring to bear on the comprehension processes.

- *Offer students many opportunities for listening so that, over time, listening becomes more and more automatic.*

Listening comprehension becomes more automatic when various processes work in an orchestrated manner that is increasingly effortless. These opportunities should enable students to recycle language that they have previously heard and engage in cognitive processes that they have previously learnt to use. Even with proficient speakers of a language, there will be occasions when processing may still be effortful and controlled to some extent. For example, when the speaker is ambiguous or vague, listeners will need to use spend more effort to draw inferences about the meaning of what is said even though they have no problem with perceiving and recognising the words in the input. Thus, language learners should also have many opportunities to apply listening strategies so that they become increasingly familiar with their use.

• *Provide students with word recognition exercises in the early stages of language learning so as to develop bottom-up processing skills.*

L2/FL learners in general have limited opportunities to hear the target language being spoken in their own countries. Even with the pervasiveness of the internet and technologies such as podcasts, many learners still find it difficult to recognise sounds in streams of speech as words that they know in print. As bottom-up processing is critical to perception and parsing, it is important to plan short exercises that can train students' hearing of words and phrases. Dictation exercises can also be useful for achieving this purpose. For example, when sentences and short texts are read out at normal speed students can practise their perception skills without the anxiety of having to cope with long texts where they can easily lose their concentration or get too fixated at the earlier parts and neglect the rest of the text. In general, bottom-up processing exercises such as lexical segmentation and recognizing key words should be based on the listening texts that students work with in other parts of the listening lesson or programme.

• *Teach students how to listen so that they become acquainted with the processes that characterize successful listening.*

Students often feel they are not in control of their listening comprehension because of external factors such as the speech rate and accent of a speaker, difficulty of a topic, etc. Many also do not understand why despite their hours of practice and concentration, they are still unable to understand the next thing they hear in class or when communicating with speakers of the target language. Listening teachers therefore should plan lessons and activities that do not test listening (which further adds to the students' anxiety) but that enable them to utilize their metacognitive abilities to improve listening.Learning-to-listen activities should be integrated into listening lessons to help learners deepen their understanding of themselves as L2 listeners and the nature and processes of L2/FL listening. When the cognitive and social demands of listening are acknowledged, learners can use their understanding to explore and practise various metacognitive and comprehension processes in their own listening. These learning-to-listen activities also provide opportunities for learners to practise and acquire strategies for managing their comprehension and learning through planning, monitoring and evaluating.

HELPING STUDENTS LEARN HOW TO LISTEN

We can help learners become more adept at engaging in cognitive processes through a metacognitive approach that combines metacognitive instruction for listening with task-based listening practice. Normal listening activities are integrated with metacognitive activities to help learners deepen their understanding of themselves as L2 listeners, the nature of L2/FL listening, as well as strategies that they can use to compensate for or enhance their comprehension. As they learn more about the cognitive and social processes of listening, learners get to explore and practise these processes in their own listening. To this end two methods are proposed below. The first, metacognitive pedagogical sequence is more suited to one-way listening activities where traditionally students listen to a spoken text and demonstrate their comprehension by completing a task or answering some questions. The second, integrated (task-based and metacognitive) lessons, can be used in both one-way and two way (interactive/participatory) listening activities.

The two methods can be used in a complementary manner in a language programme where listening is explicitly focused on. To use the two methods, teachers can develop some materials on their own or where prescribed text books are used, they can adapt the listening activities in the books to include a metacognitive dimension. When preparing or adapting materials for teaching students how to listen, teachers should also consider relevant listening strategies for the purpose for the listening task, develop additional self-directed learning materials to guide learners' thinking in extensive listening, and use only natural spoken texts or texts that have authentic features of speech (Goh, 2014b).

Metacognitive Pedagogical Sequence for Listening

This method takes learners through the process of listening by enabling them to consciously engage in some key listening processes, such as predicting, inferring and evaluating (Vandergrift, 2004). It involves student listening to a recorded audio or video text while being guided by the teacher to activate key cognitive processes through five lesson stages. The teacher begins the listening lesson by providing context for the students through visual or other forms of information about the topic, text genre, culture and relevant information that will put the students' mind at ease and prepared for listening. After that the teacher begins the first stage of the pedagogical sequence and guides the students through each subsequent stage. The five stages of instruction are as follows:

- Pre-listening-planning/predicting stage: Students discuss or predict words that they will hear based on the topic of the text.
- First listen and verification stage: Students listen and take notes, verify their predictions in 1, and compare their notes with each other.

- Second listen and verification stage: Students improve their notes from 2, reconstruct the text with another student using their shared notes and reflect on the processes they have engaged in that lead to their comprehension.
- Third listen and final verification stage: Students listen specifically to information obtained from 3 and check understanding by referring to a transcript of the text.
- Post-listening reflection and goal setting: Students reflect on their challenges and achievements, and set goals for the next listening activity.

At each stage, students will engage in one or more of metacognitive processes such as planning, monitoring, evaluating and problem-solving. Learning aids, such as checklists, pictures, advance organisers may also be used if the teacher feels that further support is needed for lower proficiency learners in particular. The teacher initially plays a major role in guiding students through the various stages, but this role will diminish with time as students develop greater familiarity with the procedures and processes involved in the sequence. The students should be able eventually to tackle listening activities by working together on their own. The teacher will continue to plan listening activities but his/her role will evolve to that of a facilitator and a more knowledgeable other for confirming comprehension and dealing with language-related questions.

Integrated Task-Based and Metacognitive Listening Lessons

In many language classrooms today, it is common to see two stages in a listening lesson: the pre-listening stage and the listening stage. Typically, students get a few minutes to discuss the topic of the listening text to prepare themselves for listening. During the listening stage, students have to complete some accompanying comprehension activities, such as completing some information gaps, making notes and answering questions. In task-based listening lessons, there should be three stages: pre-listening, while-listening and post-listening. Students listen to an FL text for a communicative purpose during the listening stage and this is followed by a post-listening activity that utilizes the information obtained for a related outcome or goal. In one-way listening tasks, students respond to listening input in a number of different ways, such as sorting, comparing, matching and evaluating the information. They use the information that has been obtained to achieve further communication goals in the post-listening stage. For example, they may use a set of notes to compose an email. (Further details on lesson procedures for each type of listening task can be found in Goh, 2014a).

While a traditional task-based listening lesson tends to focus on the content of the listening input, metacognitive approach expands the scope and purposes of the pre- and post-listening phases to include activities that develop learners' orientate towards not just language or world knowledge but also metacognitive knowledge. An extension activity can also be added after the post-listening stage to cater specifically to metacognitive processes such as evaluation and planning. The four stages are as follows:

- Pre-listening: Students predict key words or learn unfamiliar words; activate prior knowledge; anticipate challenges; prepare to use specific strategies.
- Listening: Students listen for a purpose and complete one-way listening or two-way (interactive) listening tasks.
- Post-listening: Students apply, synthesize and evaluate information and interpretation from task; analyse pronunciation, grammar and vocabulary in text.
- Extension beyond communicative listening: Students reflect on listening performance and processes in 2 and 3; plan for future listening; plan and carry out extensive listening.

COMPARING AND COMBINING TWO METACOGNITIVE INSTRUCTIONAL METHODS

Each of the two methods described above caters to specific instructional goals for L2/FL listening. A comparison of these goals and other features of the methods are presented in Table 13.1. As the table shows, the two methods serve different but complementary goals for listening development, so both should be included in a listening programmer to ensure a comprehensive approach. Each method can be used to conduct a single lesson depending on how long the lesson is. In the case of the metacognitive pedagogical sequence, it is advisable that the sequence be completed within the same listening lesson so that learners can benefit from the continual reflection and engagement. The task-based lessons should ideally be carried out in one lesson too, but as some lessons may be short, it is possible to conduct the extension stage as home work. The outlines of the procedures and processes of the methods can also be used as a guide when adapting listening activities in prescribed text books. If adaptation is not possible, teachers can use the suggestions to prepare supplementary listening lessons.

CONCLUSION

Listening involves complex cognitive processes in one's first language. For L2 and FL learners, developing listening competence in the target language can therefore be a daunting process. Nevertheless, many learners are highly motivated to improve their listening and are prepared to put in many hours of practice, yet they may still not achieve the success that they desire. One of the reasons is that these language learners have not learnt how to listen and manage their comprehension processes effectively. Compared with other language skills such as reading and writing, there is a lot less explicit teaching of listening. In many listening lessons, learners merely listen to audio recordings or watch videos and this is followed by some comprehension activities. Instead of being taught how to listen, learners are tested

Table 13.1. Comparing two teaching methods in a metacognitive approach to listening instruction

	Metacognitive Pedagogical Sequence for Listening	Integrated Task-Based and Metacognitive Listening Lesson
Instructional goal	Teaches students explicitly the processes of listening through repeated metacognitive engagement with a listening text individually and with peers.	Develops students' communicative listening skills through listening tasks and metacognitive engagement through integrated learning activities.
Comprehension Focus	Students to understand the content in the text with the help of repeated listening and application of metacognitive processes.	Students engage in a variety of listening tasks to achieve comprehension according to specific communicative purposes and supported by listening strategies.
Lesson Objectives	Students learn the metacognitive processes of planning, monitoring, evaluation and problem-solving that enables comprehension to occur. Students work collaboratively with others to develop metacognitive knowledge about L2/FL listening.	Students practice different listening skills that are appropriate for listening purposes and increase metacognitive knowledge about listening. Students work collaboratively with others to enhance listening skills and metacognitive knowledge.
Lesson Sequence	Five learning-to-listen stages with teacher scaffolding students at each stage to enhance comprehension and metacognition continually.	Three or four stages that include one main listening stage that emphasizes comprehension according to communication purpose.
Cognitive Processes	Combines top-down and bottom-up processes at various listening and verification stages.	Combines top-down and bottom-up processes at the main listening stage and offers additional opportunities for enhancing bottom-up processing and language knowledge.

on how much they can understand what they hear. Although conscientious practice can bring about improvement over time, learners can benefit a great deal more by engaging in their learning processes in an informed and meaningful manner. It is hoped that the explanations in this article of how listening comprehension works will spur teachers to consider the implications of these processes for teaching listening effectively. Key pedagogical principles and strategies identified from the theoretical perspectives presented are meant to support teachers further in this regard while the proposed instructional methods for listening will provide teachers with outlines of listening lessons. Listening improvement does not happen overnight. With clear metacognitive guidance from teachers, learners will find the journey less arduous and certainly more personally meaningful and engaging.

REFERENCES

Anderson, J. R. (2000). *Cognitive psychology and its applications* (4th ed.). New York, NY: Freeman.

Baddeley, A. (2003). Working memory and language: An overview. *Journal of Communication Disorders, 36*, 189–208.

Buck, G. (2001). *Assessing listening*. Cambridge: Cambridge University Press.

Call, M. E. (1985). Auditory short-term memory, listening comprehension, and the input hypothesis. *TESOL Quarterly, 19*, 765–781.

Dipper, L., Black, M., & Bryan, K. L. (2005). Thinking for speaking and thinking for listening: The interaction of thought and language in typical and non-fluent comprehension and production. *Language and Cognitive Processes, 20*, 417–441.

Field, J. (2008). *Listening in the language classroom*. Cambridge: Cambridge University Press.

Flavell, J. H. (1979). Metacognition and cognitive monitoring: A new area of cognitive-developmental inquiry. *American Psychologist, 34*, 906–911.

Goh, C. C. M. (2000). A cognitive perspective on language learners' listening comprehension problems. *System, 28*, 55–75.

Goh, C. C. M. (2008). Metacognitive instruction for second language listening development: Theory, practice and research implications. *RELC Journal, 39*, 188–213.

Goh, C. C. M. (2014a). Listening comprehension: Process and pedagogy. In M. Celce-Murcia, D. M. Brinton, & M. A. Snow (Eds.), *Teaching English as a second or foreign language* (4th ed., pp. 72–89). Boston, MA: National Geographic Learning/Cengage Learning.

Goh, C. C. M. (2014b, February). Five principles for teaching language learners how to listen. *TESOL MWIS Newsletter*, p. 5. Retrieved from http://newsmanager.commpartners.com/tesolmwis/issues/2014-02-19/email.html

Hulstijn, J. H. (2003). Connectionist models of language processing and the training of listening skills with the aid of multimedia software. *Computer Assisted Language Learning, 16*, 413–425.

Johnson, K. (1996). *Language teaching and skill learning*. London: Blackwell.

Macaro, E., Vanderplank, R., & Graham, S. (2005). *A Systematic review of the role of prior knowledge in unidirectional listening comprehension*. London: EPPI-Centre, Social Science Research Unit, Institute of Education, University of London.

Staehr, L. S. (2009). Vocabulary knowledge and advanced listening comprehension in English as a foreign language. *Studies in Second Language Acquisition, 31*, 577–607.

Vandergrift, L. (2003). From prediction through reflection: Guiding students through the process of L2 listening. *The Canadian Modern Language Review, 59*, 425–440.

Vandergrift, L. (2004). Learning to listen or listening to learn. *Annual Review of Applied Linguistics, 24*, 3–25.

Vandergrift, L., & Goh, C. (2012). *Teaching and learning second language listening: Metacognition in action*. New York, NY: Routledge.

Vandergrift, L., Goh, C., Mareschal, C., & Tafaghodatari, M. H. (2006). The Metacognitive Awareness Listening Questionnaire (MALQ): Development and validation. *Language Learning, 56*, 431–462.

Zeng, Y. (2012). *Metacognition and Self-Regulated Learning (SRL) for Chinese EFL listening development* (Unpublished PhD thesis). Nanyang Technological University, Singapore.

Christine C. M. Goh
Nanyang Technological University
Singapore

Larry Vandergrift[†]
University of Ottawa
Canada

RICHARD R. DAY

14. REFLECTIVE AND EFFECTIVE
TEACHING OF READING

INTRODUCTION

The first aim of this chapter is to provide an in-depth examination of reading in order to give second language (L2) reading teachers insights into effective teaching of reading. The second aim is to help you, the reader, to reflect, to think about, your beliefs about and practices of teaching L2 reading. We first look at the nature of reading, then discuss how we learn to read. The third section focuses on reading fluency; the fourth, on reading strategies.

WHAT IS READING?

In this section, we look at the nature of reading and examine three dimensions of reading. Research clearly demonstrates that teacher knowledge is a critical element of effective teaching. So it is critical to engage you about your knowledge of reading. What do you know about reading? What happens when we read? What goes on in our minds? Now, complete this sentence:

> – Reading is

When I work with teachers who are involved in teaching second or foreign language (L2) reading and ask them this question, their answers usually have something to do with *comprehension* or *understanding*. Often teachers mention *getting the meaning.* But I believe seeing reading as comprehension or understanding confuses what goes on in our minds with the result. That is, comprehension is the *product* of what happens in our minds when we read.

I prefer this way of looking at reading: *Reading is a number of interactive processes between the reader and the text in which readers use their knowledge to build, to create, to construct meaning.* This simple but helpful definition clearly shows that *meaning* is the result of a number of interactive processes.

Let's examine these *interactive processes*. One is what happens between the reader and the material (the text).In this interactive process, readers use their knowledge from the text and from their knowledge to build or construct meaning. For example, if the text begins with "*Once upon a time*", readers whose first What language (L1) is English; know that the text is a fairy tale. This knowledge directly influences their understanding of the text. Of course, knowledge of the genre of the text is not the only factor in this interactive process.

> – What other kinds of knowledge influence the construction of meaning in this interactive process?

Obviously readers' knowledge of the language (e.g., syntax, its writing system, vocabulary) is of critical importance. If readers have only a very limited knowledge of the language of the text, they would only be able to read elementary material. Also, the knowledge about the author helps readers' construct meaning. If we have read previous books by the author, then we might know to expect a surprise ending, for example.

In addition, knowledge of the topic of the text is very important in our understanding of the text.

> – Who will have a deeper understanding of a text, a reader who knows a great deal about its topic or a reader who doesn't know much?

Of course the reader who knows about the text's topic will have a deeper understanding. If a professor of English poetry and a high school student read the same poem, the professor's understanding would be deeper than the student's.

Finally, we use our knowledge of the world, including our experiences, values, and beliefs, in building meaning. Consider, for example, a student from Turkey studying English and an L1 English reader from America read a story about America's civil war. Obviously, the American will have a different understanding than the Turkish student.

To summarize, we use all of these different types of knowledge to achieve an understanding of the text. Think about this question:

> – When two people read the same book, do you think they construct the same meaning?

Most likely they would not because they do not share the same types of knowledge.

These interactive processes of building meaning are often referred to as "higher level processing" (e.g., Grabe, 2009, p. 21). There are also other processes which reading experts identify as *low level*. Grabe (2009) claims that these lower level processes include "word recognition, syntactic parsing and meaning encoding as propositions" (p. 21).

It is important to understand that these two interactive processes, lower-level and higher-level, take place simultaneously. If a reader has a problem or has difficulty with an element of either of these processes, the product of the processes, comprehension, will be adversely affected.

OTHER ASPECTS OF READING

In the previous discussion, *a cognitive view* of reading was the focus. However, there is another way of looking at reading. It can be viewed as a *cultural* event. Since reading is a human activity, it part of a culture. Think about this question.

> – Since the act of reading is done in a culture, how might this affect reading?

Perhaps the most important way in which culture impacts reading is how much, and even if, people read. There are *reading cultures* in which its members engage in reading frequently. For example, in a reading culture, people read in an airport while waiting for a plane, and then continue to read while on the plane. In a no reading culture, the opposite is true: people tend not to read. Culture also influences what, how, where, and when we read.

> – Since reading is done in a culture, how might this affect the teaching of L2 reading?

Perhaps the most challenging impact of culture on the teaching of L2 reading is when we have students from non-reading cultures. It would be difficult to motivate our students to read.

This brings us to another view of reading: the *affective*. The affective dimension is a major factor in the nature of reading because if our students do not see reading as worthwhile, as beneficial, or even as enjoyable, in their first language, then they will be very reluctant to learn to read in another language.

In this section, we have examined the nature of reading, and looked at three dimensions of reading. Before we move to the next section, learning to Read, consider these reflection questions:

> – What is the most important thing you have learned in this section?
> – Why is it important?

LEARNING TO READ

We now discuss the topic of *learning to read*. The aim of this section is to help you understand how we learn to read in either our L1 or L2. Let's start by consider how you learned to read in your L1. Answer this question:

> — How do we learn to read?

There is only one answer: *We learn to read by reading.* Reading is learned behavior; it is a skill. Like other skills, such as playing a musical instrument, driving a car, playing tennis, we learn to do the skill by engaging in it. And the more we do it, the better we become. This is true of learning to read a first language, and a foreign language.

However, the L2 reading developmental processes are similar to L1 reading developmental processes, there are differences:

- Cultural – Consider reading and nonreading cultures
- Individual – Learners' L1 reading ability; attitude toward reading; motivation to read
- Linguistic –Differences between the L1 and L2 (e.g., vocabulary, syntax) could either help or hinder learning to read the new language

However, regardless of the reading developmental processes, L2 learners, like L1 learners, have to read, read, and read some more in order to become readers.

> — Since L2 students learn to read by reading, what do you think is the L2 reading teacher's most important task?

There are a number of answers to this question. One is to give the L2 students time to read in class. Another is to make sure that the L2 students have material that interesting to them. A third answer is to motivate students to read in the L2.

We have examined how we learn to read. The next section focuses on another dimension of reading, fluency.

READING FLUENCY

We begin this section in the way that we began the chapter, by asking you, the reader, a question. Answer this question:

> — What is reading fluency?

The answer that many L2 reading teachers give has something to do with reading speed or rate. For example, *reading fluency is fast reading.* Unfortunately, reading rate is only part of what reading fluency is. There are many definitions of reading fluency; many definitions involve *oral reading* or *reading aloud.* These views of reading fluency are not really helpful to L2 reading teachers, whose primary objective is to get their students to become silent readers in the L2. Most of reading is done silently. Relatively little is done orally.

A definition that I find useful is this: *A fluent reader reads effortlessly and confidently at a level of understanding and a rate appropriate for the purpose or task and the material.* Let's examine the key words in this definition:

- Effortlessly–without difficulty, easily. A fluent reader's eyes glide smoothly across each line, seldom stopping to think about the meaning of words.
- Confidently – without worrying about the act of reading. Fluent readers know that they can read, so they don't hesitate while reading.
- A level of understanding and a rate appropriate for the purpose or task and the material – Fluent readers do not always read for 100% comprehension. They adjust their level of understanding to fit their purpose – why they are reading the text. In your L1 reading:

> – What do you read for 100% understanding?
> – What do you read for less than 100% understanding?

Fluent readers adjust their level of understanding of the materials they read; they don't read everything for 100% comprehension. Fluent readers also adjust the rate (or speed) of their reading depending on their purpose and the material. For example, when we are looking in a newspaper for the time a movie starts, our eyes move rapidly over the words, and only adjusting our rate to read more slowly when we see the time. Or consider reading a novel that we enjoy. Our reading rate is much higher than when we read an academic article such as this one.

Consider your reading rate in your L1.

> – What do you read quickly? Why?
> – What do you read slowly and carefully? Why?

Fluent reading is made possible by the *automatic recognition of words*. Automatic recognition is the immediate understanding of words quickly, without any thinking whatsoever. Fluent readers generally do not have to pause to think about the meaning of most words. They recognize them automatically, every time, correctly, regardless of the context. Words that we recognize automatically are often call *sight vocabulary*. Fluent reader has a large sight vocabulary. A word that are not in a reader's sight vocabulary but knows their meaning of a short pause are part of the reader's *general vocabulary*.

In general, L2 readers read everything slowly and carefully, word-by-word. This is because they do not have either a large sight vocabulary or a large general vocabulary. So they have to stop and think about the meaning of each word. And by the time they have finished reading a paragraph, they have forgotten the meaning of the previous sentences, so they have to go back to the beginning and read again.

Answer this question:

> – How can L2 reading teachers help their students stop reading slowly, reading word-for-word?

While there are several ways of doing this, perhaps the most effective way is to have students read *easy, interesting* material. By *easy* I mean material that is well within their L2 linguistic ability. When L2 students know most of the vocabulary in a text, they can read it without stopping to think about the meanings of most of the words. When learners read easy material, they are able to read without stopping to figure out the syntax or the meanings of words, and they do not have to translate into their L1 to understand.

Students should not be tested or asked to answer comprehension questions after they have read something that is easy and interesting. If students know that they will be held accountable for what they read, they will read it word-for-word.

When L2 reading teachers feel that they have to check to make sure that their students understand what they have read, they resort to comprehension questions or quizzes. However, there are other ways of checking comprehension. These include having students write letters to characters in the readings, tell each other about their favourite people in the reading, and rewrite the endings (see Day, 2012 for activities that students can do with their readings).

When L2 students read easy and interesting material, they are *learning to read*. In my opinion, we should not test them by asking comprehension questions. When teachers do this, it confuses *learning to read* with *reading to learn*. If the reading material is easy and interesting, then students will understand most of what they read.

In addition to helping L2 students stop reading slowly, word-for-word, L2 reading teachers need to help their students acquire a large sight vocabulary.

> – How can L2 students gain sight vocabulary?

The answer should be clear: by reading, reading, and reading some more. When students read a great deal, they read the same words over and over. They may often pause briefly to recall the meanings of some of the words, and then continue reading. When they read the same words over and over, these words gradually become part of their sight vocabulary. The more students read, the larger their sight vocabularies become. And the larger their sight vocabularies become, the more fluent their reading becomes. However, this will only take place if they are reading easy material. And when students' sight vocabularies increase, so does their reading rates.

Since reading rate is the major dimension in fluency, when reading rates increase, so does reading fluency. This is critical because reading fluency is the foundation of reading comprehension. In both L1 and L2 reading, the research clearly demonstrates that fluent readers are more efficient and effective readers than slow readers (e.g., Lightbown, Halter, White, & Horst, 2002; National Reading Panel,

2000). Slow readers cannot be fluent readers. Fluent readers understand more than slow readers.

Reading fluency refers in part to efficient, effective word recognition skills and grammatical knowledge that help readers to construct the meaning of a text. Fluency makes reading comprehension possible. When L2 readers gain fluency their comprehension increases. Slow readers, those who read word-for-word, do not understand as much as fluent readers. To sum up, reading easy and interesting material helps L2 students learn to read.

In closing this section, reflect on these questions:

> – What is the most important thing you have learned from this section?
> – How might it affect your teaching of L2 reading?

READING STRATEGIES

The final section of this chapter focuses on reading strategies. We examine two types of reading strategies, fluency and comprehension. Complete this sentence:

> – A strategy is

This is not an easy task. Many teachers confuse a *strategy* with a *skill*. One way to keep them separate is to understand that we teach *strategies*. A strategy is an action that we think about before doing it. In other words, it is a conscious behaviour. The more you use or do a particular strategy, over and over, it will become unconscious behaviour; you don't think about it before doing it. This unconscious behaviour is a skill.

Since a skill is unconscious behaviour, it cannot be taught. We teach our L2 students reading *strategies*– conscious behaviour – and give them opportunities to practice and use the strategies. Over time, with lots of practice and use, the strategies may become skills.

Are these a strategy or a skill? Before you answer, think about the difference between a strategy and a skill.

> _____ Translating from the L2 into the L1
> _____ Changing the reading rate based on the material
> _____ ignoring unknown words

All three can be either a strategy or a skill. It depends on the behaviour of the reader. If the reader thinks about ignoring an unknown word, then the reader is engaging in conscious behaviour, which is a strategy. If the reader, when coming across an unknown word, skips it and continues to read automatically, without thinking, then it is a skill.

> – Do you teach any reading strategies? Why or why not?

There are many ways of classifying reading strategies. Hudson (2007, pp. 108–111) discusses three types of comprehension reading strategies: pre-reading; while-reading; and post-reading. Most L2 reading materials include these three types. But comprehension reading strategies are not the complete picture. Often missing from L2 reading materials are *fluency* reading strategies. Some examples of fluency strategies are:

- Scanning – Scanning is an extremely rapid search for specific information (e.g., to find an answer to a question or find specific information).
- Previewing and predicting – This pre-reading fluency strategy involves looking at the title of the reading and, if there are any, illustrations, and then making a prediction (or a best guess) what the reading is about. This is very helpful strategy as research has shown that we read a text with greater understanding when we know something about the topic (e.g., Grabe, 2009, p. 47).
- Ignoring unknown words – The while-reading fluency strategy is straightforward: Don't stop reading to think about or use the dictionary for the meanings of unknown words. While it is a simple fluency strategy, L2 students often find it difficult to use, as they are addicted to their dictionaries. But when we stop to consider an unknown word, we interrupt our fluency. We have to go back and reread.

When teaching fluency reading strategies, teachers need to set a time limit (e.g., 30 seconds; one minute) for activities that they use to practice a fluency strategy. Students, who may be used to reading only word-for-word, may simply read slowly and carefully to find the information if a time limit is not given. Teachers might also want to use readings that students have already to the focus is fluency, not comprehension.

> – Do you think you might teach reading fluency strategies? Why or why not?

Comprehension reading strategies help L2 readers *read to learn* and are important. Research has shown that L2 readers need to at an intermediate level of reading ability in order to use comprehension reading strategies effectively. Fluency reading strategies, in contrast, help L2 readers *learn to read*. They can be used effectively with all levels L2 reading ability.

Regardless of the type of reading strategy, there are some very important factors that L2 reading teachers need to know about teaching reading strategies. We know from research that:

- Teachers have to explain to students why a strategy is important and when to use it.
- Teachers should plan on a great deal of practice and repetition. Students need to practice a strategy over and over. Strategy learning takes time.

> – What is the most important thing you learned in this section?

CONCLUSION

This chapter presents an in-depth discussion of the nature of reading that might be insightful to L2 reading teachers. Of particular interest is the topic of reading fluency. In general, L2 reading teachers and L2 reading materials focus on reading comprehension and ignore or neglect reading fluency. This chapter discuss the critical role of reading fluency and attempts to show how it is the basis of reading comprehension.

The final reflective question deals with what you, the reader, have gained:

> – To what extent has your teaching of L2 reading changed?

REFERENCES

Day, R. R. (Ed.). (2012). *New ways in teaching reading* (2nd ed.). Alexandria: TESOL.

Grabe, W. (2009). *Reading in a second language: Moving from theory to practice*. Cambridge: Cambridge University Press.

Hudson, T. (2007). *Teaching second language reading*. Oxford: Oxford University Press.

Lightbown, P., Halter, R., White, J., & Horst, M. (2002). Comprehension-based learning: The limits of "do it yourself". *Canadian Modern Language Review, 58*, 427–464.

National Reading Panel. (2000). *Teaching children to read: An evidence-based assessment of the scientific research literature on reading and its implications for reading instruction.* Washington, DC: National Institute of Child Health and Human Development.

Richard R. Day
Department of Second Language Studies
University of Hawai'i
Honolulu, USA

ABOUT THE CONTRIBUTORS

Maryam Azarnoosh is an assistant professor of TEFL at Semnan Branch, Islamic Azad University, Semnan, Iran. She was the dean of Faculty of Humanities for two years and has been the head of Department of English language since 2010. She is also the head of Educated Women Council of Islamic Azad University Semnan Province. She has been teaching at different universities for over 16 years and has published and presented papers in different national and international journals and conferences. She has also co-authored an ESP book for students of computer engineering and co-edited books on issues in TEFL, namely *Issues in Material Development* and *Issues in Syllabus*. Her main research interests include English language skills, materials development and evaluation, English for specific purposes, language teaching, testing and assessment.

Anne Burns is Professor of TESOL, University of New South Wales, Sydney, Australia and Professor Emerita, Aston University, Birmingham, UK. She is also an Honorary Professor at the University of Sydney and the Education University, Hong Kong. She publishes extensively on teacher education, action research, and teaching speaking. Among her recent book publications are *Doing Action Research in English Language Teaching* (2010, Routledge), which has been used by language teacher researchers worldwide, *Teaching Speaking: A Holistic Approach* (with Christine C.C.M Goh CUP, 2012), and *The Cambridge Guide to Pedagogy and Practice* (edited with Jack C. Richards, CUP, 2012). She is also the Academic Advisor (with Diane Larsen-Freeman) for the Applied Linguistics Series published by OUP, and Series Editor (with Jill Hadfield) for the Research and Resources Series published by Routledge. In 2016 she was recognised by TESOL International as one of the '50 at 50' who have made a major contribution to ELT.

Graham V. Crookes is Professor, Department of Second Language Studies, University of Hawai'i. He is particularly interested in critical language pedagogy and teachers' philosophies of teaching. His recent books are *Critical ELT in Action* (Routledge) and *Values, philosophies and beliefs in TESOL* (Cambridge).

Michael R.W. Dawson is a professor and cognitive scientist at the University of Alberta. He is the author of numerous scientific papers as well as the books *Understanding Cognitive Science* (1998), *Minds and Machines* (2004), *Connectionism: A Hands-on Approach* (2005), *From Bricks to Brains: The Embodied Cognitive Science of LEGO Robots* (2010) and *Mind, Body, World: Foundations of Cognitive Science* (2013), and *Connectionist Representations of Tonal Music: Discovering Musical Patterns by Interpreting Artificial Neural Networks* (2018).

Richard R. Day is a professor in the Department of Second Language Studies, University of Hawai'i. He is the author of numerous publications, particularly on second language reading. His most recent publications are *New Ways in Teaching Reading* (2nd edition), and *Teaching Reading*. Dr. Day is the co-author of *Extensive Reading in the Second Language Classroom*, and the co-editor of *Extensive Reading Activities for Teaching Language*. His instructional interests include second language reading, second language teacher education, and materials development. He is the co-editor of the online scholarly journal, *Reading in a Foreign Language* (www.nflrc.hawaii.edu/rfl), and co-founder of the Extensive Reading Foundation (www.erfoundation.org).

Akram Faravani is an assistant professor in Islamic Azad University, Mashhad Branch, Iran. She received her Ph.D. in TEFL from Islamic Azad University of Tehran, Science and Research Branch. She has 10 years teaching experience and has published a number of articles in national and international journals and has presented papers in some conferences. Her major research interests include SLA, language testing, syllabus designing and materials development.

Dorothy Gillmeister is a retired educator as well as a published writer and poet, holding degrees in English, adult education, and journalism. She has worked as a science writer and documentary video producer, an editor for a management consulting firm, an educational researcher, and an affirmative action officer for a large Canadian university. For the last ten years before retiring, she taught academic English to freshmen at Yonsei University in Seoul, South Korea, following a year in a remote South Korean town teaching middle and high school. She has also volunteered for community cable stations in Toronto and Sault Ste. Marie helping community groups, including native Indians, tell their stories on television by filming, editing, and occasionally hosting programs. She is now living in Sault Ste. Marie, Ontario, with her new husband, Ago Lehela, and her Korean rescue cat, Sandylion.

Christine Goh, Ph.D. is Professor of Linguistics and Language Education and holds a concurrent appointment as Dean of Graduate Studies and Professional Learning at the National Institute of Education, Nanyang Technological University, Singapore. She qualified as a secondary school teacher of English and literature with a BA (Hons) in English and a Diploma of Education in TESL. She is known internationally for her work on second language listening and speaking, and the role of metacognition in L2 learning. Her books include *Teaching Speaking: A Holistic Approach* (with Anne Burns, 2012, Cambridge University Press) and *Teaching and Learning Second Language Listening: Metacognition in Action* (with Larry Vandergrift, 2012, Routledge).

Hamid Reza Kargozari is an assistant professor at Tabaran Institute of Higher Education, Iran. His current research interests cover issues in psycholinguistics, materials development and sociolinguistics. He has been involved in a range of projects in these areas.

John M. Levis is Professor of Applied Linguistics and TESL at Iowa State University. He started the annual Pronunciation in Second Language Learning and Teaching conference, now in its ninth year. He is also the founding editor of the *Journal of Second Language Pronunciation*. He is co-editor of the Phonetics and Phonology section of the *Encyclopedia of Applied Linguistics* (2013), *Social Dynamics in Second Language Accent* (2014), *The Handbook of English Pronunciation* (2015), and *Pronunciation: Critical Concepts in Linguistics* (2017). He is also the creator of *pronunciationforteachers.com*, a website devoted to best practices in pronunciation teaching.

John I. Liontas, Ph.D., is an associate professor of foreign languages, English for speakers of other languages (ESOL), and technology in education and second language acquisition (TESLA), and director and faculty of the TESLA doctoral program at the University of South Florida. He has over 30 years of K-16+ teaching experience and research in the United States and other countries. He is a distinguished thought leader, author, and practitioner in the fields of applied linguistics, second language acquisition, and ESL/EFL and the recipient of over two dozen local, state, regional, national, ad international teaching awards and honors. He has a long-standing interest in idiomaticity and in its application in the second and foreign language classroom. He is presently involved in the design and production of a multimedia computer software program for learning English idioms called It's All Greek to Me! Learning English Idioms in Context. He is also the Editor-in-Chief of *The TESOL Encyclopedia of English Language Teaching* (published Winter 2017 Online and as a 8 Volume Print Set, http://www. tesolencyclopedia.com).

Shawn Loewen is Associate Professor in the Second Language Studies and MA TESOL programs at Michigan State University. His research interests include instructed second language acquisition and quantitative research methodology. In addition to publishing in leading SLA journals, he has co-authored two books, *Key Concepts in Second Language Acquisition*, and *An A–Z of Applied Linguistics Research Methods*. His sole authored book, *Introduction to Instructed Second Language Acquisition*, appeared in 2015.

Parviz Maftoon is associate professor of teaching English at Islamic Azad University, Science and Research Branch, Tehran, Iran. He received his Ph.D. degree from New York University in Teaching English to Speakers of Other Languages (TESOL). His primary research interests concern second language acquisition, SL/FL language teaching methodology, and language curriculum development. He has published nationally and internationally and written and edited a number of English books. He is currently on the editorial board of several language journals in Iran.

Jennifer Majorana is an ESL Senior Specialist at Saginaw Valley State University, and a graduate of the MA TESOL program at Michigan State University. Her current research interests include tracking the vocabulary size and development of students at Intensive English Programs.

Shannon McCrocklin is an assistant professor at Southern Illinois University. She completed her Ph.D. in Applied Linguistics and Technology at Iowa State University in Ames, IA. She holds an M.A. in Teaching English as a Second Language from the University of Illinois at Urbana-Champaign where she developed an interest in pronunciation teaching and applied phonetics and phonology. Shannon has taught English pronunciation to undergraduate and graduate students as well as to international faculty at Iowa State and the University of Illinois. Her research focuses on improving pronunciation training for students and CAPT (Computer-Assisted Pronunciation Teaching).

Hossein Nassaji is Professor and Department Chair in the Department of Linguistics at the University of Victoria, Victoria, BC. His recent books are *Corrective Feedback in Second Language Teaching and Learning* (2017, Routledge, with Eva Kartchava), *Interactional Feedback Dimension in Instructed Second Language Learning* (2015, Bloomsbury Publishing), *Teaching Grammar in Second Language Classrooms* (2010, Routledge, with Sandra Fotos), and *Form-Focused Instruction and Teacher Education* (2007, Oxford University Press, with Sandra Fotos). His forthcoming book is *Perspectives on Language as Action* (Multilingual Matters, with Mari Haneda). He is the co-editor of *Language Teaching Research* and the editor of the Grammar Teaching Volume of *The TESOL Encyclopedia of English Language Teaching* being published by Wiley in partnership with TESOL International.

Ulugbek Nurmukhamedov is an Assistant Professor in the TESOL program at Northeastern Illinois University. His research interests include L2 vocabulary, corpus-based vocabulary analysis, and computer-assisted language learning. Ulugbek's articles have appeared in *ELT Journal*, *TESOL Journal*, and *Writing & Pedagogy*.

Luke Plonsky is Assistant Professor at Georgetown University, where he teaches courses in second language acquisition and research methods. Recent and forthcoming publications in these and other areas can be found in *Applied Linguistics*, *Language Learning*, *Modern Language Journal*, and *Studies in Second Language Acquisition*, among other journals. He has also written and edited several books. Luke is Associate Editor of *Studies in Second Language Acquisition*, Managing Editor of *Foreign Language Annals*, and Co-Director of the IRIS Database for instruments in language learning and teaching (iris-database.org). Luke received his PhD in Second Language Studies from Michigan State University.

Nima Shakouri is an assistant professor at Islamic Azad University, Roudbar Branch, Guilan, Iran. He received his Ph.D. degree from Islamic Azad University, Science and Research Branch, Tehran in 2016 in Applied Linguistics. His research interests concern SLA and Neurolinguistics. He has published nationally and internationally. He is currently the chief editor of *Journal of Language Teaching: Theory and Practice*.

Jun Tian is an associate teaching professor of Chinese at the University of Victoria, BC, Canada. Her research interests are in the areas of applied linguistics, second language acquisition, classroom-based research, second language writing, collaborative learning, teaching Chinese/English as an additional language, and Chinese linguistics.

Laurens Vandergrift (November 10, 1946–November 1, 2015)
In Memoriam
The field of second language learner listening has lost a great scholar. Larry, as he was known to many, touched the hearts and minds of fellow listening researchers, graduate students and listening teachers all over the world. His work is read, discussed, applied and debated, and many young researchers have been inspired by it to study second language listening. In Larry Vandergrift's work shone a brilliant mind and a great heart. When he wrote this chapter, Larry Vandergrift was Full Professor at the University of Ottawa. He will be deeply missed.

Constance Weaver is Professor Emerita of English, Western Michigan University, and retired Heckert Endowed Professor, Miami University. She is best known for publications and activism in reading education (e.g., the third edition of *Reading Process and Practice*) and her books on teaching grammar as part of the writing process, beginning with *Grammar for Teachers* (1979) and including *Teaching Grammar in Context* (1996), *The Grammar Plan Book* (2007), and *Grammar to Enrich and Enhance Writing* (2008). Weaver has presented on these topics in several countries around the world, such as France, Peru, Taiwan, and Malaysia. She lives in Kalamazoo, Michigan, with her cat Sweetie.

Mitra Zeraatpishe is an assistant professor at Islamic Azad University, Mashhad Branch, Iran. She received her Ph.D. in TEFL from Islamic Azad University, Tabriz branch. She has 12 years teaching experience and has published a number of articles in national and international journals and has presented papers at several conferences. Her recent works are two co-edited books namely *Issues in Material Development* (2016, Sense Publishers) and *Issues in Syllabus* (2018, Sense Publishers). Furthermore another co-edited book will be published soon, entitled *Issues in SLA Research: Syllabus Design and Curriculum Development* (2018, Brill | Sense).

INDEX